Gary Gentile started his diving career in 1970. Since then he has made thousands of decompression dives, over 160 of them on the *Andrea Doria*. He was instrumental in merging mixed-gas technology with wreck diving. In 1994, he participated in a technical diving expedition to the *Lusitania*, at a depth of 300 feet.

Gary has specialized in wreck diving and shipwreck research, concentrating his efforts on wrecks along the east coast, from Newfoundland to Key West, and in the Great Lakes. He has compiled an extensive library of books, photographs, drawings, plans, and original source materials on ships and shipwrecks.

Gary has written dozens of magazine articles, and he has published thousands of photographs in books, periodicals, newspapers, brochures, advertisements, corporate reports, museum displays, postcards, film, and television. He lectures extensively on wilderness and underwater topics, and conducts seminars on advanced wreck-diving techniques and high-tech diving equipment. He is the author of more than two dozen books, both novels and nonfiction works, the latter on diving and nautical and shipwreck history. The Popular Dive Guide Series will eventually cover every major shipwreck along the east coast.

In 1989, after a five-year battle with the National Oceanic and Atmospheric Administration, Gary won a suit which forced the hostile government agency to issue him a permit to dive the USS *Monitor*, a protected National Marine Sanctuary. Media attention that was focused on Gary's triumphant victory resulted in nationwide coverage of his 1990 photographic expedition to the Civil War ironclad. Gary continues to fight for the right of access to all shipwreck sites.

The *Morro Castle* - from tragedy to tourist attraction.
Above: A postcard view of the wreck on the beach at Asbury Park.
Below: A night time exposure. (From the author's collection.)
See Introduction for particulars.

THE POPULAR DIVE GUIDE SERIES

Shipwrecks of New Jersey (North)

by Gary Gentile

GARY GENTILE PRODUCTIONS
P.O. Box 57137
Philadelphia, PA 19111
2000

Gary Gentile Productions
P.O. Box 57137
Philadelphia, PA 19111

Additional copies of this book may be purchased from the same address by send-ing a check or money order in the amount of $20 U.S. for each copy (postage paid). For information about GGP consulting services, workshops, presentations, and a list of available titles, visit the GGP website:

http://www.pilot.infi.net/~boring/gentile.html

Picture Credits
The front cover woodcut of the *Rusland* is from *Harper's Weekly*. The back cover woodcut of *Pliny* survivors being rescued by means of the breeches buoy is from *Frank Leslie's Illustrated Newspaper*. Every attempt has been made to contact the photographers or artists whose work appears in this book, if known, and to ascertain their names if unknown; in some cases, copies of pictures have been in public circulation for so long that the name of the photographer or artist has been lost, or the present whereabouts are impossible to trace. Any information in this regard forwarded to the author will be appreciated. Apologies are made to those whose work must under such circumstances go unrecognized. Uncredited pho-tographs, including all marine life examples typical to the area, were taken by the author.

The author wishes to acknowledge Drew Maser, Bonnie Yurga, and John Yurga for proofreading the galleys.

International Standard Book Number (ISBN) 1-883056-08-X

First Edition

Printed in Hong Kong

CONTENTS

INTRODUCTION

I wrote the original edition of *Shipwrecks of New Jersey* as my swan song to local wreck-diving. By 1988, the year of the book's publication, I had been researching and diving New Jersey wrecks for nearly two decades. It was time for me to move on to distant waters. As I traveled farther afield - diving shipwrecks along the eastern seaboard from Newfoundland to the Dry Tortugas, in the Great Lakes, and in other parts of the world - I left behind the wrecks on which I had first found so much excitement and adventure. Sometimes, an entire year would pass during which I did not make a single local dive, yet I never quit researching New Jersey shipwrecks, anticipating the time when my interest in them would be re-stimulated.

Quite consciously, I entertained hopes that the trenchant historical accounts related in the initial slender volume would inspire others to conduct some primary research on their own - commencing where I had adjourned - and that the book would provide a stimulus for divers to search for wrecks whose existence I had firmly established but whose locations lay undiscovered. Happily, both of these optimistic prospects have come to pass.

In the original introduction, I wrote, "What I have written will supply answers to the curious, and pose questions to the inquisitive. I hope to spark on those who would like to add a piece of the nautical puzzle to the fabric of human privity." Thus, I included shipwrecks that were little known or practically unheard of, lest they be forgotten. Even the most insignificant of wrecks might provide a rare insight into the cultural evolution of the human species, from individual heroic action to the way opportunists sometimes responded to terrible tragedy.

The first edition was abbreviated in text and content. Due to space constraints imposed by the publisher, many wrecks that I would like to have included were not mentioned at all. Likewise, most of the wrecks that I did include received far less coverage than was demanded by either their historic significance or story depth. Some wrecks were de-emphasized because of their lack of popularity, and received only superficial treatment. The result was an unbalanced cross section, horribly abridged content, loss of substantial detail, and the exclusion of certain wrecks based upon a perception of obscurity.

Later, the publisher declined to issue a revised, updated, and expanded edition of *Shipwrecks of New Jersey* because of the additional costs that would have been incurred: for typesetting, layout, paste up, and so on. According to my contract, publishing rights would not revert to me unless the book went out of print, and stayed out of print for six months. Authors generally are not happy when one of their books is no longer on the market. I am no exception. However, after years of eager anticipation, I was ecstatic when the publisher sold off all remaining copies and decided against another printing. By then I owned my own publishing business, enabling me to rewrite and reprint the book the way I wanted.

The multiple volume format makes it possible to correct the deficiencies of the first edition. Unfortunately, with more than 4,000 authenticated wrecks lying off the coast of New Jersey, I am still forced to exclude the majority of them. But the extra space permits the addition of those wrecks which I think possess the most importance and dramatic appeal.

In the years that have passed since the original publication, previously unlocated wrecks have been discovered - by myself as well as by others. This has come about by continued research, the examination of "hang" numbers, and the advent of technical diving. The latter has made some shipwrecks more accessible to a growing multitude, because breathing mixtures containing helium have made it possible for divers to go deeper than ever before. Enterprising boat captains - with bigger, faster, and better equipped boats - cater to these deep-water explorers by taking them to sites that lay far out to sea. Thus wreck exploration has expanded in two directions: deeper and farther offshore.

Deterioration - an Ongoing Process

To wreck-divers is it evident that shipwrecks undergo a continual process of collapse. Academics and archaeologists would make the public believe that sunken wrecks exist in a state of perpetual preservation, as if they were frozen in time like fossils in rock. But wiser heads accept that long-term immersion in a hostile and dynamic environment is destructive. From the moment a ship is built the process of deterioration begins. This process does not end until the wreck is no longer recognizable, until nothing of man's original handiwork remains.

In the thirty years that I have been diving I have witnessed this slow deterioration. The changes on older wrecks have been subtle, but nevertheless consuming. But on more recent wrecks - from World War Two and later - I have observed major structural collapse as well as the accelerating disintegration of metal. Since much of this deterioration has occurred since the original publication, this updated edition affords the opportunity to compare my wreck descriptions of yesteryear with the way the wrecks appear today, and to demonstrate the deleterious changes that have occurred.

Never-ending Research

Research is defined as collecting bits and pieces of information from a multitude of sources. In an effort to save these findings for posterity, the historian rewrites the assembled data in a comprehensible format which is more concise and less repetitious than a simple compilation of materials. Thus, the historian does not create history, he records it. However, the historian *is* charged with the responsibility of separating fact from fiction, noting possible exaggeration, and, from the perspective of his expertise, indicating his doubt about the veracity of previously recorded accounts.

Notwithstanding the above, if only a single source of evidence remains extant, the historian cannot be held accountable for lack of veracity or misrepresentation should this sole original document contains errors of fact which cannot be corroborated. If this is the case, the historian can do no better than to present the records that exist and let the reader decide what to believe. This is not a cop-out, but a recognition of reality.

In other cases, a source may have been so clear, so accurate, and so concise that its content could not be improved. To rewrite such a story might obliterate or garble important particulars.

Whenever I repeat passages which I did not create or reword, I have placed those passages in quotation marks. Sometimes I put a short phrase or even a single word in quotes as a way of informing the reader that the phrase or word is part of an original construction and not one of my own making. I did this also as a way of signifying a vague or uncertain fact when corroboration was lacking - so the reader knows what I know, and understands that the vagueness or confusion is a matter of primary documentation, not something that I misinterpreted.

In addition, I have quoted passages as a way to flavor contemporary events with the language that was prevalent at the time. Furthermore, for those who are interested in linguistics, the usage of words, grammatical constructions, and unwieldy punctuation combine to demonstrate the evolution of English toward its present form.

The chronicles that follow are based upon primary source materials - largely gathered by this author, but in some instances collected by fellow researchers. I would like to thank those who have shared with me their experiences and the efforts of their research: John Bandstra, Jack Fullmer, Dan and Terry Lieb, Frank Litter, Howard Rothweiler, and Al Vogel.

I would like to express further thanks to Howard Rothweiler for sharing his extensive knowledge of beach wrecks and for drawing sketches of their land ranges, and to Dan Lieb for meticulously redrafting these sketches in an exciting and artistic format.

The *Morro Castle*

One of New Jersey's most infamous shipping catastrophes is conspicuous by its absence. I refer to the conflagration and subsequent stranding of the *Morro Castle*, a tragedy in which 124 people perished. The burning liner drifted aimlessly until it grounded off Convention Hall in Asbury Park, on March 6, 1934. For months the scarred hull was a tourist attraction. The burned out hulk was then pulled off the beach and towed to a scrap yard, where it was dismantled. Since at least three books have been written about the *Morro Castle*, and because I could not do justice to the story in a single chapter, I refer curious readers to these books. They are referenced in the bibliography.

New Jersey Historical Divers Association

Government sponsored archaeological work on shipwrecks off the New Jersey coast has been lacking. The work of discovering, surveying, and identifying shipwrecks has been conducted primarily by recreational divers in their spare time.

The latest organized addition to this coterie of volunteer researchers is the

New Jersey Historical Divers Association. The NJHDA began informally in 1992 when founder John Bandstra set a goal for himself: to learn the identity of the Manasquan Wreck. As a youngster in the area, he had been led to believe that the wreck was the *Thistle*, cast away on Squan Beach in 1813. After three years of prodigious effort, he and a small group of determined wreck-divers concluded that the Manasquan Wreck was instead the packet ship *Amity*, lost in 1824. The story of how that identification was established is told in the appropriate chapter.

Inspired by the fulfillment of successful historical research and shipwreck documentation, the NJHDA became incorporated as a nonprofit organization in 1995, and began the publication of a quarterly journal, which disseminated information about the various shipwreck investigations in which the members were involved. Thus the NJHDA became the first *organized* wreck research group in New Jersey.

The NJHDA lent valuable assistance to the U.S. Corps of Engineers during the investigative phase of the Beach Replenishment Project, and continues to function in an advisory capacity in other areas of historical preservation. Ongoing projects include surveying and mapping unidentified wrecks, artifact recovery and restoration, and photo and video documentation. Perhaps the biggest project the association has tackled is the establishment of a shipwreck museum. At the time of this writing, the association is looking for an existing building which can be converted to a facility in which New Jersey's shipwreck history can be told through the display of artifacts recovered by avocational historians and archaeologists.

Beach Replenishment Project

Beach erosion is a natural process that is caused suddenly by a storm or incrementally by wind and tides.

Storm damage can be severe and is exceedingly noticeable. A hurricane or a northeast gale can create changes in beach front property literally overnight, not only by knocking down structures and uplifting boardwalks, but by scouring deep grooves in the beach between the tide lines and by depleting vast tracts of sand. A beach may be drastically truncated when the barrier dunes are undermined and collapse into the waves, the sand then being washed away by the undercurrent. In severe cases, the ocean may wash completely over the height of land and create a new inlet.

Sand that is blown off the beaches by wind, or that is carried away by moving water such as rip tides and cross currents, moves subtly over such long spans of time that alterations are not immediately obvious. Gauges must be erected in order to ascertain the changes. Often, these gauges are not scientific devices but structures such as houses and boardwalks. Homeowners may watch their front yards disappear, or sunbathers may notice that the distance from the parking lot to the ocean becomes perceptibly shorter from year to year. These changes are gradual but no less insidious.

In keeping with the first law of thermodynamics, sand is neither created nor destroyed - it is simply moved from one location to another. Nothing is lost or gained. Furthermore, nature works in phases: an erosional phase followed by a depositional phase, which is followed by another erosional phase. Nor does nature care about this constant shift of sand. Those who care are those who have a vested interest in a particular contour of the beach: property owners.

In 1995, the State of New Jersey began a project to add sand to beaches that were being washed away by natural erosion. This effort to halt - at least temporarily - the natural movement of sand was called the Beach Replenishment Project. In this project, sand was taken from offshore where its presence or absence was inconsequential (in human terms), and was placed in the surf zone to shore up the beach front.

Several active and well-known wreck sites were blanketed with sand in this manmade process, and undoubtedly many other wrecks, as yet unlocated, were interred. The impact on these surf-zone wrecks was tremendous in terms of loss: the loss of dive sites, fishing grounds, and historic and archaeological material. Largely through the efforts of the New Jersey Historical Divers Association, the State of New Jersey was convinced to survey the established dive sites, and to conduct a minimal search for unknown wrecks in the regions to be buried.

The U.S. Corps of Engineers was charged with the responsibility of implementing the project. The Corps hired an out-of-state archaeological firm to conduct electronic remote-sensing surveys of certain locations. These surveys were conducted chiefly by means of side-scan sonar and magnetometer. This phase of the project was not methodical, but rather a helter-skelter operation in which areas chosen seemingly at random were fully investigated, while adjacent areas were not investigated at all. The pattern of investigation was based largely upon word-of-mouth knowledge or vague notions of where shipwrecks were believed to exist. Afterward, selected sites were dived, wreckage was explored, site plans were drawn, and, in some cases, sample artifacts were recovered.

The beach wrecks from Sandy Hook to Manasquan - along some fifty miles of coast line - were covered by a thick shroud of sand. Those that were examined to various degrees prior to entombment were the *Antioch, Malta, Rjukan, Western World*, Dual Wrecks (*Adonis* and *Rusland*), Firing Range Wreck, Manasquan Wreck (*Amity*), Sea Girt Wreck, and Tin Wreck. Other wrecks were buried as a matter of course, but not investigated.

Those wrecks for which site plans were drawn can now serve as sand gauges for beach replenishment engineers. The original relief, or "height of exposure," of each wreck is a quantity that is known. By determining how fast and how much of a wreck's structure reappears, the movement and erosion of sand can be measured against time.

The descriptions of beach wrecks given in the following pages refer to a time prior to interment by the Beach Replenishment Project, and are noted thus. The project is not completed but, when it is, beaches south of Manasquan will also be rebuilt.

ADONIS

Built: 1853
Previous names: None
Gross tonnage: 550
Type of vessel: Wooden-hulled full-rigged ship
Builder: Johann Lange, in Vegesack, Germany
Owner: F. Reck & Company, Bremen, Germany
Port of registry: Bremen, Germany
Cause of sinking: Ran aground
Location: 26950.2

Sunk: March 7, 1859
Depth: 20 feet
Dimensions: 122' x 29' x 17'
Power: Sail

43598.8
(Off the southern end of St. Alphonso's Retreat, in Long Branch)

Back in the early days of pull rods and double-hose regulators, Bill Skripko, a skin diver who turned to scuba, spearfished on an old broken-down wreck thought to be a steel-hulled tug. (In actuality, the hull plates were made of iron, but the difference between steel and iron is difficult to determine under water.) One day in 1960, his buddy Chuck Tucker asked him for directions to the site.

From *Harper's Weekly*.

With appropriate land ranges, Tucker went out to the wreck, and discovered that it was made out of wood, not steel (or iron).

Skripko was perplexed when he heard this. Together, the two went back to explore the wreck more thoroughly. They soon discovered that there were *two* wrecked vessels at the same location: an iron-hulled steamship whose engine, boilers, and propeller shaft were exposed, and a wooden-hulled windjammer whose remains lay perpendicular to the after end of the iron ship like the horizontal slash of a T.

The tips of wooden ribs that protruded from the sand were reminiscent of a stubby skeleton. "Sitting in the center of the hull were enormous grindstones. Some were about five feet high and six feet around, shaped like a hat. Others were a scant two feet across, flat and five inches thick." They also found stacks of 115-pound lead ingots, stamped "Locke Blackett & Co."

Skripko and Tucker did some research and eventually identified the wooden hull as "the Bark *Adonis*, a Dutch ship." This short description contains two errors: the *Adonis* was not a bark, but a full-rigged ship; and she was not Dutch, but German. The *Adonis* was on a passage from Liverpool to New York when she was cast away in a fierce gale onto New Jersey's bleak and, at the time, largely uninhabited shore. She was under the command of Captain Diedrich Bosse.

Her cargo consisted of seven chains, 96 casks of ground flint, 124 grindstones, 100 casks of alkali, 501 casks of soda, 160 casks of bleaching powder, 600 pigs of lead, 130 casks of "b carb soda," 200 casks of venetian red, 500 kegs of "carb soda," and 380 packages of merchandise "to order."

Several weeks after the stranding, an account of the accident was published in *Harper's Weekly*: "On 7th inst. the ship *Adonis* went ashore, shortly before midnight, at Long Branch. A correspondent of the Monmouth *Democrat* gives the following thrilling description of the manner in which the crew were saved:

"Mr. Green, the station-keeper, was on the spot the following morning with a crew of wreckers. They launched the surf-boat, boarded the ship, and brought the captain ashore. The captain insisted upon returning to the ship, but, the wind breezing up, it was found impossible to do so, as upon the second attempt the surf-boat was filled. All haste was then made to shoot a line over the vessel; the first attempt the line did not reach the ship; the second line parted; and the third was successful. A larger line was then secured to the ship, and then a hawser, which was properly made fast to the mainmast head. The crew soon understood the working of the life-car upon the hawser, and five of them landed the first voyage to the shore. The life-car was again dispatched upon its errand of mercy; this time, better satisfied, six of them got into the car, but, when within about thirty yards of the shore, the line attached to the shore end of the car gave way. Then there was a universal shout of agony, the men on the beach running to and fro. There was quite a number of ladies present, who, as they looked upon the scene, turned from it with a shudder. Thus the car was at one moment upon the top of a large wave, and at another in the trough of the sea. The daring and impulsive boat's crew could not stand tamely by and see a car-load of human beings in this doubtful condition, but rushed in up to their armpits, seized the car, and brought

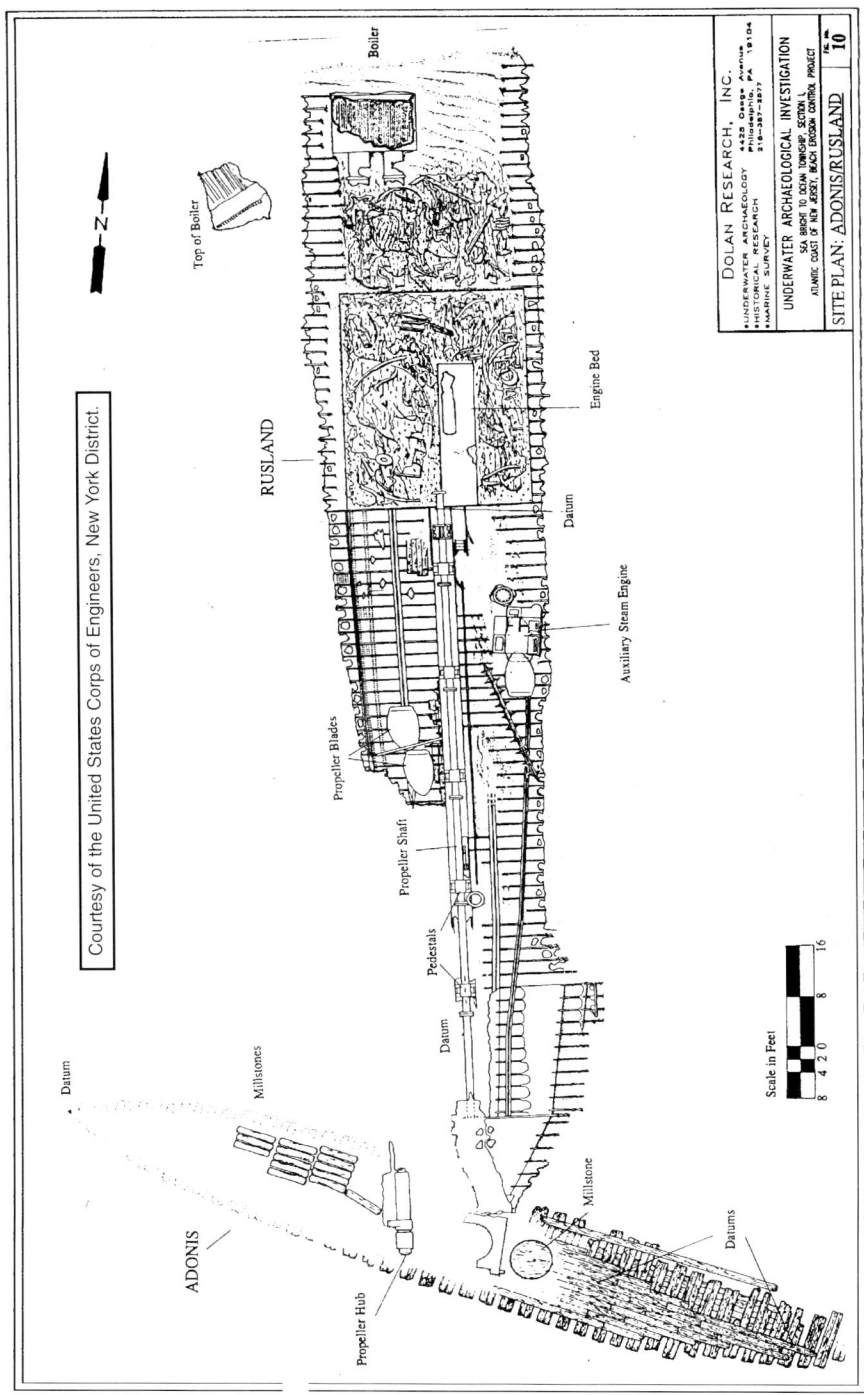

Courtesy of the United States Corps of Engineers, New York District.

RUSLAND

ADONIS

Boiler

Top of Boiler

Engine Bed

Datum

Auxiliary Steam Engine

Propeller Blades

Propeller Shaft

Pedestals

Datum

Datum

Millstones

Millstone

Datums

Propeller Hub

Scale in Feet

DOLAN RESEARCH, INC.
• UNDERWATER ARCHAEOLOGY
• HISTORICAL RESEARCH
• MARINE SURVEY

4425 Osage Avenue
Philadelphia, PA 19104
215-387-2877

UNDERWATER ARCHAEOLOGICAL INVESTIGATION
SEA BRIGHT TO OCEAN TOWNSHIP, SECTION I,
ATLANTIC COAST OF NEW JERSEY, BEACH EROSION CONTROL PROJECT

SITE PLAN: ADONIS/RUSLAND

FIG. 10

it ashore. The name of Joseph West and his crew should be written in letters of gold upon the record of the Life-Saving Association. Upon examination it was found that the ring-bolt on the end of the life-car, to which the shore end of the line was attached, was imperfect, and thus the breakage was easily accounted for. The damage was repaired, and again the car was dispatched, and the remaining seven were soon upon the beach."

Not a life was lost. Hopes were strong that the ship could soon be pulled off her precarious perch. It was next reported that the ship "now lies, with her head to the northwest, on the outer bar. The steam-pump was got to work this morning, and reduced the water some three feet on the rising tide. She is badly hogged. Another steam-pump will be sent down by the schr. *Ringgold*, and, if the weather proves favorable, Capt. Merritt expects to get her off."

Alas, such was not to be. Overnight the ship filled with water and went to pieces during a heavy southwest gale. What remained of the *Adonis* was sold at a public auction that was held on the beach adjacent to the wreck. The battered German ship fetched only $25. Even in antebellum dollars that was not a lot of money.

The *Adonis* next came to mind on March 17, 1877, when the Red Star liner *Rusland* ran aground at the same spot and raked over the grindstones that had been too heavy to salvage. The *Rusland* swung around in the storm until she lay broadside to the beach. In the process she tore up what was left of the hull of the *Adonis*. As the iron ship was worked over by the waves, the grinding action of iron on wood ripped timbers and planking out of the hulk of the *Adonis*, and spread floating debris for miles along the coast. For further details of the Belgian liner, see *Rusland*.

Not much of the *Adonis* lay exposed before the Beach Replenishment Project completely covered the wreck: a few wooden ribs, three rows of giant grindstones, and, if one dug deep enough, an occasional lead ingot. Previously, the exposed ribs offered numerous hiding places for small bottom dwellers, and provided a substrate for sessile marine organisms such as barnacles, anemones, and seaweed. Winter storms often stripped the wreck naked, but as the summer season progressed, marine growth reattached itself, attracted other denizens, and the wreck became alive.

The chief attraction of the *Adonis*, besides the sense of history that it conveys, is its proximity to the iron-hulled *Rusland*, whose propeller and stern lay on top of some of the mangled wooden remains. These combined sites constitute one of the most popular beach dives along the entire Jersey shore. The *Adonis* and the *Rusland* together are known as the Dual Wrecks.

The Dual Wrecks lie off the southern end of St. Alphonso's Retreat. The retreat resides on private property but the beach itself is public. If the residents of St. Alphonso's deny permission to access the beach from the grounds of the retreat, you will have to gain access to the beach elsewhere and carry your gear along the water's edge to the entry point. Alternatively, you can enter the water upcurrent and drift along with the current. A small boat makes the dive less physically challenging.

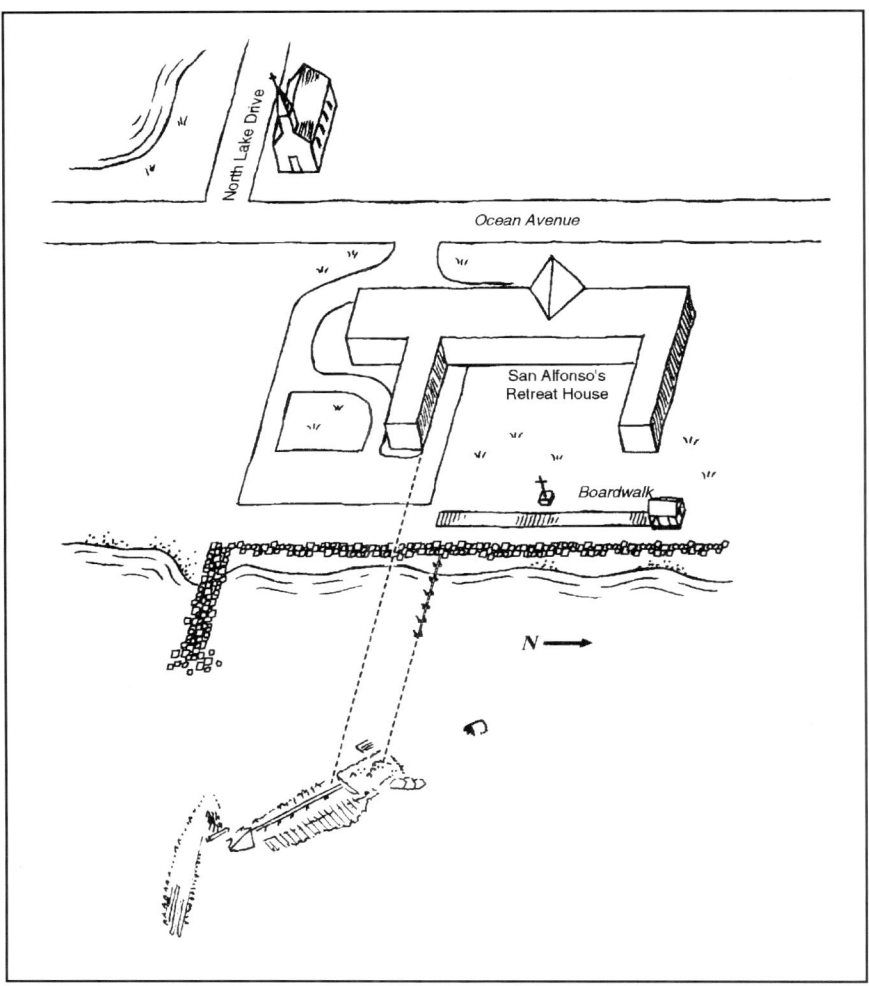

Enter the water from the north side of the base of the jetty. Swim north to an imaginary extension of the north side of the south wing of the retreat. Submerge and follow a compass bearing due east until you bump into the wreckage of the *Rusland*; or swim east on the surface until you can align the northeast corner of the condominium tower (not shown above) with the air-conditioning unit on the adjacent roof, then submerge directly on top of the *Rusland*. To find the *Adonis* from this point, follow the *Rusland's* propeller shaft beyond the propeller to the rudder. To find the *Rusland's* noncontiguous boiler, swim on the surface from the north end of the wreck and in line with the wreck until you are directly in front of the cross, then submerge.

ALVENA

Built: 1870
Previous names: *Glengyle*
Gross tonnage: 1,741
Type of vessel: Iron-hulled freighter
Builder: London & Glasgow Company, Glasgow, Scotland
Owner: Atlas Steam Ship Company
Port of registry: Liverpool, England
Cause of sinking: Collision with SS *British Queen*
Location: Unknown

Sunk: January 19, 1897
Depth: Unknown
Dimensions: 274' x 32' x 24'
Power: Coal-fired steam

A misunderstanding of signals was given as the cause for the collision in which the *Alvena* was sunk by the *British Queen*. "There was a clear sky, little wind, and a smooth sea, and every buoy was visible at a long distance." The time was mid-afternoon.

The *Alvena* was outbound for Haiti and other West Indian ports, her holds crammed with 2,000 tons of general cargo. She also carried two passengers. Captain Dow held the bridge watch as the freighter slipped through New York harbor toward the open ocean.

Inbound from Antwerp, Belgium was the Phoenix Line steamer *British Queen*. At 4,388 tons and 410 feet in length, she was a modern Goliath compared to the aging Atlas Line steamer. Her master was Captain Smith.

The *Alvena* "proceeded down the bay through the ship channel, turned into the Swash Channel, which affords a short cut to the bar for vessels of her draft, and was approaching the intersection of the Swash Channel with the Bayside Main Ship Channel, when the *British Queen* was seen coming across the bar, in Gedney's Channel. The incoming vessel, on reaching the point where Gedney's Channel meets the Bayside Channel, of which it is a continuation, blew her whistle to indicate which side she would pass the *Alvena*, and the latter responded.

"The *British Queen* came on then through the Bayside Channel, while the Alvena's path was at right angles, so that in the ordinary course of events she would have passed out of the Swash Channel, across the Bayside Channel to the South Channel, which forms a continuation of the Swash. There had been a misunderstanding of signals - "cross signals" the pilots called it - and the *British Queen*, instead of crossing the bow of the Alvena, as she was evidently trying to do, or of going astern, as Capt. Dow, of the *Alvena*, intended she should do, struck the Atlas Line steamship.

"Capt. Smith had ordered the engines of the *British Queen* reversed as soon as he saw the collision was imminent, and his helm was put hard to starboard, to bring the vessels as near parallel as possible and avert a head-on blow, while the *Alvena* was steaming full speed ahead to clear the other vessel if possible, and her helm was put hard aport, to keep her off. These manoeuvres (*sic*) were executed too late to be of any avail, but the *British Queen* struck nearly head-on.

"There was great excitement on the *Alvena*, but the Captain managed to have his men close the watertight bulkheads. Then all hands scampered to the upper deck, and some of the seamen began cutting away the boats. There were various steam craft about at the time, including the ocean-going tug *Edwin Luckenbach*, the tug *Emperor*, and the steam pilot boat *Walter Adams*, the last-named in charge of Capt. Owen Hennessey. The *Emperor* was the first alongside.

"The *Alvena* began to settle aft, and Capt. Arnold of the *Emperor* shouted to Capt. Dow to make for the bar and beach his vessel. The advice was followed. The inner side of the bar was about three-quarters of a mile distant to the eastward. The closing of the bulkhead compartments had thus kept water out of the engine room, and the stokers and fireroom crew returned to work. The vessels had got clear of each other within two minutes, and twenty minutes later the sunken stern of the vessel grated on the bottom in twenty feet of water. The engines were then stopped, and the men in the fire and engine rooms were glad to get out, as the water had begun to come through the ill-fitting bulkhead doors.

"The *Alvena* had been drawing about twenty feet of water, and the forward end soon settled also, so that she rested on an even keel. It left her main deck just above the water, then at low tide. Her crew, however, in their fear had jumped to the *Emperor*. Capt. Dow ordered them back and they returned.

"The *British Queen* had come to anchor meantime, but, finding that life was not in danger, owing to the presence of so many other craft, weighed anchor and proceeded to her berth in Hoboken." Damage to the *British Queen* was slight: dented plates above the waterline, and a gash where the fluke of her own anchor had been driven through the hull.

The collision did not go unnoticed by those on shore. The Marine Observer at Sandy Hook, Count De La Motte, telegraphed news of the event to the city. In due course the Chapman Derrick and Wrecking Company dispatched the wrecking steamer *Hustler* to the scene. Captain Patterson and the crew of the Sandy Hook Life Saving Station launched a boat which was towed to the *Alvena* by the tug *Ordinance*. "His assistance was not required, but his men helped the Alvena's crew in lowering away the steamer's four boats, which were then tied alongside for use in emergency."

The *Alvena* was resting easy and not in immediate danger. The pilot boat *Walter Adams* came alongside and "offered to take off all hands and any property. The mails, navigating instruments, a quantity of furniture and baggage, and thirty-three of the officers and men and the two passengers were accordingly transferred to her." Also taken off was Mrs. Cameron, the stewardess. Captain Dow and a dozen seamen held the fort - or the ship.

"By 6 o'clock the rising of the tide had covered the decks with two feet of water throughout the greater part of the vessel's length, but leaving her awash forward and aft, while the deckhouses were above the water about four feet. They were nearly awash at 8:30 o'clock, when the tide was flood. The Captain and men made themselves as comfortable as possible in the pilot house and about the bridge, which were still dry. There was fortunately little sea, and the wind was blowing only a light breeze."

The Atlas Line hired the tug *Wendell Goodwin* to house and feed the crew members who remained aboard overnight. Had conditions remained calm, the *Alvena* likely could have been lightered and pulled off the bar. Salvage operations did not begin right away, however, because the Atlas Line's American agents were waiting to hear from the owners in England about how they wanted to proceed, and to authorize expenditures for salvaging the cargo.

Atlas Line representative Mr. Kellock stated, "We have cabled the details of the accident and are waiting for instructions, which will probably come tomorrow. The Merritt and Chapman wrecking companies have tugs down there, but we have made no agreement with any of them, and no work will be done until we hear from the other side." By "the other side" he must have been referring to England across the Atlantic Ocean, not to a spiritualistic voice from beyond.

No action was taken the following day. Tha night a fierce storm arose, forcing the men to abandon the *Alvena* to her fate. Waves battered the grounded ship like giant rams, playing "havoc with her superstructure. Her deck houses were wrenched off and sent drift, her cargo, derricks, and bridge were gone, and boatmen reported that the lower bay was strewn with drifting wreckage and cargo. One tugboat picked up seventy-eight boxes of soap. Another picked up a lot of pillows and mattresses, which came from her staterooms, and quantities of dried herring. A large amount of wreckage also floated ashore on the Jersey beach. The hull of the vessel had settled somewhat in the sand.

"The Lighthouse board, which affixed lights to her rigging, reported that she lay in twenty-five feet of water on the easterly side of the southern channel." Elsewhere it was reported that the *Alvena* lay "off the tail of the Romer Shoal, which forms one of the banks of the Swash Channel."

It was reported officially that the *Alvena* "will prove a total loss." No follow-up reports appeared.

Neither Captain Dow nor Captain Smith was responsible for the collision. This was because the commands of both ships were relinquished to harbor pilots. When a pilot took control of a vessel he made all navigational decisions, gave steering and engine orders, and was held accountable for any accidents that occurred. Not unexpectedly, conflicting stories erupted about who did what and who had the right of way, each side contending that the other was in the wrong. The hub of doubt centered not on the actions taken, but on the signals given.

Just as vehicles must give braking and turning signals, so must vessels communicate their intentions. At sea, this is accomplished by giving whistle blasts. A code has been developed in which the number of toots and the spacing between them signal an action that is being taken: a turn to port or starboard, reversing engines, and so on. It was the contention of witnesses on each of the vessels that the signal that was heard from the other vessel was not the signal that witnesses on the other vessel claimed was given.

Since both vessels were British, any resulting settlement or lawsuit would have taken place on "the other side."

Rescue by breeches buoy. (From the author's collection.)

ANTIOCH

Built: 1876

Previous names: None

Gross tonnage: 987

Type of vessel: Wooden-hulled barkentine

Builder: D. Clark, Kennebank, Maine

Owner: John S. Emery & Company, Boston, Massachusetts

Port of registry: Boston, Massachusetts

Cause of sinking: Ran aground

Location: Off the northern end of the boardwalk in Manasquan

Sunk: March 27, 1913

Depth: 20 feet

Dimensions: 183' x 35' x 21'

Power: Sail

What should have been only another routine voyage from Savannah, Georgia to New York City ended precipitously and prematurely when the *Antioch* ran aground in a storm less than half a mile south of the Squan Beach Life-Saving Station. Aboard the barkentine were ten exhausted men and a rich cargo of prime southern lumber.

The tide was low when the *Antioch*, on the port tack and west of her intended course, stranded on the outer bar some five hundred yards from shore. The time was 4:50 a.m. Only ten minutes later a surfman noticed the plight of the barkentine and ran to the station to raise the alarm. The life-saving crew was galvanized to action. They dragged the beach apparatus into the dark and along the dunes to a point opposite the stranded windjammer. Keeper Andrew Longstreet reported that "the sea was high and the wind was blowing heavily from the south-southwest, with very thick weather by spells. A bad cut of the tide - the worst I ever saw - was running north."

The life-savers set up the Lyle gun (a line-throwing gun). The first and second shots fell short. "In both of these instances the wind prevented the line from carrying to the vessel." The rising tide was gradually working the *Antioch* toward shore. The third line fell across the barkentine's deck. Eager hands secured the whip to the donkey engine, but before the hawser could be pulled aboard, "the shot line parted from the heavy strain put upon it by current and seas. On the fourth discharge of the gun the projectile struck the sheer pole of the vessel, cutting it off. The crew got the line, nevertheless.

"About this time the crew from the Spring Lake Station appeared, and, my force being increased, I sent to my station for the practice gear. When it arrived I bent the practice whip line on the whip line already in use, so as to pay out as the current forced the line down the beach. The ship's crew hauled the tailblock on board and made it fast. They were then given the hawser, with another hawser bent on, as in the case of the whip line. This work could not have been accomplished with one hawser, for it would have been impossible to hold the shore end against the current. Tide and wind were steadily increasing, and in order to forward the work a team of horses was employed to haul the hawser tight.

"At 9:30 a.m. the first man was landed. Everything worked smoothly until the third man left the vessel, when the hawser parted from chafing against the ship's wire rigging. Fortunately the man managed to stay in the buoy while we dragged it ashore. Following the breaking of the hawser someone on board cut the whip line in two in the mistaken belief that it would enable us more readily to haul the sailor out of the water."

Omitted from Longstreet's matter-of-fact account were many graphic details of the rescue operation. This bare narrative style was a trademark of the majority of Life-Saving Service reports. In this instance, however, newspaper reporters, who were accustomed to describing events in somewhat purple prose, may not have needed to resort to exaggeration in order to sell copy. In fact, their depiction of events may have gone a long way toward providing a balance for Longstreet's strictly factual and self-effacing report. Furthermore, newspaper articles provided a broader perspective to the narrative by relating concurrent activities on shore.

According to the *Asbury Park Evening Press*, "In the heavy fog she narrowly missed, about 3 o'clock, a south bound steamer. Shortly after that she fouled in a fishing pond, and then, out of control, swung entirely around and drifted in upon the beach. She struck at 4.30 and a few minutes later a distress rocket was fired. . . . Seas were running high and wild and a gale was howling from the southeast. . . . Giant waves were washing the decks and it was only with the greatest difficulty and at great hazard that First Mate [Harry] Anderson made the line and pulled aboard the heavy hauser [sic] on which the breeches buoy was run out. Then came the made scramble among the colored men to be first in the chair." The Life-Saving Service report made no racial distinctions, but the newspaper noted - blandly and without discrimination - the same way it would report nationality or sex, that "the three who were saved this morning were negroes." The newspaper also noted that the last person to reach shore had been dragged through the pounding surf for a quarter of a mile, arriving on the beach unconscious, and was revived without much difficulty.

Asbury Park Evening Press: "At 2 o'clock, when the line was got out the second time there were fully 1,000 people on the beach. Rain was pouring down as if the flood gate of heaven had opened and it seemed as if the shipwrecks men would be literally washed from the rigging. The ship was then working shoreward and to the north and the tide was going down. Anderson said they were so desperate after the breaking of the breeches buoy line this morning that they probably would have taken their chances in a life boat had there been one. The ship's boats, however, were washed away soon after the vessel struck this morning, all but one, a small gig which would have held but four men and in which it was certain suicide to venture from the ship."

The Squan Beach Station had no more shot line, so Keeper Longstreet sent to the Spring Lake Station for "one of suitable size; also for an extra hawser and whip line." While some of his men were absent on this errand, the remainder tried to re-establish contact with the *Antioch*. The next line "parted 3 fathoms from the shank of the projectile. I tried it again and the line broke off in the eye of the shank."

The life-saving crews from the Bay Head and Mantoloking stations lent assistance. After the men returned with more line a successful shot was made. Longstreet: "We now landed 5 men in a thunderstorm. When the last of the five

Reaching the wreck in calm weather. (From the author's collection.)

was about two-thirds of the way in the hawser parted again, due to the cause previously mentioned, letting the occupant of the buoy down into the surf. He was hauled out, however, as his shipmate had been. Luckily the two men still on the wreck kept their hands off the whip, and we were able once more to haul the hawser on board without having to do our work all over."

Now the only two men left on board were "Captain David Morrell and one negro of the crew." It eventuated that the "negro" was in fact a dark-complected native Hawaiian. Both men took to the rigging to await the re-establishment of the breeches buoy. They were soaking wet and suffering horribly from exposure to the cold, west wind. First the Hawaiian and then the captain were pulled ashore. They "were taken to the life saving station, where Druggist Edward Sweeting administered a brandy rubdown to both and they were put to bed."

The following day, the Asbury Park Evening Press noted that "the captain's story of the disaster coincided with that of the other rescued men as told in yesterday's Press with the exception that he stated that he knew the boat was destined to meet with trouble when they left Savannah because every rat on board had taken to land before she sailed."

Keeper Longstreet concluded his report thus: "We returned to the station at 5.30 p.m., having spent 12 hours on the beach. In all my 29 years' experience as a life-saver I never worked under such discouraging conditions as surrounded this case."

Every man was saved, but not so the barkentine. By the next day the seas had calmed down enough to permit Captain Morrell to return to his erstwhile command by boat in order to survey the damage. He found the *Antioch* broken in two amidships. With no hope of saving the vessel intact, salvage operations commenced the following day. William Blodgett and Harry Height "arranged with John S. Emery, owner of the ill-fated Antioch, to dismantle and dispose of the wreck and her cargo on a 50 per cent basis." On March 29, "men employed by Blodgett and Height dynamited the deck in an effort to get at the cargo of timber more readily."

It was reported that "thousands of autoists and others visited the scene of the wrecking of the barkentine *Antioch*. . . . The forward hull of the barkentine is firmly embedded in the sand, but the stern is free, permitting the vessel to swing with the wave."

Captain Morrell oversaw the salvage operations. He remained a guest of the Squan Beach Life-Saving Station until the job of dismantling the *Antioch* was complete. The vessel was estimated to be worth $12,000, the cargo $5,500. The total value saved was $2,750.

Researchers should note that the Lloyd's Register of Ships lists the *Antioch* as a bark, while Life-Saving Service reports and newspaper accounts called her a barkentine. The *New York Times* claimed that the *Antioch's* cargo was railroad timbers.

Divers and anglers should note that the remains of the *Antioch* was completely covered with sand as a result of New Jersey's Beach Replenishment Project. But who knows how much wreckage the next northeaster might expose?

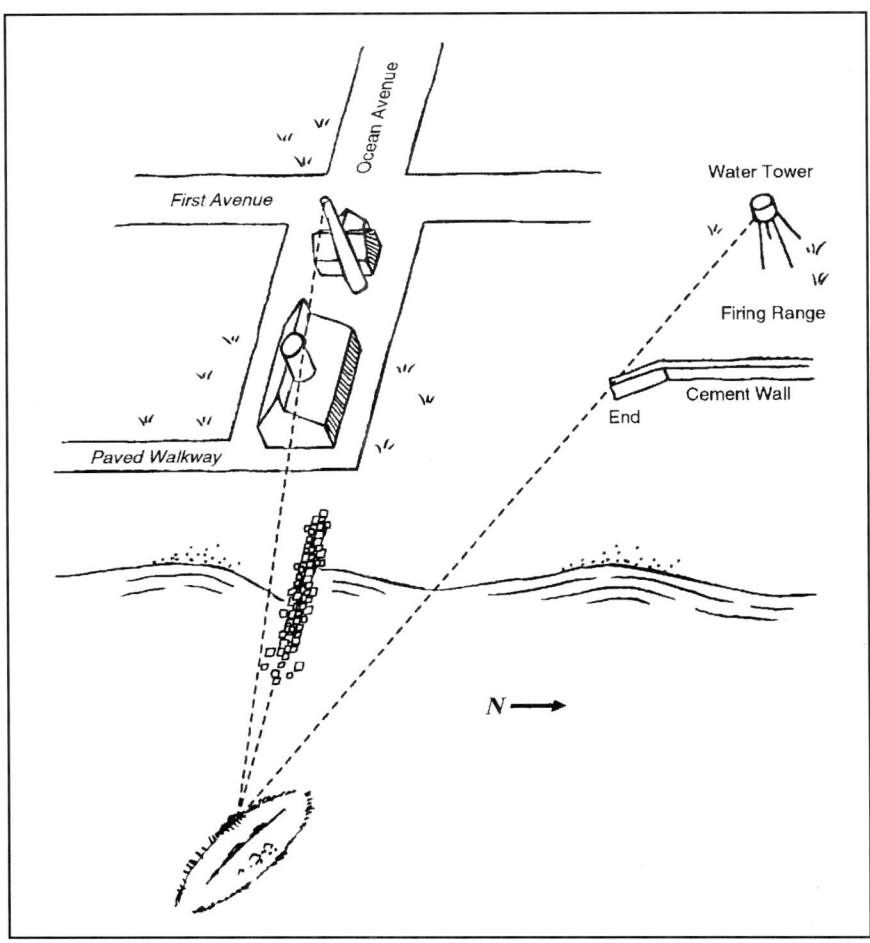

The center of the wreck lies roughly off the tip of the jetty. Swim east from shore along either side of the jetty. Align the standpipe of the westernmost building with the raised roof of the bathroom building (the easternmost building). When the south end of the firing range wall is aligned with the water tower, you will be directly above the wreck.

This photograph was taken only days before the *Arundo* departed on her final voyage. Notice the locomotives on the after deck. (Official U.S. Coast Guard photo.)

ARUNDO

Built: 1930   Sunk: April 28, 1942

Previous names: *Petersfield, Cromarty*   Depth: 130 feet

Gross tonnage: 5,163   Dimensions: 412' x 55' x 26'

Type of vessel: Freighter   Power: Coal-fired steam

Builder: Northumberland Ship Building Company, Newcastle, England

Owner: N.V. Maats, Zeevaart

Port of registry: Rotterdam, Holland

Cause of sinking: Torpedoed by *U-136* (Kapitanleutnant Zimmermann)

Location: 26792.4   43515.1

By spring of 1942, the U-boat war along the U.S. eastern seaboard was in full swing. American troops were headed for both theaters, and military cargoes left New York on a regular basis. In the *Arundo's* holds, the cargo bound for Alexandria, Egypt via Capetown, Africa was comprised of such delectables as 2,000 cases of evaporated milk, 7,000 cases of canned herring in tomato sauce, 4,500 drums of lubricating oil, 55,000 bags of nitrate of soda, 123 3-ton GMC trucks, and, as deck load, a pair of 2-8-2 coal-fired steam locomotives and their tenders. Oh, and 5,000 cases of beer.

Captain A.C. Trdelman, the *Arundo's* Dutch master, had already lost one ship to enemy action, when she was bombed in European waters. But everything seemed bright and cheery this fine spring morning: "the weather was clear, sea calm with slight swells, wind, little or none, visibility excellent." From the bridge Trdelman noted two tankers and a U.S. destroyer four miles to the south, and two other merchantmen close to the horizon. He must have felt like a fish in the middle of the school - safety in numbers.

For a freighter and non-combatant, the *Arundo* was armed to the teeth: a 4-inch gun mounted on the after deck, two 20-mm antiaircraft guns, two twin Marlins, and two 30-caliber Hotchkiss guns.

At 9:30 a.m., only four hours out of port, Chief Officer Akkerman and Third

Officer Van Rhee spotted the wake of a torpedo. Instantly, a tremendous explosion tore out the starboard hull just under the bridge. The violent concussion shook the ship and a column of water shot up into the air. "The hull at #2 hold was extensively damaged, the hatch covers in #2 hold were blown off, #1 lifeboat destroyed, and the radio equipment damaged. The only hold known to have flooded was #2. No fires were started."

The U-boat was not seen, and there was no time for the gunners to man their weapons. The *Arundo* took an immediate starboard list. It took only five minutes for the vessel to tilt to 90 degrees. Then she plunged bow first beneath the waves.

The scrambling crew launched three lifeboats and two rafts. One of the lifeboats was pulled under as the ship sank; the other two were damaged. Most of the men ended up donning life belts and leaping into the frigid water. Of the crew of forty-three, six were lost: "Two individuals, a trimmer and a fireman, were not seen subsequent to the attack, and the other four men may have lost their lives either in the lifeboats that were faultily launched or because one of the locomotives, which were a part of the deck load, tipped into the water among the swimming survivors."

The men spent two hours floating aimlessly about until the destroyer USS *Lea* picked them up. All the officers agreed that "the installation of a convoy system was necessary to protect merchant shipping along the East Coast of the United States."

Notice the square survival rafts stowed on angled launching platforms for immediate deployment. (Official U.S. Coast Guard photo.)

Boats from the Shark River and Manasquan lifeboat stations were dispatched to search for survivors. They found "some wreckage, lifeboats and liferafts. Searched waters, picked up body identified as ship's cook. Picked up inflated tire, found capsized lifeboat, attempted to tow it in, but cast it loose. It was later towed in the CG 4344 from Manasquan Light Station." No other bodies were found.

No salvage was attempted. The wreck was marked with a buoy until it was demolished, and cleared to a least depth of 63 feet. During a 1950 survey, the wreck was again wire-dragged, this time to 72 feet.

Because of its huge size, the *Arundo* is one of the most fascinating wrecks to explore. Although the hull has been blown apart, huge sections remain intact. In several places, sections of the superstructure sit on slightly tilted angles, their rooms readily accessible but not complicated enough to be dangerous. Truck chassis are strewn about, as are axles and differentials; the metal bodies have long since rusted away. Rubber tires lie strewn about the wrckage. Clear glass one-quart beer bottles abound by the thousands. Miscellaneous brass parts lie scattered throughout the jumbled debris.

The remains of the locomotives can be found in the sand on the starboard side, about fifty to one hundred feet forward of the propeller. They lie on their sides and are difficult to recognize because the cabs are gone and the external metal components have long since turned into rust. Essentially, what you can expect to see are just the long, narrow boilers, with the train of wheels.

Interestingly, when the ship's bell was recovered by John Dudas, George Hoffman, and Mike de Camp, the name cast in bronze was *Petersfield*, the *Arundo's* christened name.

Fish practically blanket the wreck, and the convolutions of broken hull plates offer almost infinite hiding places for lobsters. Hardly anyone comes back from the wreck empty handed. There is always something to bring up.

The *U-136* survived only another couple of months. On its next war patrol, while operating off the west coast of Spain against a Gibraltar-bound convoy, it was sunk by the HMS *Spey*, the HMS *Pelican*, and the RF *Leopard*. There were no survivors.

Yellow sponge, sea raven, and ling.

This photograph was taken early in the war, prior to the emplacement of the stern deck gun and emergency life rafts. (Official U.S. Coast Guard photo.)

AYURUOCA

Built: 1912

Previous names: *Roland*

Gross tonnage: 6,872

Type of vessel: Freighter

Builder: Akt. Ges. "Weser," Bremen, Germany

Owner: Lloyd Brasileiro, Rio de Janeiro, Brazil

Port of registry: Rio de Janeiro, Brazil

Cause of sinking: Collision with MV *General Fleischer*

Location: 26814.8

Sunk: June 10, 1945

Depth: 170 feet

Dimensions: 468' x 58' x 29'

Power: Coal-fired steam

43547.2

Despite the large size of the vessel and the expensive cargo of lend-lease supplies, the *Ayuruoca* received scant notice when she went down. Then she lay dormant for decades. The amount of fishing on the wreck was evident when I first starting diving it (in the early 1970's): monofilament draped over the hull and superstructure like thick spider webs. Because the intact hull and midship superstructure rises so far off the bottom, the wreck has long been a high profile reef which is excellent for attracting pelagic game fish.

According to the cargo manifest, the *Ayuruoca* left New York for Brazil with general merchandise in her holds: tea, cement, newsprint, tools, machines, assorted metal products, and (divers take note) a case of compasses. In addition, four tow trucks were lashed to the upper deck immediately in front of the wheel house, and two more were tied down near the stern, just forward of the after mast and dog houses.

The *Ayuruoca* was still in the harbor approaches, some fifteen miles south of Ambrose Light, in a dense fog at night, when the 5,138-ton Norwegian motor vessel *General Fleischer* ran her down and cut her in two.

During the half hour that the ship stayed afloat, the sixty-six man crew got into lifeboats and were picked up by the U.S. Navy sub chaser *SC-1057*. When a head count was taken later, one man was reported missing. The Norwegian merchantman, inbound from Europe and in ballast, was holed above the waterline and not in danger of sinking. She proceeded into New York harbor under her own power.

Two days later a lighted buoy was established over the wreck. It was painted red and black in horizontal bands, showing an *interrupted quick flashing red* light of 40 candlepower, and stood 13 feet above the water. The italicized words were printed that way in the Notice to Mariners, along with the latitude and longitude, and the advice that "vessels are cautioned to stand well clear of this buoy," likely because the masts stood close to the surface and presented a hazard to navigation. Today the masts are broken off above crow's-nests, probably because the wreck was wire-dragged in order to reduce the height of its profile.

Despite the buoyed position and the wreck's established identity, the site was placed on the Navy Wreck List as an unknown.

The *Ayuruoca* is one of the most intact and exciting wrecks off the Jersey coast. The depth keeps most divers away, and the commonly poor visibility turns off many who pay the wreck a visit. Because it lies in the Mud Hole, floating sediment can reduce visibility to only a few feet, sometimes less than arm's reach. Once, when I was still on the surface above the wreck, I could not see my own knees. Even when the water is clear, so much light may be absorbed by particulate matter and suspended silt that the bottom has the appearance of a night dive. Along with the profusion of high-strength monofilament, any dive can be potentially dangerous. It is what I call a "two knife" wreck. In the 1970's I used to

This aerial photo was taken later in the war, probably from a patrolling blimp. Notice that the lifeboats are swung out, ready to be lowered in an emergency. The square life rafts lying on the angled platforms rest on chocks which are secured by means of pins that can be knocked out in an instant, allowing the rafts to float off by themselves. (Courtesy of the National Archives.)

swim along the decks with a sharp knife in my hand, slashing as I propelled myself along, much as if I were wielding a machete through a South American jungle. The situation is not as bad today because generations of divers have cut away much of the fishing line, but hooks continue to snag the wreck and monofilament keeps accumulating. Divers should take extreme precautions.

The wreck is broken into nearly equal lengths abaft the wheel house. Both sections sit upright about one hundred feet apart. In the early 1970's, because we usually grappled into the bridge, we had a rope stretched between the two sections from one high point to the other. Without the rope, it is possible to locate the stern from the bridge by

dropping to the muddy bottom at 170 feet and swimming at a slight angle to port or north northeast, but I don't suggest you try it without tying a wreck-reel line at your point of departure. Better to grapnel each section separately.

On the forward section, the upper bridge level, which was made of wood, is gone: apparently swept away by a trawler net, which still partly shrouds the starboard side of the bridge. The teredo eaten decking is still in place, as are the steel railings. The depth of the uppermost deck is 110 feet. A staircase leads down the port side to the next level ten feet lower, and here one can enter a large compartment and paw through the debris for artifacts. The next two levels are similar. They each have a door at either side. The rear panels are partially or largely collapsed, and the glass ports have been removed. Many small items can be scooped up out of the muck that covers the interior decking. The remains of a radio set can be seen, complete with vacuum tubes, as well as a porcelain bathtub.

At the main deck level, at 140 feet, one can see where the ship was sliced in two immediately abaft the bridge. On the port side are two rooms; the after room is partially crushed from the rear as a result of the collision.

Directly in front of the midship superstructure sit two tow trucks, each complete with rubber tires, a steering wheel, and winch assembly. Forward of the trucks gape the open hatches of one of the cargo holds. Beyond the mast sit two more trucks and more open cargo holds. Forward of the next mast looms the forecastle with its rooms still intact, and above it the anchor machinery laid out perfectly.

On the stern section, the midship rooms can be entered with ease from the break. Working aft, one can pass over top of these rooms, then duck inside where the casemate drops to the deck level. At this point the depth is 150 feet. By swimming aft, one passes two open cargo holds, another pair of tow trucks, and two dog houses whose doors face each other inboard, creating a roofless corridor.

At the fantail, a deck gun is mounted on a raised pedestal, the barrel slightly elevated and pointing aft. Under the gun platform is the auxiliary steering station: originally consisting of two wooden wheels which were five and a half feet in diameter. Only the after helm now remains, as John Chatterton and John Yurga removed the forward helm in 1993. They cut through the shaft with a Broco torch.

In the 1970's, visibility was generally from bad to horrendous. One time, the grapnel fell through an open hatch, and several divers found themselves swimming around in the holds without knowing it. They barely escaped with their lives. On the other hand, there were days when the visibility was good, and exceptionally rare days on which the visibility was excellent. On one occasion I had fifty feet of ambient light on the main deck.

Nowadays, visibility averages ten to twenty feet. Truly bad visibility is seldom seen (a contradiction in terms, but you know what I mean). This increase in visibility is the result of strict - and strictly enforced - environmental laws which prohibit the dumping of pollutants, raw sewage, and industrial waste into the Hudson River, which place restrictions on the cleaning of bilges in New York harbor, and which disallow the dumping of trash in the harbor approaches. Modern environmental awareness has done a great deal to clarify the water. Once seen in bright natural light, the wreck earns the awe and respect which it so justly deserves.

In the 1960's, Mike de Camp, George Hoffman, and Walt Krumbeck recovered a wooden thingamajig from the wheel house. The object was nearly the size of a phone booth. They believed (or hoped) it was the captain's desk. When the mysterious object was lifted out of the water, it "smelled to high heaven," according to de Camp. It stank so bad, in fact, that boat captain Joe Galluccio would not let them bring it aboard. He cut it free from the winch and let it drop back into the sea. The "desk" turned out to be a water closet!

The *Ayuruoca* is popularly called the Oil Wreck. The name is a holdover from the 1960's, before the wreck was identified by Mike de Camp. At that time,

fuel oil leaked prodigiously from the *Ayuruoca's* deep tanks. The nickname has stuck, probably because it is easier to pronounce than the wreck's real name. The leakage of oil has diminished with the passage of time - and with the passage of oil from the bunkers - but when the ocean is flat a slick may still be observed on the "oily" calm surface above the wreck.

BALAENA

Type of vessel: Wooden-hulled three-masted sailing ship   Depth: 170 feet
Location: 26799.8   43521.8

The only fact known about this nearly intact sailing vessel is the name. And even that is somewhat of a presumption.

During one of the initial explorations of the wreck in the late 1960's, Joel Entler found the ship's bell where it had fallen from the mast. He put the bell in his mesh bag but, because he was near the end of his dive, he had neither enough time or air to secure and inflate a liftbag. After decompressing, he climbed onto the boat and told his buddies about his find and the condition in which he left it.

A moment later, George Hoffman splashed into the water. He followed Entler's directions, located the bell, secured a liftbag to Entler's goodie bag, and sent the precious item to the surface. The name cast in bronze read "Balaena."

The unfortunate continuation of this story is that after Hoffman removed the bell from the bag, he handed the bag to Entler and announced that he was keeping the bell for himself. This incident occurred at a time before any respectable code of ethics existed in the wreck-diving community. Hoffman believed in the "Law of G. Magnus," a law that he devised for his own benefit. He claimed that his middle name was Magnus. The Law of G. Magnus was simplistically defined in Hoffman's own words: "He who floats it, owns it." By this he meant that no matter who discovered an artifact, no matter how much effort the finder put into working on it, no matter how close the finder was to recovering it, the artifact could ultimately be taken away by an opportunistic diver who lurked in the background waiting to dispossess the finder of his hard-earned efforts by sending the artifact to the surface and claiming ownership.

In the march toward civilized behavior, the time of such self-serving mentality has passed. Today, a higher code of ethics prevails, although code breakers with aberrant behavior exist.

A shipwreck researcher rejoices when the name of a sunken ship is discovered. The name is usually the starting point for successfully tracing a ship's history. Such was not the case with the *Balaena*. Tracking the ship through the registers has proved enormously frustrating. "Balaena" is a common name in Norway, in whose language the word means "whale." John Leavitt, assistant curator of the Mystic Seaport Marine Historical Society, found four vessels named *Balaena* in various ship registers. None of the vessels seem to fit the bill for the wreck in question.

"In 1872, a bark rigged steam auxiliary whaler was built in Draman, Norway, under the name of *Mjolner* and was later sold to England and her name changed to *Balaena*. She was in service until the outbreak of the second war.

Another steam auxiliary bark by that name was built at San Francisco in 1882 but she was lost in the Pacific about 1900. The last one was a huge steam whaler of 15,760 ton, 539.7' long built by Harland & Wolff Ltd. in 1846. I am sure she would have had no three-masted rig."

Leavitt's most likely choice was "a wooden whaling bark by that name built at New Bedford in 1818 and was owned in New Bedford and Sag Harbor until 1872 when she disappears from the registers." This information is inconclusive, for "disappearing from the registers" can mean a number of things. The vessel's name may have been changed, in which case she may have been listed elsewhere in the register under her new name. (In the early registers, name changes were not noted, although previous names, if any, were listed.) The only way to track down the vessel's new name in the early registers is to read the entire register in order to determine if any vessels were noted as having once been named *Balaena*. Since tens of thousands of vessels were registered in any one year, looking for such a tiny bit of information would be an onerous task.

Furthermore, "disappearing from the registers" could mean that the vessel was scrapped or scuttled, not sunk accidentally. Then again, the bell might have been taken off another vessel and hung on the "Balaena" in order to comply with maritime regulations, in which case the wreck in question might not be the *Balaena* at all.

The wreck sits upright with the bases of the masts in place. The hull is partially intact, and the holds are full of coal. Large deadeyes are found around the wreck, indicating that the ship was still under sail at the time of her loss. (Generally, ex-windjammers that were placed in service as barges were dismasted and their rigging was removed.)

No steam machinery exists within the hull of the wreck. Nor is it possible to determine how the vessel was rigged - whether the masts were square-rigged or fore-and-aft rigged. The question of rigging leaves doubt as to what kind of vessel the *Balaena* was originally: ship (square-rigged), schooner (fore-and-aft rigged), or bark, barkentine, brig, or brigantine (all of whose rigging consisted of various combinations of square-rigging and fore-and-aft rigging).

Ships are given a registration number during construction. The registration number on wooden-hulled sailing ships was cut into a deck beam, generally one that served as a cross-thwart timber of a hatch. The number generally faces aft, so that one would see it when looking toward the vessel's bow. Ships sunk in fresh water may sometimes be identified by finding the relevant timber. But in the ocean environment, wood is attacked by teredoes (wood-boring mollusks) and wood-reducing bacteria, so that if the bulk of the timber remained after a century under water, the number might be illegible.

The *Balaena* requires more investigation.

BRUNETTE

Built: 1867   Sunk: February 1, 1870
Previous names: None   Depth: 75 feet
Gross tonnage: 274   Dimensions: 133' x 23' x 14'
Type of vessel: Iron-hulled coastal freighter   Power: Steam engine
Builder: Pusey & Jones Yards, Christiana River, Wilmington, Delaware
Owner: Jacob Lorillard, Jr. (Lorillard Line)
Port of registry: New York, NY
Cause of sinking: Collision with SS *Santiago de Cuba*
Location: 26916.4   43476.0

When divers first started working this snag, comprising little more than a winch, a pair of boilers, a small steam engine, and a propeller shaft with an iron prop, it yielded vast quantities of porcelain doorknobs, some brown and some white, each with a round white porcelain escutcheon plate. For that reason it became known as the Doorknob Wreck.

As the sand shifted and exposed other artifacts, divers began digging and recovering such relics as Norwalk locks and keys, oil lamp parts, pewter flatware, yardsticks, ax heads and handles, mother-of-pearl shells, and intricate folding rules. When crates were found buried in the sand, crowbars quickly opened the wooden lids. One crate contained double-pan balance-beam scales with brass weights.

Divers soon found artifacts that helped with the wreck's eventual identification. A bronze bilge pump was stamped "Pusey, Jones, & Sons, Wilm. Del". Brass valves were brought up bearing the seals of "Cooper, Jones & Cadbury, pat. Sept 11, 1866, Phila." and "A.W. Metcalf, NY". Obviously the ship was of American construction.

The ship's time span was narrowed down when Trueman Seamans brought up a case of Missisquoi Spring bottles which were still corked and full. After he brought the bottles home, his wife Nike looked up Missisquoi in the family atlas and found that it was the name of a town in Vermont, situated on the bank of the Missisquoi River. By researching the Vermont manufacturer, Trueman ascertained that the company ceased bottling spring water in 1870.

Additionally, Jon Hulburt recovered a door latch with a patent date of March 29, 1869. The Seamans and the Hulburts took this accumulated information to the National Archives to corroborate it with official records. The Hulburts poured through the records of the Steamboat Inspection Service for the two-year period. It was Jon's wife Judy who came across an entry for the *Brunette*, which sank off Squam Beach, New Jersey. (The "m" in Squam was later corrupted to "n", and Squam became known as Squan. Manasquan is the latest derivative.) Coincidentally, the Hulburts lived in Wilmington, close to where the *Brunette* initially slipped down the ways.

Taking a different tack independent of the Seamans and Hulburts, Joe Milligan scanned the *Encyclopedia of American Shipwrecks*, by Bruce D. Berman, looking for casualties that fit the location. He found the *Brunette* listed as a steel-hulled vessel lost off Squan, New Jersey. He then went to the newspapers of the day and found articles describing the calamity.

The February 3, 1870 edition of the *New York Tribune* gave a concise account of the collision and sinking under the headline "The Steamer *Brunette* Run Down by the Steamer *Santiago de Cuba*--Two Lives Lost."

"On Tuesday afternoon at 6 o'clock the steamer *Brunette*, Capt. Doane, left the Lorillard Steamship Dock, bound to Philadelphia. She was laden with an assorted cargo, and about three-quarters full. Including officers, there were thirteen souls on board. Nothing of interest occurred until about 20 minutes past 10, when a steamer was noticed bearing down for the *Brunette*. She proved to be the *Santiago de Cuba*, Capt. Jones, bound from Havre, France, to this port, going at the rate of about six knots an hour, and having on board a cargo not exceeding 600 tons. The statements respecting the immediate cause of the collision, which took place about 10 1/2 o'clock, are conflicting, but it seems the *Brunette* attempted to cross the bows of the *Santiago de Cuba* and, failing to do so in time, the two vessels collided, and the former sank in less than ten minutes. The disaster occurred off Squam Beach, but a little distance off shore. The *Santiago de Cuba* had crossed the Atlantic Ocean by the southern route and fell in with the land to the southward, working her way up along the beach, while the *Brunette* was taking the inshore route going down.

"Every effort was made on board of both vessels to avoid the disaster by reversing the engines, but the orders were given too late, and the *Santiago de Cuba* struck the *Brunette* a terrific blow in the port broadside, completely crushing her in and keeling her over to starboard. Stout as the *Santiago de Cuba* is, she trembled from stem to stern with the concussion, while the *Brunette* splintered with the thrust like match sticks. Within a minute four of the *Brunette's* people clambered over the bows of the *Cuba*, and were safe. In another minute both crews busied themselves in lowering each a boat. Seven of the crew of the *Brunette* entered their boat, and with the boat of the *Santiago de Cuba* they went in search of any who might be in the water, as all hands left in such a hurry that it was not known at the time who really were missing. Scarce had the boats been launched when the *Brunette* went down. Nearly an hour was spent in pulling around listening for distress hailings, but at the end of that time the boats were hoisted on board of the *Santiago de Cuba*, and she headed for New York. On mustering the crew of the *Brunette*, it was found that George A. Coleman and James McCarthy, one a seaman and the other a fireman, had perished.

"Soon after the collision occurred the pumps of the *Santiago de Cuba* were sounded, and it was found that she was leaking. The donkey was set to work and full speed given to her. She arrived yesterday morning, and made fast to the dock of the Liverpool and Great Western Steamship Pier. Most of the crew of the *Brunette* are Philadelphians, and they left for that town last night."

Two photographs of the same bottle. In the photo at left, the embossing is clearly legible but the glass appears black because of the dark background and the contents in the bottle. In the photo at right, I am holding the bottle against the sun so that the true green color of the glass becomes apparent.

The *Brunette* was a screw steamer, the *Santiago de Cuba* a paddle wheel steamer. The merchandise on the *Brunette* was consigned to John F. Ohl, and was reportedly insured.

The Steamboat Inspection Service duly investigated the case, "but the testimony was so conflicting that it was impossible to decide who was at fault. We are, however, of the opinion that the accident was caused by an error of judgment on the part of both masters."

More than a century later, the *Brunette* was the cause of another collision at sea.

On the morning of January 26, 1980, the *Sea Lion* grappled into the wreck of the *Brunette* in order to let divers explore the site. Captain George Hoffman raised the diver's flag to alert all traffic that divers were in the water and that the boat could not maneuver. A couple of hours later, after some of the divers had returned from their first dive and were waiting out their surface interval before making a second dive, Hoffman entered the water. While he was on the bottom a tugboat appeared on the horizon towing a string of two barges, one behind the other. Both barges were carrying construction equipment.

The tugboat *Margaret G.* passed the *Sea Lion* at a distance of more than one hundred feet - the safe distance required by the Rules of the Road. But due to the howling west wind and the current, the barges did not follow directly in line with the tug's direction of travel. Instead, the barges were being towed at an angle to the direction of travel, like a pair of cork balls tied to the end of a string in a wind storm - and the barges were being swept unerringly toward the *Sea Lion*. Those aboard the dive boat recognized the imminent peril. Observers who stood outside on the deck of the *Sea Lion* shouted for those who were keeping warm in the cabin to get out.

The first barge passed barely fifty feet away, casting a shadow over divers who were decompressing on the anchor line. The thrumming of the tug's diesel engine was clearly audible to divers in the water, because water propagates sound waves faster than air. No one topside could doubt the proximity of the second barge in tow, or that collision was inevitable. Joe Milligan, who was standing next to the starboard rail, added his voice to the general tumult by shouting a warning to those in the cabin below. Mike Boring had just returned from his dive and was leaning against the starboard side. He shrugged out of his tanks, doffed his mask and fins, and was sitting halfway on the rail when he heard the shouts of alarm. The cabin was in the way so he could not see the oncoming barge. He paid scant attention to the excitement because he was still reminiscing to himself about the dive.

The second barge then struck a glancing blow against the *Sea Lion's* port bow. The force of the collision drove in the railing and splintered the planks at the gunwale and in the hull above the waterline. The Seamans' cooler full of beer was also stove in. Several people were knocked off their feet when the *Sea Lion* rolled and was bumped aside. Milligan was thrown off the dive boat's deck into the water; fortunately he was wearing his drysuit at the time. The jolt caused Boring to lose his balance. He toppled over the rail and hit the sea with a splash, still wearing his lead weight belt! There was hardly any air in his drysuit. He ditched the weight belt before the lead dragged him under the surface. Both he and Milligan eventually reached the ladder and managed to climb back onto the boat.

The moving barge continued to exert pressure against the *Sea Lion*. Being tethered to the wreck, the dive boat was pushed aside like a weight at the end of a pendulum. To the people on board it seemed as if the *Sea Lion* might go down. Nike Seamans was particularly concerned because she was bubble watching that day and did not have her drysuit.

The situation under water was every bit as perilous. Trueman Seamans was decompressing at the time of the collision, as was Jon Hulburt, who ascended the anchor line shortly after Seamans and who was decompressing below him. Several events occurred simultaneously. According to Hulburt, the anchor line got taut and his liftbag, which was floating nearby with a recovered deck plank, disappeared. He was irritated because he believed that several people must have been jerking the anchor line. As a precaution, he started to descend backward while looking up at the *Sea Lion*. A shadow approached very fast from the port side of the boat. Hulburt then saw a dark hull form heading straight for Seamans. Hulburt was conscious of the fact that the hull form made no sound. He sped down the anchor line, but traveled only a few feet before the line began dragging him sideways at high speed. After what seemed like ten seconds but was probably less, the line became slack. Hulburt considered this "as more evidence that a UFO had gulped the *Sea Lion*."

Seamans recalled that the water went pitch black, then got light again. The anchor line started pulling them down at a 45° angle: the result of the awful sheer force that was exerted against the anchor line as it was dragged through the water because of the barge's forward motion against the dive boat's hull. Seamans could not clear his ears so he let go of the anchor line. Hulburt hung on to the anchor line and pulled himself down like a descending rocket. Seamans then followed Hulburt's bubbles down at a pace that was established by the clearing of his ears. He caught up with Hulburt on the bottom near the wreck. (Hulburt thinks that Seamans caught up with him at 30 or 40 feet, not on the bottom.)

On the *Sea Lion*, Chuck Wine cut the anchor line with a knife. This relieved the stress against the boat. No longer tethered to the wreck, the Sea Lion was then pushed out of the way of the barge. John Moyer checked the bow and determined that all the damage occurred above the waterline. Carl Fenton, mate for the day, radioed the Coast Guard.

On the wreck, Hulburt and Seamans held on to the running portion of the severed anchor line, which was still secured to the wreck. They re-ascended within minutes and completed their decompression by maintaining positive buoyancy and keeping the anchor line taut. While decompressing, they pulled in the rope until they reached the frayed end. Hulburt then tied his sisal upline to the cut end so they would have plenty of scope to enable them to float easily on the surface. In order to lighten his load, Hulburt clipped his eight-pound hammer to the anchor line and let it slide to the bottom, where it struck the wreck with a clang.

By the time they completed their decompression, the *Sea Lion* had drifted a long way off. Although Hulburt spun around twice, he could see nothing but whitecaps and houses on the shore. Then Seamans surfaced. Looking beyond Hulburt he spotted the *Sea Lion* far, far away. A sport fishing boat called the *Hel-Dor* approached them, and the operator yelled for them to climb on board. This was easier shouted than done because the boat possessed no ladder. Worse yet, the boat hove to upwind and kept pressing down on the two hapless divers, pushing them under the surface. Instead of dumping their equipment and attempting to climb over the gunwale, Hulburt and Seamans found themselves drifting directly toward the *Sea Lion*. With some dedicated fin kicking action they eventually caught up with the dive boat.

Meanwhile, George Hoffman, the *Sea Lion's* captain, returned to the spot where the grapnel was hooked to the wreck. He found the anchor line lying limp on the bottom, surmised that it had been severed from his boat, and made a controlled ascent to the surface. The *Sea Lion* was adrift but in no danger of sinking. By the time Hoffman surfaced, the wind and current had swept the *Sea Lion* too far away for him to catch. The *Margaret G.* hove to and dropped anchor. Alerted to the accident, two Coast Guard cutters from the Manasquan station and a marine police launch were dispatched to the scene. Hoffman was taken in tow by a Coast Guard cutter and was trolled all the way to the *Sea Lion*. He swam the last few feet to his boat's ladder, climbed aboard, doffed his dive gear, surveyed the damage, then motored back to the *Brunette*, which was marked by Jon Hulburt's still-floating liftbag. Hoffman sent a diver down to retrieve his anchor line and grapnel, as well as Hulburt's hammer. Hoffman then piloted the boat to the dock under escort.

There were no fatalities or injuries. It was an exciting day for all involved. Hulburt admits that he guzzled the remains of the Seamans' beer until he was too drunk to drive.

The *Brunette* remains an interesting dive because of the artifacts that are continuously being found beneath the ever-shifting sands. The best way to work the wreck is with an airlift, but even fanning the sand with a Ping-Pong paddle or a large clam shell may expose interesting and well-preserved antiques. Only those who seek, will find.

An artist for *Harper's Weekly* drew this picture of the *Santiago de Cuba* when she ran aground on Absecon Beach on May 21, 1867. Absecon Beach is near Atlantic City, and about fifty miles south of where the paddle wheeler collided with the *Brunette* nearly three years later. Six people drowned during rescue operations when their lifeboat capsized in the surf. More than three hundred passengers and crew were saved. The steamer was refloated on a high tide. (This is the same *Santiago de Cuba* which, commissioned as a gunboat during the Civil War, captured the *Ella Warley* (q.v.).)

CATAMOUNT

Built: 1929

Previous names: None

Gross tonnage: 67

Type of vessel: Cutter

Builder: Luders Marine Construction Company, Stamford, Connecticut

Owner: United States Coast Guard

Port of registry: New York, NY

Cause of sinking: Explosion

Location: Possibly in the vicinity of the "HA" Buoy

Sunk: March 27, 1943

Depth: Unknown

Dimensions: 85' x 15' x 7'

Power: Twin 8-cylinder gasoline engines

The *Catamount* was built as a private yacht and was owned by George F. Trommer until the outbreak of World War Two. When the coastal U-boat offensive created a drain on Naval reserves, the U.S. Government commenced acquiring private vessels for conversion to patrol craft. The *Catamount* was bought, armed, and designated *CG-85006*.

Her troubles began shortly after noon on March 26, 1943, when one engine's fuel line clogged. She lay dead in the water for an hour while the line was cleared. The *CG-85006* resumed her patrol throughout the night until 4:04 a.m. on the 27th, when a terrific explosion "blew the bottom out of the ship."

Five men who were topside at the time were blown into the water. Six men sleeping in their bunks below were never seen again. "The vessel itself had likewise completely disappeared, though bits of wreckage floated about on the surface."

The surviving night watch gathered on a large piece of wood, and clung to it throughout the remainder of the night. "Three slipped off into the darkness and drowned, but two remained as morning broke over the sea." At 10 a.m., the U.S. cargo ship *Charles B. Aycock* came upon the wreckage, and effected a rescue. By that time, only Chief Boatswain's Mate Beal was still alive. He and the deceased seaman were taken aboard the freighter.

Due to a Navy directive to maintain radio silence, the incident was not reported until 2 p.m., when the *Charles B. Aycock* arrived at the Sandy Hook Pilot Station. "The CGC *Kimball*, the *SC-683*, a Hall boat, and the blimp *K-3* were dispatched to search the area but no survivors were found, though at 1700 another blimp, the *K-4*, on patrol sighted hatch covers, planks, and papers at the position of the sinking." Searches the next day turned up three more bodies, but six men remained unaccounted for.

During the search, the tanker *Esso Manhattan* was steaming only a few miles away when "a great shock was felt throughout the vessel." The ship split apart, and the captain ordered abandon ship. Upon seeing plumes of smoke from the broken tanker, the *Kimball* suspended her search and rescued every one of the twenty-five gun crew and forty-eight merchant marines. It was fortunate that the *Kimball* happened to be operating nearby, or there may have been a great loss of life among the men of the *Esso Manhattan*. In the event there were no fatalities.

These two incidents, occurring so close together in time and space, indicated the presence of U-boats. The two explosions were interpreted as possible evidence of either torpedo action or enemy mine laying. Accordingly, the port of New York was closed.

However, "investigation established the fact that the Coast Guard Reserve vessel had in all probability been blown up by an internal explosion, caused, perhaps, by the engine trouble which had interrupted her patrol of the day before."

The *Esso Manhattan* folded up like a jackknife, her bow touching her stern. The two sections separated then drifted apart. Each section stayed afloat. Surveyors determined that the tanker split apart due to structural weakness, perhaps because the hull was fractured when she grounded on a shoal off Aruba the previous October.

Investigators decided that the sinking of the *CG-85006* and the break-up of the *Esso Manhattan* were coincidental occurrences, each brought about by natural causes instead of enemy action. The U-boat scare was ended as of noon on March 30, and the port of New York was reopened. Both halves of the *Esso Manhattan* were later towed into dry dock and reunited.

The sinking of the *CG-85006* was reported to have occurred "28 miles bearing 130 degrees true from Ambrose," at 40-08 north latitude and 73-23 west longitude. In August 1943, the local Notice to Mariners reported the location as 40-09 and 73-21. In 1951, a U.S. Coast and Geodetic survey corrected the position to 40-08-04 and 73-21-54. Operating in 122 feet of water, the survey vessel's wire-drag hung at 120 feet, but cleared at 118 feet. "The obstruction did not show on the fathometer." Because "the area is frequented by vessels dredging on the bottom for scallops and bottom obstructions may cause them to lose their gear," the field examination officer recommended placing a wreck symbol on the chart as a warning.

Over the years, many people (including this author) have tried to locate and identify the elusive wreck of the *Catamount*. So far none has been successful. The Navy Wreck list, published in 1957 by the Hydrographic Office, gives the *Catamount's* position as 40-08-09 N and 73-21-40 W. A wreck indeed exists at that location. Local skippers call it the "HA" Buoy Wreck, after the navigational buoy moored half a mile to the southeast. How Navy hydrographers made the identification went unrecorded. I suspect the designation of the name was arbitrary - based, perhaps, upon military intelligence and without any research into pre-war marine casualties.

The *Catamount's* hull was constructed of wood. Probably not much remains except the gasoline engines and other metal parts. The "HA" Buoy Wreck consists of a single steam engine, and is more likely to be the remains of the *Coastwise* (q.v.). The location of the *Catamount* is a chimera which will undoubtedly intrigue shipwreck historians for years to come.

Brand new as the *Helga*. (Courtesy of the original owners, J. Lauritzen A/S.)

CHOAPA

Built: 1937

Previous names: *Helga*

Gross tonnage: 1,700

Type of vessel: Freighter

Sunk: September 21, 1944

Depth: 200 feet

Dimensions: 292' x 41' x 16'

Power: Oil-fired steam

Builder: Helsingors Jernsk & Msk., Elsinore, Denmark

Owner: Chilean government (Cia. Sud Americana de Vapores, Managers)

Port of registry: Valparaiso, Chile

Cause of sinking: Collision first with SS *British Harmony*, then with SS *Voco,* and finally with SS *Empire Garrick*

Location: 26863.4   43590.8

In 1944, wartime shipping traffic in the approaches to New York Harbor was intense. Whenever vessels in motion are concentrated in a confined area or along narrow sea lanes, the opportunity for accident is abundant. At that time, harbor traffic routing coordination was further complicated by the convoying of outbound ships as protection against marauding German U-boats, and by the arrival of inbound convoys. Convoying meant the amassing of large numbers of ships. When outbound convoys departed at the same time inbound convoys arrived, the harbor became a place where accidents were bound to happen. It was a mariner's nightmare.

In the present instance, four collisions involving five ships were so interrelated that it took six years of legal proceedings to unravel the complicated chronology of events, to ascribe liability for each collision, to rule on the actions taken subsequent to the collisions, and to apportion damages. The massive amount of live testimony and submitted evidence has left for posterity a comprehensive, detailed record of this multiple mishap: something that is often lacking in accounts of other accidents at sea.

According to the findings of the court, the saga began like this: "On the evening of September 20th, in a dense fog, the *Choapa* was proceeding fully laden into New York as part of a convoy consisting of a port column of seven ships and a starboard column of six. The *Choapa* was maintaining her position as the fifth ship in the port column. The master of the *Choapa* knew that there was a swept channel, marked by mid-channel buoys, in the approaches to New York harbor, but had not received any instructions as to the exact position of the buoys or the compass direction between them. For some time before the collision the *Choapa* proceeded at the convoy speed of 8 knots and followed the courses signalled from time to time by the commodore, maintaining her position in the port column by the bearing of signals of the vessels ahead, astern and to the starboard. Her master could not recall her precise compass heading at the time the vessel with which she subsequently collided was sighted. His recollection was that the *Choapa's* heading lay between 310 and 320 degrees. Visibility was less than 1,000 feet, and the *Choapa* was showing her navigating lights, sounding regulation fog signals and maintaining a proper lookout forward. Suddenly a fog blast was heard off the *Choapa's* starboard bow which seemed to come from a vessel other than one of the convoy units. The *Choapa's* engines were immediately stopped. As soon as the white masthead light of a vessel came into view close off the starboard bow, approximately 900 feet away, the *Choapa's* engines were put full speed astern and her rudder hard astarboard in an effort to avoid collision by a port to port passing. When the loom of the other ship was seen she appeared to be moving across the path of the *Choapa* at an angle of about 45 degrees and was too close to be avoided by the *Choapa's* starboard rudder, whereupon the *Choapa* put her rudder hard aport in order to minimize the contact. By her prompt engine movement the *Choapa's* 8 knot headway had been largely reduced when the collision occurred at 7.53 p.m. The stem of the other vessel, identified at the time as a tanker, struck the starboard side of the *Choapa* abreast of the forward end of No. 4 hold, and struck and demolished the *Choapa's* starboard lifeboat, which was hung outboard as a wartime precaution. The tanker then disappeared along the starboard side off the stern of the *Choapa* into the fog. Following the collision, an investigation by the chief officer and first engineer disclosed that the damage to the *Choapa* was not serious, and the convoy commodore was so advised by wireless. The commodore thereupon instructed the master of the *Choapa* by radio to anchor well clear to starboard and to proceed at his discretion when visibility permitted. Thereafter, at 8.47 p.m., the *Choapa* dropped her anchor in compliance with the commodore's instructions."

It was later determined that the vessel in the other corner was the tanker *British Harmony*, grossing in at 8,452 tons. "The *Harmony*, fully laden and acting under naval orders, took her departure from Gedney buoy in New York harbor at 3.30 p.m. Preceded by a convoy patrol vessel and followed by two merchant ships, she proceeded in single-column formation outbound through the swept channel . . . On account of the dense fog the *Harmony* proceeded at speeds varying between three and five knots and sounded regulation fog signals. Her master, chief officer and helmsman were on the bridge, and a lookout was stationed on the forecastle head. . . . At 6.57 p.m. . . . . the navigation lights of the

Harmony were turned on and her course was altered to 133 degrees true, which was the channel course between buoys E and C. At this time the *Harmony* was maintaining a speed of 3 to 4 knots. . . . At about 7.44 1/2 p.m., upon hearing a fog whistle bearing approximately two points off her port bow, her engines were stopped. They remained stopped until 7.50, at which time a slow ahead order was given for the purpose of maintaining steerageway. That order, however, was countermanded by a full astern order about twenty seconds later when a white light with a green light underneath were observed bearing about four points on the *Harmony's* port bow. The vessel sighted to port continued across the *Harmony's* bow from port to starboard, bringing her starboard side lightly into contact with the *Harmony's* stem at 7.52, the angle of collision being between 80 and 90 degrees. At the time of impact the *Harmony* was 'practically stopped' and starting to go astern. After the initial light impact the colliding vessel proceeded ahead, scrapping her starboard side against the *Harmony's* stem for some distance before disappearing off the *Harmony's* starboard bow. While the two vessels were in contact, estimated to be twenty seconds, the master and chief officer of the *Harmony* observed that the colliding vessel appeared gray with a white funnel, but subsequent efforts to communicate with the vessel and learn her identity were unsuccessful. Thereafter the *Harmony* dispatched an 'S.O.S.' message, giving notice of the collision, and, because the other ship did not appear to be damaged, resumed her outbound course."

I have the distinct impression that the *British Harmony* - as well as other convoy vessels whose testimony was not solicited - maneuvered like a getaway car bucking two lanes of traffic on a crowded interstate highway during a Hollywood high-speed chase scene. With two convoys converging, meshing, and passing through each other, it is astonishing that only a single collision occurred.

Meanwhile, aboard the anchored *Choapa*, "her crew shifted some of the cargo in No. 2 hold and made temporary repairs to the area damaged by the *Harmony*. There was some leakage into the starboard bilge of Nos. 2 and 3 holds through a cracked plate and some displaced rivets, wetting a few bags of sugar which were stowed next to the damaged area, but the leakage was at all times controlled by the *Choapa's* pumps and never rose higher than 18 inches in the three-foot bilge. At about 4.15 a.m. on September 21st, the *Choapa* weighed anchor and proceeded northward for about fifteen minutes, when the dense fog required her to re-anchor. She got under way again at about 10.55 a.m. and, guiding herself by the radio bearing of Ambrose Lightship, moved cautiously in a northerly direction. . . . Because fog signals were heard at this time from what seemed to be an outbound convoy and the visibility was not good" the *Choapa* anchored some "900 to 1200 feet in a sidewise direction to the eastward" of the swept channel.

It is important to keep in mind the meaning of "swept channel": a shipping lane that was swept free of mines, or a cleared path through a defensive mine field whose purpose was to protect the harbor from the encroachment of enemy submarines. In this case, the swept channel was a zigzag course of varying compass headings to which convoy commodores had access, but not the masters of the vessels within the convoy.

The *Choapa's* captain (whose name was not given in any official documents) found himself in a precarious position with difficult decisions to make. He did not want to proceed under the condition of heavy fog, nor drop anchor in the swept channel where his ship would be a menace to navigation. Nor could he afford to stray too far from the swept channel, for that would place his vessel in the mine field.

"The *Choapa* displayed in her forerigging a black ball, the regulation daylight signal for a vessel at anchor, and hoisted two additional 'shapes' above her bridge as an extra precaution. She also began sounding regulation fog bells, both fore and aft, one alternating with the other."

On the fog shrouded afternoon of September 21, Convoy HXF 310 flowed out with the tide and headed for an escorted Atlantic crossing via Halifax, Nova Scotia. One member of the convoy, the SS *Voco*, experienced minor mechanical difficulties which forced her to drop out of formation to let the following vessels pass while repairs were effected. After ten minutes, her engines were restarted and she proceeded along the course that was laid out the previous day at the convoy conference, which was attended all the masters. "Heavy fog having been encountered, the *Voco* was blowing regulation fog signals and trailing a fog-buoy. Her master and second officer were on the bridge, and lookouts were stationed forward, on top of the wheelhouse and at the stern." In compliance with convoy instructions, the *Voco* altered course several times in order to follow the crooked path of the mine-swept channel.

The *Choapa's* convoy, KN 338, had long since entered the harbor safely. At this time, the damaged straggler was still waiting for the fog to disperse before proceeding to New York. A shift in the wind caused the *Choapa* to swing on her anchor chain until unknowingly she lay athwart the swept channel.

"At about 3.00 p.m. the bow of the *Voco* was sighted looming out of the fog and heading approximately at a right angle for the starboard side of the *Choapa*. The *Choapa's* fog bells, which up to the time had been sounded alternately, were then rang continuously, and her master, noticing that the *Voco* was not changing her course, ordered full speed ahead in an effort to pull clear. The *Choapa* succeeded in moving only 70 or 80 feet before the *Voco* crashed into the starboard side at the forward end of No. 4 hold at an angle of nearly 90 degrees. The force of the impact was such that it caused the *Choapa* to roll 15 to 20 degrees to port and broke some steam connections in the engine room, flooding the engine and boiler rooms with live steam and making it impossible for the crew to remain there and keep up steam or operate the pumps. About a minute after the *Voco* collision, and while *Choapa's* fog bells were still being sounded continuously, the *Empire Garrick* loomed out of the fog off the *Choapa's* starboard side, crossed the *Choapa's* bow, and in so doing, sideswiped the stem of the *Choapa* with her port side. Soundings taken of the *Choapa's* after hold a few minutes later disclosed that they contained about four or five feet of water. After learning that the water in these holds was rising rapidly and that the steam from the engine room prevented the crew from operating the pumps in the stern part of the ship, the *Choapa's* master ordered her abandonment. All of her personnel thereupon were transferred safely to the *Voco*, which was standing by. At about 5.00 p.m. the *Choapa* sank stern first."

From the *Voco's* point of view, "The fog lifted somewhat and the *Voco* sighted a ship about a half mile ahead." She maneuvered at various speeds "until 2.50, when she sighted the stern section of the *Choapa* ahead off her port bow at a distance of approximately 1500 feet. When first sighted, the *Choapa* was at a right angle to the course of the *Voco*, showing her starboard side, and appeared to be crossing the channel with some headway on her. The *Voco's* wheel was immediately put hard aport and her engines reduced to slow ahead in an effort to avoid collision by passing under the *Choapa's* stern. About a minute later, however, the *Voco* observed two black balls and an anchor ball on the *Choapa*. The *Voco's* engines were then immediately put full speed astern. By this time the *Voco* had swung three degrees to her left under her port helm, but her full astern movement checked this swing and caused the *Voco* to come back to the right, so that she was heading approximately 164 degrees true at about 2.53, when the two vessels collided at an angle of 90 degrees. At the time of the collision the *Voco* had a headway of approximately two knots and the contact between vessels was comparatively light. Immediately after the impact the reverse movement of the *Voco's* engines backed her away from the *Choapa*. At the request of the *Choapa*, however, the *Voco* went ahead again and put her stem up against the starboard side of the *Choapa*. Shortly thereafter the *Voco's* stern lookout reported the approach of a vessel astern, and the *Voco's* master observed the *Empire Garrick* about a point on the starboard quarter at a distance of about two or two and one-half cables heading straight for the *Voco's* bridge. The *Voco* immediately went full astern, pulling clear of the *Choapa*. The *Garrick*, proceeding at considerable speed, started to swing off to starboard, and her port side forward struck the starboard bow of the *Choapa* a heavy blow. Immediately after this collision the crew of the *Choapa* began abandoning ship and were taken on board the *Voco*, which returned them to New York after the *Choapa* sank stern first at about 5.00 p.m. The damage sustained by the *Voco* as a result of the collision was very slight and confined to her stem. . . .

"According to the *Garrick*, her collisions with the *Choapa* and the *John P. Poe* that afternoon occurred in the following manner: After dropping her pilot the *Garrick* proceeded down the swept channel at a speed of approximately 9 1/2 knots in the port line of two staggered columns. She had a lookout posted on the forecastle head, a deck watch consisting of her master, second mate, helmsman and a cadet, and sounded regulation fog signals whenever the fog closed in. According to her master, . . . he heard a backing signal of three short blasts coming from a point fine [sic] on the port bow. The *Garrick* immediately stopped her engines and went full speed astern at 2.57 p.m., sounding three short blasts. Almost immediately thereafter the forecastle lookout reported two ships ahead, which were observed by those on the bridge practically simultaneously about 1000 feet away. Upon sighting these vessels, which proved to [be] the *Choapa* and *Voco* and which were in collision at the time, the *Garrick*'s helm [rudder] was put hard astarboard. The *Choapa*'s bow was pointing in a westerly direction and her starboard side was practically beam on to the *Garrick*. The *Voco* was on the *Garrick*'s port bow, nearly stern on to the *Garrick*, showing her starboard side slightly. As a result of her engine and rudder action the *Garrick* swung off to starboard, but not sufficiently to avoid collision, and at 2.58 her port side just forward of the bridge struck the stem of the *Choapa* a glancing blow and scraped past at an angle of 70 to 80 degrees. The *Garrick*'s master estimated that her speed had been reduced to 7 or 8 knots when the collision occurred. . . . After her collision with the *Choapa*, the *Garrick* blew two long blasts for a ship underway but stopped in the water, and was about to anchor when the *John P. Poe* came into sight over two ship lengths away approaching the *Garrick*'s starboard side. Thereafter, at 3.03 p.m., the flare of the *Poe*'s port bow, about in line with her No. 1 hatch, struck the starboard side of the *Garrick* abreast of her foremast at an angle of about 70 degrees. The *Garrick* then returned to New York for repairs. . . .

"According to the *Poe*, after leaving Gedney buoy at 1.30 that afternoon she assumed her assigned position in the starboard column of the convoy and started down the swept channel. Her master, second mate, helmsman and naval gunner were on the bridge, two naval gunners were on the forward gun platform and a lookout was stationed on the bow. . . . At the time the *Poe* was proceeding at a speed of approximately 7 1/2 knots and blowing fog signals of about five seconds duration every minute. After passing buoy G the *Poe* heard a number of different whistles, including a danger signal, which seemed to come from three or four ships well off the port side and clear of the *Poe*. The vessels were not seen at the time, but a few minutes later, at 2.58, the shadow of the *Empire Garrick* was observed about one or two ship lengths ahead, moving across the channel at an angle of 45 to 50 degrees with very slight headway on her. The *Poe* immediately stopped her engines, went full speed astern and put her rudder hard astarboard, but was unable to avoid collision, her port bow striking the starboard bow of the *Garrick* at about an angle of 22 degrees at 3.00 p.m. Thereafter the *Poe*, unable to contact the *Garrick* because of the dense fog, returned to New York for repairs."

This freak shipping occurrence involving so many ships and collisions is the maritime equivalent of a highway pile up. Vessel crashes are much like vehicle crashes in that the courts do not recognize the term "accident" to mean "an act of God" or "an unavoidable circumstance in which no one is to blame." The purpose of the court proceeding was not to describe the incidents in excruciating detail as a heritage to history, but to determine who was at fault, and, by extension, who was blameless. Courts do not entertain the concept that circumstances can occur which are beyond anyone's power to control.

After a convoluted discourse which filled six pages of the final ruling, the court determined that fault for the initial collision between the *Choapa* and the *British Harmony* lay solely with the *British Harmony*, for straying across the channel markers into the inbound lane of traffic (despite extenuating circum-

The *Choapa* in her wartime guise. This photograph was taken two and a half months prior to her loss. The *Choapa* carried no deck gun because Chile remained neutral throughout the war. In the early years of the war, the *Choapa's* hull was painted white, and both her name and her country of registry were painted in large black letters on both sides amidships. This was done to announce her neutrality to lurking U-boats - a stratagem that seldom worked. U-boat commanders were often more concerned with their tonnage records than with adherence to neutrality laws. Thus the drab gray paint pictured above. Notice the emergency life rafts astern, the cargo net hung over the side, and lifeboats swung out in position for rapid lowering. (Offical U.S. Coast Guard photo.)

stances). However, that collision was not held to be the cause of the *Choapa's* ultimate sinking. The *British Harmony* was held liable only for damage done to the *Choapa* and her cargo as a consequence of the initial collision. That amount was estimated and then subtracted from the value of the *Choapa* and her cargo at the time of their actual loss on the following day.

The court then determined that the sinking of the *Choapa* and the loss of her cargo were due solely to the collision between the *Choapa* and the *Voco*. Another ten pages of reasoning (in some parts, rationalizing) were required to explain which vessel lay at fault for this second collision. Counsel for all parties submitted diagrams which depicted the relative positions of the various ships with respect to the channel buoys. These diagrams were based upon log book entries, compass bearings, and personal observations. Many important facts, though, were either lacking or contradictory. Nonetheless, the court could not decline to state an opinion due to inconclusive evidence. A court must make *some* determination in order to resolve the legal issues involved, if only to satisfy the raison d'être of the judiciary process. The court admitted to the unreliability of the evidence pertaining to the various ships' positions with respect to the channel buoys, but decided that the *Voco* was at fault for "proceeding down the easterly side of the channel at an excessive rate of speed." At the same time, the court ruled that the master of the *Voco* was not negligent in attempting to regain his position within the convoy as per the commodore's previous instructions.

However, "the court is of the opinion that the *Choapa* contributed to the collision by maintaining a dangerous heading across the channel while at anchor." The court ameliorated this finding by exonerating the *Choapa's* master from blame for his decision to drop anchor within the confines of the swept channel, because of the greater potential threat to his ship from the surrounding mine field. "Nevertheless, the *Choapa* must be held at fault for permitting herself to swing on her anchor to a position where she constituted an unreasonable obstruction in the channel."

As to whether the *Empire Garrick* contributed to the sinking of the *Choapa*, the court noted that "inasmuch as any leakage occasioned by the *Choapa*'s collision with the *Garrick* was confined to the *Choapa*'s forepeak and concededly was not vital, it follows that the heavy inrush of water into the *Choapa*'s after holds was the direct result of the *Voco* collision. It was the flooding of these holds, coupled with the fact that the escape of live steam in the engine room prevented pumping operations, that caused the *Choapa* to sink. For this the *Harmony* bears no responsibility. The court is of the opinion that the collision between the *Choapa* and the *Garrick* resulted from the combined negligence of the *Choapa*, *Voco* and *Garrick*."

The court's line of reasoning with respect to the *Empire Garrick*'s involvement was stated in two pages. In summation, "The *Garrick* was at fault for navigating on the east side of the swept channel and for failing to take prompt avoiding action."

The *John P. Poe* was absolved of all blame.

"With respect to the apportionment of damages, the owners of the *Choapa*'s cargo are entitled to recover the full amount of their losses from the *Voco*, less the value of any cargo damage resulting from the *Harmony* collision, subject to the *Voco*'s right to limit. . . . The *Choapa*'s claim in the *Voco* limitation proceeding is allowed to the extent of one half her total loss, after deducting damage sustained as a result of her collision with the *Harmony* which is recoverable from the *Harmony*. The *Choapa*'s libel against the *Garrick* must be dismissed because the *Choapa* was already doomed as a result of the fatal blow dealt by the *Voco* when the *Garrick* ran into her. The *Voco* is entitled to a decree against the limitation fund of the *Choapa* in the amount of one-half her damages. The *Garrick* is entitled to recover two-thirds of her damages; one-third from the *Choapa* and one-third from the *Voco*, subject, of course, to their right to limit. . . . Inasmuch as the *Poe* did not assert any claim against the *Garrick*, she may only recover two-thirds of her damages, these to be equally assessed against the *Choapa* and *Voco*, subject to their right to limit. Since neither the cargo owners nor the *Poe* were at fault in any respect, their claims should be given priority."

Various versions of the numerous collisions that resulted in the sinking of the *Choapa* have been presented throughout the years: embellishments that have given rise to tales of almost mythical proportions. I don't know if these renderings were deliberate mistellings, or if they resulted from inadequate research: perhaps research that relied solely on anecdotal, word-of-mouth information instead of on official, primary source materials. In some accounts, the actual circumstances were altered without authentication, then blurred into a tale in which truth became subservient to dramatic appeal.

Another apocryphal story has the *Choapa* being sunk deliberately. This version came about because of the coincidental double meaning of "Voco." Voco, or more precisely, VOCO, was a contemporary military acronym which meant "by vocal order of the commanding officer." If a reporter thought that *Voco* was an unlikely name for a vessel, he might have honestly misinterpreted a succinct official statement such as "CHOAPA sunk by VOCO" to mean that the *Choapa* was scuttled on the unwritten authority of a military commander.

Although ships' names are italicized in published documents that have been typeset, typewritten reports printed ships' names either capitalized underlined - this because a typewriter could not type italics. In manuscript protocol, underlining is the writer's or editor's means of instructing the printer to place certain words in italics. Official reports that were composed on a typewriter relied upon capitals as a way to make ships' names stand out on the page for easier scanning.

Rest assured that the Lloyd's Register of Ships duly authenticates the existence of the British tanker named *Voco*, 5,090 gross tons. In fact, two years earlier, the *Voco*, owned by the Socony-Vacuum Oil Company, rammed and sank the British freighter *Gypsum Prince* off Lewes, Delaware. See *Shipwrecks of Delaware and Maryland*, by this author, for details.

The *Choapa* was called the Junior before it was identified. I don't know why. The wreck lies in a deep trench that connects the Hudson River with the Hudson Canyon, and which fans out at the edge of the continental shelf. This trench is called the Mud Hole. At various times in the geologic past, sea level was lower than it is today. This was because a great deal of water was bound in the form of ice, which accumulated on land and at the Earth's poles: the Ice Ages. During those times the Mud Hole was a river trough.

Now the trough is submerged, but it still carries the outflow of effluvium, garbage, industrial chemicals, and heavy particulate matter from New York City's sewers and waste treatment facilities. The Mud Hole is in effect an underwater sewage system which provides nutrients for waterborne algae and microbial life forms: the bottom of the food chain on which filter feeders and predatory fish survive. Game fish proliferate in this biotic miasma, which explains the profusion of monofilament that enshrouds the wrecks that lie there.

Divers describe the Mud Hole succinctly: deep, dark, and dangerous. The wrecks in the Mud Hole can justifiably be considered the most challenging dives on the eastern seaboard, perhaps in the world. I have often said, "If you can dive the *Choapa* you can dive the *Doria*. But just because you've dived the *Doria* doesn't mean you're ready for the *Choapa*." I still hold to this sentiment.

The *Choapa* sits upright with its bow pointing north. The muddy bottom lies beneath 200 feet of often turbid water. The hull is largely intact, with the bridge rising to a depth of 165 feet. The smokestack stands immediately abaft the bridge, rising higher, and close enough to touch from the after bulkhead of the midship superstructure. The wooden bulkheads that once enclosed the wheel house have long since collapsed.

Thick monofilament covers the wreck like a pall, and is extremely dangerous. Visibility is usually poor: in the five to ten foot range with a light but pitch black otherwise, much like a night dive.

Once I became so entangled in monofilament that I felt like a fly in a spider's web. Silver strands gripped my tanks with incredible tenacity, and my fins were wrapped as tight as a doughnut box. Visibility was only a few feet. I slashed away at the heavy-duty line around my ankles, but was unable to reach far enough over my shoulders to clear my tank valves. By good fortune, I happened to be hovering above the deck behind the bridge and next to the stack on the port side. Secured to the stack were ladder rungs that climbed the cylindrical metal casing.

I gripped a rung to stabilize myself. Then I grabbed the rung above it and pulled myself up. Taut strands snapped. I grabbed a higher rung, pulled, and felt the release of more tension as the strands of monofilament broke. I climbed half a dozen rungs before I was free from entrapment. I oriented myself through the blackness to the top of the bridge, located the anchor line, and made my ascent. After decompressing, I climbed onto the boat with long strands of monofilament streaming from my fin straps and tank tops. My ashen face telegraphed my experience to those on board.

This incident occurred in the early 1970's. In 1997, I had an experience of a different kind. The grapnel snagged on what appeared to be the side of the wreck. Visibility was bad to awful - about three feet. I secured a guide line to a beam next to the grapnel, then dropped over the edge to the sand some twenty feet below. I found myself in a debris field. Unreeling the line, I worked my way across the debris field for a couple of minutes until I bumped into a vertical stanchion. I ascended a couple of feet to clear a pile of twisted beams, and banged my head on something overhead.

When I looked up I saw an overhang - a metal lip that extended behind me. I had swum underneath a steel plate. Since I couldn't see much farther away than arm's length, I followed the bottom of the overhang while reeling in my line - then discovered that I was not exploring off the edge of the wreck at all, but was in the bottom of a hold! The guide line was my salvation.

The *Choapa* is an ugly dive at best. Divers go there because there are still artifacts to be recovered. China and glassware can be dug out of the lower levels of the bridge. Portholes are occasionally found in the debris around the wheel house. Tom Packer recovered most of the ship's bell - the brittle brass had snapped in two, but he got the part with the name. Divers should note an observation made by the *Voco*'s master: "After the *Choapa*'s decks were awash she tipped up to a nearly vertical position and went down very quickly stern first." This nearly upright posture would cause anything loose to slide down toward the stern. Artifacts are more likely to be found in the after corners of the compartments than in the forward corners.

Furthermore, in case you missed the point, the court records made repeated mention of the fact that the *Choapa* rang two bells continuously after the collision with the *Voco*: one bell forward and one bell aft. (". . . the seaman who was ringing the fog bell at the *Choapa*'s stern . . .") Whether or not this stern bell was stamped with a name remains to be seen.

Because of the evident hazards, much of the wreck remains largely unexplored. If the grapnel happens to fall far forward or aft of the bridge, it is difficult to determine the precise position - or even if the location is forward or aft of the bridge. And because of the profusion of monofilament, the wreck is definitely a two-knife dive - maybe even a three.

COASTWISE

Built: 1900
Previous names: None
Gross tonnage: 268
Type of vessel: Wooden-hulled screw tug
Builder: Perth Amboy, New Jersey (probably by Hugh Ramsay)
Owner: Neptune Line, Inc.
Port of registry: New York, NY
Cause of sinking: Foundered
Location: 40-20 North

Sunk: July 19, 1920
Depth: Unknown
Dimensions: 109' x 24' x 15'
Power: Steam engine

73-18 West

The loss of the *Coastwise* received little notice except among those who survived her sinking. Witness this cryptic paragraph published in 1920: "New York, July 23 - Tug *Coastwise*, of the Neptune Line, foundered off Fire Island late last Tuesday night. All of the crew were saved and are aboard tug *Roger Williams*, which was sent out Wednesday night to pick up the barges which the *Coastwise* had in tow."

The inference is that when the *Coastwise* started to founder, her captain notified the tug company (by some means not specified), then he and the crew scampered aboard the barges to wait for a replacement tug to rescue them and to continue with the voyage. When the tug's enrollment was surrendered in New York, on August 6, 1920, the following reason was given: "Vessel sank during storm, 10 miles S.W. from Fire Island, N.Y; on July 19, 1920[.] Total loss, 17 persons on board, no life lost." At the time of her loss the *Coastwise* possessed a forward deck house, a midship deck house, and an aft deck house.

Elsewhere, I found evidence that the *Coastwise* foundered thirty miles off Long Branch, New Jersey. These two locations - off Fire Island and off Long Branch - are not necessarily contradictory. Thirty miles east of Long Branch is almost far enough off the Jersey shore to be south of Fire Island. Newspapers commonly gave place names that were familiar to its readers. Thus a New York paper might give a location off a New York landmark, while a New Jersey paper might give a location off a New Jersey landmark.

I once read an account in a New York newspaper in which the position of a ship was given as "190 miles off Ambrose." No direction was noted. The position of the ship could have been on the beach of Nantucket Island, which is part of Massachusetts; the coast of Virginia; or anywhere along an arc in between.

The latitude and longitude given in the statistical sidebar are suspect. The position was undoubtedly not calculated from a sextant sighting. At best it was an approximation based upon dead reckoning (the nautical term for "guesswork") - and probably after the fact.

Two official sources place the *Coastwise* at 40-20 N and 72-18 W. These sources are the Wreck Information List, published by the U.S. Hydrographic Office in 1945, and the Navy Wreck List, published by the U.S. Navy Hydrographic Office in 1957. The 1957 list is probably a derivative of the 1945 list, and cannot therefore be used as corroboration.

I have long tinkered with the notion that the *Coastwise* might be the wreck which lies in the position given for what local skippers call the "HA" Buoy Wreck, or the *Catamount* (q.v.), so called because of the navigational buoy moored half a mile to the southeast. This site is twelve miles from the position given by the hydrographic offices, both of which gave an accuracy rating of one to three miles. Furthermore, no accounts state that the tug foundered quickly. She could well have drifted away partially submerged after the crew found her too dangerous to remain aboard.

The "HA" Buoy Wreck is definitely *not* the *Catamount*, because the private yacht turned Coast Guard cutter was driven by twin gasoline engines. The large steam engine at the site of the "HA" Buoy Wreck could very well be the propulsion unit of a powerful ocean-going tug.

The depth of the "HA" Buoy Wreck is 120 feet. The engine rises twelve feet off a bright white sandy bottom. Scattered wreckage consisting of worm-eaten timbers extend twenty to thirty feet both fore and aft of the engine. One-quart liquor bottles that litter the area might explain why the tug foundered so mysteriously - a hushed up tragedy from rum-running days, when more than one vessel ran afoul of the law. The wreck lies in an area of extremely clear water, with visibility generally exceeding fifty feet. The abundance of large lobsters keeps divers returning for more.

Official U.S. Coast Guard photo.

CONTINENT

Built: 1931
Previous names: *Castor*
Gross tonnage: 466
Type of vessel: Freighter
Builder: N.V. Scheepswerf Voorheen, Gebr G & H. Bodewes Martenshoek, in Papendrecht, Netherlands
Owner: Joe Brothers & Co., Ltd.
Port of registry: St. Johns, Newfoundland
Cause of sinking: Collision with SS *Byron D. Benson*
Location: 26884.7

Sunk: January 10, 1942
Depth: 130 feet
Dimensions: 149' x 25' x 9'
Power: Diesel engine

43637.4

    The Bureau of Marine Inspection and Navigation, which held the inquiry on this accident, found that "the collision was due to the failure of the *Continent* to keep out of the way of the *Byron D. Benson* which was the privileged vessel under the circumstances. The failure of the *Continent* to do so, in our opinion, may be attributed to the neglect in not having a competent person in charge of the navigation on the bridge of the *Continent* prior to and at the time of the collision." This strong indictment left little room for doubt about which vessel was at fault.

    In one corner was the 7,953-ton American tanker *Byron D. Benson*, bound from Port Arthur, Texas to New York with a cargo of bulk fuel oil. On the bridge were John MacMillan, master, and First Officer James Lundbeck. In addition to the helmsman, two seamen were on lookout. "All of these men were lawfully certified by the Bureau of Marine Inspection and Navigation." In the other corner was the 466-ton British motor vessel *Continent*, outbound from New York with meat, vegetables, and produce. She was under command of a boatswain and a seaman. "These two men held no qualifying papers from the British Board of Trade. The testimony further disclose that there was no legally qualified officer on the bridge in charge of the navigation of the *Continent* at the time of the collision."

The sea was rough, the sky clear with a slight haze. By 7:15 p.m. it was already dark. The two ships converged with "the navigation lights of each vessel clearly indicating a crossing situation." By the time the *Byron D. Benson* sounded a blast from her whistle, followed by a danger signal, the situation was already in extremis. "The *Continent* attempted to cross the bow of the *Benson* from port to starboard, and made no change in course until shortly before the collision, at which time the rudder was put hard left, tending to bring the *Continent* across the bow of the *Benson*."

In an attempt to avoid hitting the much smaller freighter, the *Byron D. Benson* swung hard to port, contravening the usual port-to-port passing due to the existing circumstances. The *Byron D. Benson*, a 465-foot-long Tidewater tanker, could not respond quickly enough to her helm.

"The master of the *Continent* arrived on the bridge after the collision, at which time the engines on the *Continent* were stopped." The ship went down immediately. Second Assistant Engineer William Lang "apparently lost his life subsequent to the embarkation of a lifeboat." No explanation for this fatality was forthcoming from the thirteen survivors, who were picked up by lifeboats launched from the *Byron D. Benson* and subsequently taken into port.

The wreck was marked with a buoy. Because of its small size it did not pose a threat to navigation, so no further action was taken.

The wreck is dark and poor visibility is common. It offers little of particular interest, either in the way of lobsters or the recovery of artifacts. The bow is completely intact. The steering quadrant on the stern is the highest point of relief, standing about twenty feet above the bottom. The deck is gone, so the wreck is wide open. Very few artifacts have been recovered, and those that have been brought up were of poor quality. The portholes were made of steel. Monofilament abounds, so the wreck must be a good fishing spot. Spearfishing advocates take note.

The *Byron D. Benson* did not long survive the *Continent*. Less than three months later, on April 3, 1942, she was torpedoed off North Carolina by the *U-552* (Oberleutnant zur See Erich Topp). For details, see *Shipwrecks of North Carolina: from the Diamond Shoals North*, by this author.

DAGHESTAN

Built: 1900

Previous names: None

Gross tonnage: 3,466

Type of vessel: Steel-hulled freighter

Builder: Short Brothers, Sunderland, England

Owner: Hindustan Steamship Company, Sunderland, England

Port of registry: Sunderland, England

Cause of sinking: Collision with SS *Catalone*

Location: 26932.3

Sunk: December 18, 1908

Depth: 70 feet

Dimensions: 353' x 45' x 18'

Power: Coal-fired steam

43707.0

New York harbor was bound by thick fog on December 18, 1908. Fog seldom forces vessels to stop in the shipping lanes, any more than fog causes vehicles to stop on the highways - it merely reduces the speed of traffic. And fog at sea, as fog on land, is often the cause of accidents.

The British freighter *Daghestan* was outbound with a cargo of grain loaded by the Seager Trading Company and slated for delivery to Marseilles, France. (Researchers note: newspapers reported that "she had on board a valuable cargo of miscellaneous merchandise.") She passed slowly through the Gedney Channel, groping her way through clinging fog that was thick enough to choke a horse. Captain A.M. Haig peered ahead from her tall bridge. Somewhere to starboard lay Sandy Hook, invisible from the wheel house.

Inbound came the *Catalone*, another British freighter, under the command of Captain Glover. About one quarter mile from the sea end of the Gedney Channel, her lookouts spotted the *Daghestan* dead ahead. At the same time the *Catalone* was spotted by lookouts on the *Daghestan*.

Both vessels played a chorus of telegraph bells as their engines were thrown frantically into reverse. Adding to the din were the deep-throated blasts from their steam whistles. Time and distance were too short. Captain Haig threw his helm hard over. Neither vessel slowed nor changed course perceptibly before they converged with a crashing grind of British steel. Sparks shot into the air as the *Daghestan* was speared by the larger freighter like a captured moth on a pin. The men on deck were knocked off their feet like tenpins.

The *Daghestan's* port side was crushed by the *Catalone's* sharp stem. Hull plates tore like tissue paper. The two ships bounced apart almost at once. In the short time the hulls were pressed together, some of the *Daghestan's* deck crew managed to leap onto the *Catalone's* bow. They must have intuited that their ship was doomed and that the other ship offered a better chance at survival. Immediately, water poured into the cavernous opening in the *Daghestan's* side. The rising flood chased the machinery crew out of the boiler and engine rooms.

By the time the stokers, firemen, and engineers reached the open air, topside personnel were already launching the lifeboats. There was hardly a moment to spare.

The lifeboats were away in minutes. Miraculously, no one was killed in the collision or hasty abandonment. The men pulled at the oars until they were a safe distance away from the *Daghestan*. The ship drifted out of the channel until her keel came to rest on a bar in thirty feet of water, with her upperworks exposed.

A cacophony of steam whistles cut through the fog as craft of all sizes, alerted by the clanging of bells that preceded the collision, drove in to render assistance. The rattle of iron chains pierced the fog as the *Catalone* dropped her anchor. The steel plates on her bows were dented, but, other than those slight dueling scars, there was little evidence that she had been involved in a major collision and sank another vessel.

The men in the lifeboats were not yet saved. A stiff breeze was blowing and a heavy sea was running. Cold air and sleet were dashed against their faces. Only superb seamanship enabled them to reach the *Catalone* and clamber aboard. There they remained only a short while until the pilot boat *New York* appeared on the scene, took them off, and conveyed them to the dock.

The Merritt Chapman Wrecking Company was notified of the accident, and was hired to save the cargo and raise the hull. The next day, the company dispatched the wrecking steamer *I.J. Merritt* to the scene, some two miles off the *Scotland* lightship, only to learn that overnight the *Daghestan* had slipped off the bar and had sunk in 60 feet of water. The ship was given up as a total loss, and later demolished as a hazard to navigation.

In 1967, Frank Litter and friends began diving an unidentified wreck which they called the Evergreen. The wreck earned its name from the vast quantities of brass items which lay strewn among the twisted beams and hull plates. The brass was covered with a green patina that was caused by the oxidation of the copper in the alloy. The wreck yielded portholes, silverware, unmonogramed china, keys, door handles, a three-foot-tall steam whistle, valves, pumps, and other odds and ends including a worm-eaten stoker shovel handle. According to Litter, the ship's bell was recovered in 1970. The name was inscribed on the bell, positively identifying the wreck as the *Daghestan*.

The wreck lies in an area of strong current and dark water, at a depth of 70 feet. Divers beware: despite the shallow depth, this is a challenging wreck to dive because of normally adverse conditions. It would be best to check the tide tables before scheduling a visit to this seldom-dived site. Litter advised me that prior to diving the wreck, his group used to call the New York-Sandy Hook Pilots Association to request permission. They did this because the wreck lay in the shipping channel and they wanted to ensure that they could complete a dive between vessel passings.

DELAWARE

Built: 1880
Previous names: None
Gross tonnage: 1,646
Type of vessel: Wooden-hulled passenger-freighter
Builder: Birely, Hill & Streaker, Philadelphia, Pennsylvania
Owner: W.P. Clyde & Co.
Port of registry: Philadelphia, Pennsylvania
Cause of sinking: Fire
Location: 26928.4

Sunk: July 9, 1898
Depth: 70 feet
Dimensions: 250' x 37' x 17'
Power: Coal-fired steam

43467.5

George Hoffman called the *Delaware* the Money Wreck. Because the site was located so close to Manasquan Inlet, he could get there in all but the worst

Courtesy of the Mariners Museum, Newport News, Virginia.

weather conditions and thereby fulfill his charter obligation - even on days when the Coast Guard flew small craft advisories. More than a few divers have paid to barf over a wreck which should be dived only on days when the sea is calm. Due to its proximity to shore, storm-driven swells stir the silt on the bottom and turn the wreck into a black soup of sediment and particulate matter.

During the Spanish-American War, the Clyde Line chartered some of its newer vessels to the U.S. Army for the transportation of troops. This left the line short of passenger ships. The *Delaware*, a Clyde Line freighter that previously saw service in the East India trade, was hastily refitted to accommodate passengers. On July 8, 1898 she departed New York on her first voyage with paying customers. On board were sixty-six souls: thirty-two passengers and thirty-four officers and crew.

In addition, "she carried a miscellaneous cargo of groceries, provisions and dry goods - much of which is supposed to have been supplied under Army contracts." Her destination was Jacksonville, Florida, with a stop at Charleston, South Carolina along the way.

The first obstacle the *Delaware* encountered upon leaving the harbor was the protective mine field off Sandy Hook. Captain A.D. Ingram, "the youngest man ever given a master's license out of New York harbor," plied the oak and yellow pine steamship out of the harbor in the middle of a sunny afternoon. The sea was "unusually calm."

A brass door latch and a spigot. A cask or barrel was tapped by placing the tapered tube of the spigot against the bung, then driving in the bung by slamming a mallet against the peg on the spout of the spigot.

At 10 p.m., after most people had turned in for the night, a seaman reported to the bridge officer that smoke was seeping through the after hatch. By that time the blaze in the hold was already out of control. The entire crew was roused, and holes were drilled in the deck so that fire hoses could be inserted in order to extinguish the flames. The men even rolled up the carpet in the saloon and cut through the deck underneath, but the "smoke came through in such overpowering masses that it was deemed time to notify the passengers and prepare for the worst."

Then "First Officer, B. McBeth, and the stewardess went quietly from room to room and awakened such as were asleep, and notified all in a way not to excite alarm that there was a fire in the hold, and all hands were to go on deck as a precautionary measure. . . . All save ten or twelve got into their clothes."

Said passenger I.P. Ward: "The passengers evidently understood the emergency of the summons. They flung open their stateroom doors, and thronged into the hallway. Yet there was no excitement, only the confusion of hurry. One man cracked his door, and thrusting his head out, asked what the trouble was. I told him I thought the ship was on fire. 'Oh, is that all!' he said, and he closed the door again. Later, I saw him on the upper deck, fully dressed and smoking a pipe."

The *Delaware* was cruising south some ten miles off the coast. With a fire in the hold, Captain Ingram did not deliberate for long before he turned the ship toward shore. He also fired rockets, to alert other ships and to signal to the life-saving stations. Ordinarily the life-saving stations were shut down during the summer and their crews disbursed to other jobs. But, owing to the war, they were manned and fully operational "for signaling purposes."

Captain Ingram remained very much in charge of the situation. When the *Delaware* approached to within two miles of the beach, he directed the four lifeboats to be swung out on their davits, then gave the order to abandon ship. "The women and children first," he said.

Ward: "The male passengers turned their attention to the women, and assisted them up the steps. When I got back to the deck nearly everybody was grouped forward watching the flames, which were then burning fiercely. I rushed back down to get my grip, in which was a gold watch, a diamond bracelet, and a set of diamond studs I had just bought, but the passage had become filled with smoke, and I found it impossible to reach my stateroom. I again went on deck. With me were two or three men who had evidently gone below,

The intensity of the heat is literally cast in bronze in what appears to be a piece of modernistic art. Only the threads reveal that this must have been a deck flange which melted into a curious, bloblike shape.

like myself, to secure their baggage. When we reached the deck for the last time the boats were swinging clear, and the women and children being handed in. A man came running toward the first boat and tried to get a seat. Capt. Ingram caught him by the collar and flung him prostrate on the deck. Two or three other men stepped up to where he lay and warned him to be still if he valued his life. I do not know what this man's name was, but somebody told me he was a Cuban doctor.

"In a minute another man dashed toward the boat. He, too, was a Cuban, I understand, and he met the same consideration as his fellow-countryman. I asked an officer why the hurry was so great, as the danger from the flames did not even then seem pressing. He told me because there was a lot of ammunition for Sampson stored below, and the Captain was afraid it would explode and blow everybody up." (Admiral Sampson was in command of the American fleet that was besieging Cuba.)

The first boat to leave the *Delaware* held nine women and children passengers, as well as a stewardess.

Ward: "When my turn came to get in a boat, a fellow dragging a trunk pushed past me and flung the trunk into the little craft. Four men, who were already seated, calmly and of one accord, picked it up and tossed it overboard. Then they invited the trunk owner in, and afterward explained to him the fact that there wasn't room enough for his baggage.

"We all pulled away a short distance and watched the steamer burn. Directly there came two explosions in rapid succession, and following a display of fireworks of such magnificence as I have ever seen."

Another passenger, R.P. Marsh, confirmed Ward's statement about the consignment of ammunition, "and that it did explode afterward. Mr. Marsh had along with him his two sisters. They saved nothing except their nightdresses and one shoe. As they were being helped up the steps to the deck, Mr. Marsh ran back to the hallway and seized a pair of blankets from a bunk in one of the forward staterooms. These he gave to the young women.

"Mr. Marsh's statement about the behavior of passengers and crew is, like Mr. Ward's, a story of coolness and courage and discipline. The sailors worked quietly and rapidly at cutting away the boats, and wherever the passengers could be of assistance they tendered their help. And where their aid was not needed, they withdrew in order to avoid being in the crew's way. The men, he says, stood about in little groups, quietly smoking and talking about the chances of being blown to atoms any second."

The women acted as calm as the men. One woman, Mrs. Claussen, "declined to go in the first boat and leave her husband." She boarded the second boat with her husband - the only woman among fifteen men. "She wanted to help at the oars." This boat "afterward pulled back close to the burning ship to take three men off of a raft. Two of these men were engineers and one an oiler, all of whom had waited for the passengers to get off the vessel before trying to leave themselves."

Another life raft, stowed on the after deck, was cut off from the other crew members by flames. So they jury-rigged two hatch gratings into life rafts. "On these the remaining members of the crew and finally the Captain took refuge. The Captain left last, lowering himself by a rope. Two of the boats then took the rafts in tow and pulled out of danger." By then the Delaware was "a mass of fire, the flames having swept up the rigging, ignited the deckhouses, around which they licked viciously, and even wrapped themselves about the masts."

The *Delaware* was abandoned in generally exemplary fashion. The only behavior that was considered unacceptable to some of the survivors was exhibited by the two Cubans. "These were quickly and sternly made to realize that Americans did not approve of the Latins' principle of safety in time of danger." Anti-Cuban sentiment undoubtedly ran high at the time because of the war.

"Meantime the patrol of the Cedar Creek Life Saving Station had discovered the fire at sea and a surf boat was put off to the rescue. She relieved some of the boats of their passengers and then happily the fishing smack *Samuel B. Miller* of New York came up. She took all of the occupants of one boat aboard.

"Captain Ingram, as soon as all the boats were off, had warned them to keep offshore to avoid the breakers, and this admonition was repeated by the life savers, who said it would not be well to attempt to reach the beach until after day-break.

"One boat, in charge of Second Officer Hill, got separated from the others for a time, but she turned up all right, having been only hidden in a cloud of smoke. Some of the men and some of the women were scantily clad, and all got wet by the dashing of spray over the sides of the boats, but this discomfort was not seriously considered since all were at least safe."

About three o'clock in the morning the tug *Ocean King* hove into view of the burning ship. The tug had three barges in tow, bound for Norfolk, Virginia, but promptly anchored them and "took aboard all hands from boats and schooner, save the Captain and twelve of his officers and men, who boarded the schooner and remained to cruise about the wreck and hold possession if it should prove that she would remain afloat and could be towed to the city. The Captain and crew were subsequently taken ashore by the life savers, and they came to the city by rail." The Pennsylvania Railroad furnished them transportation.

The *Ocean King* arrived at the Clyde pier at about 10:30 in the morning. Most of the passengers were taken to the United States Hotel, "where they were quartered at the expense of the Clyde Company." C.H. Warburton, the Clyde Line's Eastern Passenger Agent, said that "his company would do, and was doing, everything that could be expected of it for the relief of the Delaware's passengers." He spent an entire day with them, "buying shirts and underclothing and trousers, and articles of feminine wear. Not only will they be taken care of here at our expense until they can make a new start toward the South, but, when they are in shape to go we shall offer them their choice of rail or water. As for their lost baggage, of course I can't replace that. But, when these people get home we will leave them at liberty to take steps to indemnify themselves."

With respect to charges that the *Delaware* carried a cargo of ammunition, other "passengers said they heard explosions and were sure there was ammunition aboard, but the officials of the company deny this, and think that the passengers, in their nervous fright, got exaggerated impressions of the noises of combustion going on aboard the ship." To my knowledge, no sign of ammunition - bullets, shell casings, and the like - have ever been seen or recovered from the wreck.

The Merritt-Chapman Derrick and Wrecking Company dispatched the wrecking tug *W.S. Chapman* to the scene. "The hulk of the *Delaware* was found still afloat and still burning despite the heavy rain of the morning." The ship was taken in tow. Thousands of people on shore watched curiously as the *W.S. Chapman* chugged slowly northward with the *Delaware* engulfed in flames. The valiant effort was in vain, however, for the *Delaware* finally took the plunge to the sandy bottom. The *W.S. Chapman* went on to New York alone.

The *Delaware* was insured for $125,000.

Flotsam drifted ashore for weeks after the catastrophe. Beachcombers raked in whatever souvenirs they could find. Half-burned timbers were used for firewood after their brass bolts were removed. Pelts and bolts of cloth washed up soaked, but still usable. One man even found half a dozen silk umbrellas that were undamaged by smoke and fire. Most of the merchandise, though, went down with the ship.

Today the *Delaware* is known as a digging wreck. Any items that were once exposed have long since been recovered by divers who are, in one sense, underwater beachcombers.

The highest part of the wreck is the engine, abaft of which the propeller shaft leads to a four-bladed iron propeller. Very little of the wooden hull remains in the stern. It is along both sides of the shaft where the sand-fanning diver will unearth the most relics: bottles, ink wells, and brass lamps among them. A small dredge or airlift will help immeasurably in uncovering artifacts.

Much of the wooden hull remains along the sides of the engine and forward to the bow. This is a good place to look for hand-blown soda pop bottles embossed "Jacksonville Steam Bottling Works, Jacksonville, Fla." Because the wreck is dived so frequently, lobsters are few and far between, and usually shorter than legal size.

The best prize of all was recovered by Bill Davis in 1989. From his open runabout, he hooked a small piece of wreckage that lay east of the main hull. He went down to take a look and found the ship's bronze bell. The *Delaware's* name and date of construction were engraved above the bell's flared lip.

From a painting at the Maryland Historical Society.

ELLA WARLEY

Built: 1848
Previous names: *Isabel*
Gross tonnage: 1,169
Type of vessel: Wooden-hulled sidewheel steamer
Builder: Levin .H. Duncan, Baltimore, Maryland
Owner: F.W. Reynolds & Company of Providence, Rhode Island
Port of registry: New York, NY
Cause of sinking: Collision with SS *North Star*
Location: 15 miles south-southeast of the Highlands light

Sunk: February 9, 1863
Depth: 42 feet
Dimensions: 210' x 34' x 17'
Power: Coal-fired steam

The *Ella Warley* began her career as the *Isabel*, the first ocean-going steamship ever to be built in Baltimore. Her wooden hull was constructed by Levin H. Duncan, her machinery by Charles Reeder's Marine Engine & Iron Works. Her primary means of propulsion consisted of a side-lever engine whose seventy-two-inch cylinder had an eight-foot stroke and delivered 500 horsepower to the paddle wheels at her sides. Her hull lines were modeled after the Baltimore clipper, and she was rigged for sail in the same full style.

The launching of the hull was marred by a melancholy accident in which three people were killed and thirty more were injured. Contemporary accounts did not state the nature of the accident or how the fatalities and injuries occurred.

The *Isabel* was named after the reigning queen of Spain. Her interior appointments were as queenly as her name suggested. "Her staterooms were of mahogany, inlaid with porcelain. She was the first ship to have a bell pull system connecting from staterooms to ward room. She had accommodations for 150 passengers." She was issued a temporary enrollment in Baltimore in 1848. (A vessel enrollment is equivalent to a vehicle registration.)

Captain William Rollins took first command. He steamed the *Isabel* to Charleston, South Carolina, where she received her permanent enrollment. According to her papers she boasted three masts, one deck, a round stern, no galleries, and an eagle head. (In this case "head" did not refer to toilet facilities, but a figurehead.) Her dimensions at that time were given as: length of 209 feet, breadth of 33 feet 6 inches, and depth of 16 feet 7 inches. Her tonnage was listed as 1,115 and 85/95 (a fraction of one ton). She was owned by M.C. Mordecai & Company. For thirteen years she operated between Havana and her home port of Charleston, as originally intended, except for a time when she ran between Havana and New York. In addition to transporting cargo and passengers she also carried mail.

The *Isabel* had the misfortune to be docked in Charleston when the Civil War broke out - misfortune, at least, for her owners, because the Confederate government requisitioned the steamer and changed her name to *Ella Warley*. Soon the paddle wheeler's quiet career as an peaceful transport assumed a new and exciting identity. When the Union threw a naval blockade around Charleston harbor, the *Ella Warley* became a bold blockade runner.

The *Ella Warley's* first run of the blockade began on January 2, 1862. A few days earlier, she was docked in the Bahamian port of Nassau, on New Providence Island: a safe haven for blockade runners because the Union navy was powerless to detain suspicious vessels in foreign waters - the navy's authority ended at another country's three-mile territorial limit. Due to its proximity to Southern ports, Nassau served as a transfer point for goods and war materiel arriving from overseas - principally from England - and which were ultimately bound for the Confederate States of America. Confederate ships arrived in Nassau laden with cotton to trade for guns, ammunition, and a host of machine parts and manufactured items that could not be fabricated in the non-industrialized South. Nassau officials knew that the Union resented the protection offered by international treaty, but maintained a staunch position of neutrality with respect to taxable commercial exchange. The result was that Nassau was a very busy port during the War between the States, and subsequently commerce soared.

The Union kept a warship patrolling off Nassau harbor in hopes of catching a blockade runner entering or leaving the port. The *Flambeau* drew this onerous duty for so long that she ran out of coal. The Union dispatched a pair of coaling schooners to refuel the cruising gunboat, but Nassau authorities refused to let the warship enter the harbor in order to coal. So as to avoid an international incident, the *Flambeau* was forced to steam to Key West for recoaling - a lengthy and arduous process that could not be carried out in the open ocean, without protection from wind and waves.

The *Ella Warley* took advantage of the *Flambeau's* absence. She steamed straight for Charleston and arrived at dawn on January 2. According to the *New*

York Tribune she "was chased and ineffectually shelled by the blockaders." The *Charleston Courier*, a Southern newspaper, was a bit more expressive. "The good people of Charleston woke up yesterday morning to be hugely delighted with the news that the fine ocean steamer *Ella Warley*, Capt. Swasey, from Nassau, N.P., had entered our harbor with the first rays of the rising sun, and was already safely moored to our wharves. At early dawn she appeared off Charleston entrance, in full view of the blockading vessels. These immediately gave chase, and commenced a rapid fire of shot and shell, all of which, however, fell short. After passing for several miles under the enemy's fire unharmed, the noble steamship finally came within the protecting range of the guns of Fort Sumter, and swept majestically up to the city. How far the Yankee naval officers indulged in profane expletives as they beheld what would have been a very plump prize slip from their grasp, we leave to the imagination of our readers. . . . What Lord Derby, and the owners of the English cotton ships, and John Bull generally, will say when they hear of the *Ella Warley* having run into Charleston harbor in broad daylight, with the Southern flag flying, and in willful and contumelious disregard alike of stone and paper blockades, is, likely, we imagine, to be a little stronger than anything they have yet said."

A Florida newspaper, the *Quincy Dispatch*, vied with the *Courier* in exuberant description of the *Ella Warley's* bold dash through the Union blockade, and added a few details that were lacking in the *Courier*. "Just ere the peep of dawn, came up in front of the bar off Charleston. The whole horizon was shrouded in a dense fog, and they were compelled to heave to until the rising sun should clear up the mist and open the way to the harbor of their hopes. But, as the sun began to rise and the mist to vanish, the lifting of the murky veil revealed to their astonished gaze the threatening aspect of the two war steamers blockading the port, distant about a mile. It was no time then to pause for wonder and speculation, but every hand, passenger, crew and all, were beat to quarters and put to work. Wood, tar, pitch, turpentine - everything combustible - was thrown into the furnaces, till, reaching a white heat, away the steamer flew. Quick chase was given, and peal after peal of shot and shell came thundering after them; but the noble ship sped on her way unharmed, crossed the bar, keeping up the full power of steam, till, safely passing beneath the protecting guns of Sumter, she was greeted by the garrison with loud and repeated shouts of triumphant welcome."

A different light was shed on the subject from Union Flag-Officer S.F. Du Pont in an official dispatch to Secretary of the Navy Gideon Welles. "The *Isabel*, I am sorry to say, has got into Charleston, in a fog. The *Mohican* slipped her chain instantly on the lookout vessel of that channel firing a gun, but the *Isabel* was too swift. The *Mohican* blew her stern off by a shell; this we have from deserters from Stono to-day, brought down by the *Pocahontas*. She had coffee on board; no arms. The *Mohican* chased her until she drew the fire of the forts."

Commander S.W. Godon, the *Mohican's* captain, excused the inability of his ship to catch the *Ella Warley* on account of lack of maintenance due to the exigencies of war. "I regret to say that the *Mohican* has quite lost her speed in the last six months, and now I can only obtain 6 or 7 knots under the same steam and same revolutions which formerly gave me 9 and 10. The engines and boilers have been in use without an overhauling for more than two years. This and a very foul bottom may account for the sluggishness, but does not relieve me from the serious annoyance of having a very slow vessel to do duty requiring the greatest speed. I have now placed the ship to within half a mile range of a long gun on Sullivan's Island, below Fort Moultrie, but at least three steamers should be here, and one, at least, very fast, and they must ride out all gales except southeasters. Then they will be obliged to go to sea."

If Southern accounts are to be believed, the *Ella Warley* carried not only a valuable cargo of arms, ammunition, blankets, shoes, medicines, and so on - worth some $700,000 - but a Mr. B.T. Bisbie who had important dispatches which immediately upon landing he proceeded to take to Richmond by train.

The *Ella Warley's* vaunted career as a blockade runner was short-lived. After several other successful runs through the South Atlantic Blockading Squadron, Confederate smugness gave sway to humble pie when she was captured in April by the Union gunboat *Santiago de Cuba*, some one hundred miles north of Abaco (a Bahamian island north of Nassau). The cargo which was lost to the Confederates - and which gives an indication of the kinds of necessities which the South found lacking - consisted of pig lead, sheet copper, iron in bundles, slabs of zinc, cases of Enfield rifles, swords, nautical instruments, cotton cords, drugs, quinine, potash, soda, cream of tartar, castor oil, potash, soap, paper and stationary, cigars, candles, tallow, codfish, herring, mackerel, butter, cheese, bread, tea, alcohol, gin, carboys, and toothbrushes. It is interesting to note the cotton cords; although the South grew great crops of cotton, it did not have the technology needed to process it. Cotton shipped to England often returned in the form of clothing or other woven and manufactured products.

The *Ella Warley* thus became a legal prize of war. "Legal" is a word whose meaning is subject to interpretation. Like a card game with different sets of rules, what was considered legal in one country was not considered legal in another. Nor might either form of legality necessarily be recognized by a third or any other nation. Legality has meaning only in the context of a government's system of jurisprudence. Ten feet away, across an invisible political border, legality may be entirely different. Legality should never be confused with morality or with the concepts of right and wrong, or good and evil.

Captain Alex Swasey, his officers and crew, and the passengers on board the *Ella Warley* at the time of her capture, all became prisoners of war. A prize crew under the command of Lieutenant Gibson took the steamer to New York, where she was docked at the Brooklyn Navy Yard. The prisoners were held in the army stockade and the cargo was discharged. According to the dictates of the U.S. government, foreigners and passengers "having no connection with the intent to evade the blockade" were released. The officers and crew of the *Ella Warley*, and citizens of the United States, were held in custody.

During the next several months the *Ella Warley's* cargo was sold or auctioned by the U.S. Marshall, and the ship herself was put up for sale. According to Union prize rules, the proceeds were to be distributed among the officers and

Erik Heyl drew this picture of the *Ella Warley* as the *Isabel*. (From *Early American Steamers*.)

crew of the capturing vessel, in this case the *Santiago de Cuba*. This policy of distributing the proceeds of a capture offered a mercenary incentive to naval personnel that went far beyond the intangible notion of patriotism. Profit was often the motive for audacity. (See *Brunette* for more on the *Santiago de Cuba*.)

According to one account the *Ella Warley* was purchased by Trujillo & Vining, of New York City. But the certificate of enrollment was registered under the name of William H. Reynolds, who represented the F.W. Reynolds & Company of Providence, Rhode Island. The steamer's vital statistics differed slightly from those given in her original documentation. Her three masts still carried sails, but now she boasted two decks, a square stern, a round tuck, and no head. (Again, this did not mean that the toilet had been eliminated, but likely that the eagle figurehead had been removed.) Her length was given as 210 feet 10 inches, breadth as 34 feet 2 inches, depth as 17 feet 1 inch. Her tonnage was recalculated to 1,169 and 38/95. Her boilers had been replaced in 1857.

The certificate of enrollment was dated December 2, 1862. Two months later, on February 9, 1863, the *Ella Warley* departed New York at 5 p.m. She was bound for New Orleans with thirty passengers and a cargo of dry goods, provisions, leather, hay, and "a large amount of express matter. Adams Express Company had one safe containing $5,000, and a passenger had in his possession $8,000 in gold. Her cargo is valued at $175,000."

The side wheeler churned past Sandy Hook at 7:15, "the Highlands light bearing west." An hour later, Captain George Schenck spotted a green light to starboard. In the lingo of the day he put his "wheel a-starboard," which meant that he turned the ship to port. He maintained this course for half an hour when, according to his account, "the *North Star* struck us just forward of the starboard wheelhouse, at right angles, cutting us half through, and carrying away our starboard boiler and steampipe, and causing the *Ella Warley* to sink in about eight minutes."

Live steam engulfed the boiler room crew, cooking them like lobsters in a pot. In addition to the six men who were scalded to death, several others were injured. Captain Schenck "fell from the hurricane deck through the gap made by the collision, down among the freight, was badly bruised, and, his coat getting fastened in something, was nearly drowned by the water pouring in on him." Despite the captain's unheralded precipitation, after being helped to his feet by Chief Engineer Charles Skidmore, he waded into the cabins through waist-deep water to make sure that all the passengers had escaped.

The *Ella Warley's* lifeboats were launched without delay. The first boat to depart carried eighteen women and children - all wearing night clothes as they had already retired. Henry Brastow, the purser, "having by this time got into the nearest boat, alongside the ship, took them into it, and passed them to the outer boat, while others were filling the forward part of the boat which he occupied."

While the women and children were abandoning ship on the starboard side, First Officer Oliver Hazard and several male passengers were launching the boats on the port side. Captain Schenck remained on board, shouting over the cacophony of escaping steam "to know if the women and children were safe." It so happened that Mr. Reynolds, one of the owners, was on board. He informed Captain Schenck that the women and children had already departed, and that he - the captain - was the only living person still on board. Whereupon Captain Schenck then permitted himself to be helped into Mr. Brastow's lifeboat, the last to leave the steamship.

At the time of the collision the *North Star's* engine had been reversed. She hove to at once. Her stem was considerably damaged and her cutwater was almost entirely torn away. She was leaking badly. Powerful steam pumps ejected the inrush of water with a comfortable margin of safety. Captain Lefevre ordered two of his lifeboats lowered, and sent them toward the *Ella Warley* to assist in the rescue. These boats met the *Ella Warley's* boats in the dark, then guided or towed them back to the *North Star*. "Mr. Hazard, after placing his passengers on board the *North Star*, returned again to the *Warley*, rowed around her, hailed to know if there was any one still on the wreck or in the water, and having received no answer, he returned to the steamer."

By that time the deck of the *Ella Warley* was level with the water. She soon sank "in seven fathoms of water." Captain Schenck stated that when the collision occurred "the Highlands light was bearing N.N.W., about fifteen miles."

The usual recriminations ensued. Each captain maintained that he attempted to avert disaster by turning his ship away from the approaching vessel, and that the other ship veered in the same direction instead of veering away. Long-winded and contradictory statements did nothing to clarify either ship's position relative to the other. Accusations that the *Ella Warley's* officers were intoxicated were unfounded - more likely an offensive maneuver from an indefensible position. The suggestion that the pilot on the *North Star* mistook the *Ella Warley's* lights for those of the lightship - made by Oliver Hazard - was not corroborated. In the final analysis, it appears that each ship was proceeding upon an identical but reciprocal course, and that each captain attempted to avoid collision by turning to opposite sides - one to port and the other to starboard. (Today, international Rules of the Road suggest that whenever two vessels are plying a potentially collision course, both should turn to starboard for a port-to-port passing.)

The *Ella Warley's* last position noted by the captain was five miles east of Shark River Inlet. On February 12, the pilot boat *James Avery* located the wreck in 13 fathoms (as opposed to 7 fathoms noted above) and "brought up a passenger's trunk and the foretopsail." Several days later the Coast Wrecking Company fitted out the wrecking schooner *Henry W. Johnson* "with steam-pumps, divers, &c., for the purpose of recovering the cargo of the steamship *Ella Worley* [sp.]."

This curious item appeared in the newspaper on February 23: "The pilot-boat *Washington*, No. 4, came to the City today, and reports the steamer *Ella Warley*, that was sunk by collision with the *North Star*, as having parted amidships, and rose to the surface, and is now entirely afloat, but is still held in the same place by (probably) the anchor; would have boarded her but for the tremendous high sea at that time."

This intelligence is open to speculation, especially as no follow-up was published. A literal translation would lead one to believe that the hull was successfully salvaged. Yet how was it possible for a vessel to part amidships yet be entirely afloat? What was meant by "parted amidships"? And how could salvors raise a completely submerged steamship by means of pumps alone? In order to raise a sunken ship the hull first has to be sealed, so that more water does not enter the compartments when the existing water is ejected. Wooden-hulled sailing vessels possessed a certain amount of reserve buoyancy; not so a paddle wheel steamer with heavy iron machinery - the weight of the engine and boilers constituted nonremovable ballast.

Many wrecks are known to be sunk in the area in which the *Ella Warley* was lost: the ferryboat *Vega*, the barge *Druid Hill*, the barge *Pocopson*, *Barge # 10*, the barge *Marion*, as well as other wrecks and obstructions that have never been identified. One wreck that was hung by a trawler lay at 26889.0 and 43528.9. The ferryboat *Vega* had a hull made of steel and so did some of the barges. But other barges were constructed of wooden timbers. The Spanish bark *Corbella* went down in the same area, in 1857, and she had a wooden hull. However, no one has ever reported the wreckage of an aged sidewheel steamer.

Extensive wire-dragging has been conducted in the vicinity because the coastal lanes are heavily traveled. As the draft of modern ships deepened, shoals and obstructions were investigated and subsequently cleared to greater depths. During one such survey conducted in 1939, in search of a sunken dredge that was a hazard to navigation, the dredge was not located but three other wrecks were hung! Undoubtedly others exist.

Perhaps the *Ella Warley's* most distinctive features - her paddle wheels - have been wire-dragged to pieces, making the wreck no longer recognizable as a sidewheeler to the nondiscerning eye. A diver may very well have grabbed a lobster from a shelter that was formed by worm-eaten paddle blades, and never gave it a thought! Or perhaps the wreck was raised and towed away, to be scrapped. No one knows.

Possibly under a mound of unidentified wooden debris lies a rusted side-lever engine, an ancient iron safe containing $5,000, and a conglomerate consisting of $8,000 in gold. Or possibly not.

FORT VICTORIA

Built: 1913
Previous names: *Willochra*
Gross tonnage: 7,784
Type of vessel: Passenger liner
Builder: W. Beardmore Co., Ltd., Glasgow, Scotland
Owner: Bermuda & West Indies Steam Ship Company
Port of registry: Hamilton, Bermuda
Cause of sinking: Collision with SS *Algonquin*
Location: 40-28-35 North

Sunk: December 18, 1929
Depth: 50 feet
Dimensions: 411' x 56' x 34'
Power: Oil-fired steam

73-53-10 West

Undoubtedly the two hundred six passengers who boarded the *Fort Victoria* on December 18, 1929, anticipated a welcome escape from the cold, rainy, and unhealthy winter environs of New York City, and looked forward eagerly to the warm, sunny weather of Bermuda. The liner proceeded slowly through the thick fog of the Lower Bay, sounding her horn at intervals, then halted momentarily in mid-channel to debark the pilot. As the pilot stepped from the ladder to a bobbing dory, the bow of the Clyde-Mallory Line steamer *Algonquin* - 5,945 tons, and outbound for Miami, Florida and Galveston, Texas - loomed out of the clinging mist and slammed into the *Fort Victoria's* port side amidships. The time was 3:45 p.m.

The *Algonquin* was brought to a dead stop. Coincidentally, some of her passengers were already wearing life belts and were standing near their lifeboat stations, where they had assembled for an abandon ship drill. Charles Ciliberti and Wilfred Trustill saw the *Fort Victoria* moments before the crash, and grabbed onto stanchions to keep from being thrown off their feet. Other passengers reported their experiences of the moment with differing accounts of the severity with which they felt the collision.

Jane Sweibell told of crockery and loose chairs being scattered about the tea room, but said that the crash was not violent enough to knock down any passengers. Pearl Buckley was asleep in her cabin and was awakened by the crash (apparently, attendance for lifeboat drills was not mandatory); she rolled over and went back to sleep. William Crear thought so little of the collision that he retired to his cabin and went to sleep. Calmness prevailed.

The *Algonquin's* engines were reversed. The liner backed away from wounded *Fort Victoria* and was soon lost in the fog. Damage was slight: "Several dents and a few torn plates six feet above the water line showed on her bow, and an overhanging guard rail of sheet iron, two feet wide, along the prow had been crushed back."

The situation on the *Fort Victoria* was worse. The *Algonquin's* stem pene-

trated some eight to ten feet into the *Fort Victoria's* hull. Rushing water quickly flooded her boiler room, dousing the fires and rendering the vessel without power. The watertight doors between the boiler room and engine room were closed promptly, thus preventing flooding of the engine room. An emergency dynamo came on line. The *Fort Victoria* soon filled the airwaves with calls for help. Tugs, police launches, pilot boats, and Coast Guard cutters were already on the way, however, in response to the *Algonquin's* radio distress calls. The pilot boat *New York* remained alongside the stricken liner. The pilot boat *Sandy Hook* arrived shortly thereafter. Searchlights cut through the fog.

The message transmitted by the *Fort Victoria* was clear: "Ship listing. May have to abandon any minute now."

The pilot returned to the bridge and advised Captain A.L. Francis, master of the *Fort Victoria*, to drop anchor in order to prevent the ship from drifting out to sea or into any other vessels that might be anchored nearby because of the fog. The darkened ship, totally without lights, swung into a steady position.

What followed was a textbook evacuation that was so cool and deliberate that it could have been a practice drill or exercise. Passengers abandoned ship with more courtesy and aplomb than if they were disembarking at their intended destination at Hamilton, Bermuda.

"In addition to the accommodation ladders many of the passengers left the stricken steamship by lifeboats. The passengers were directed to the boats by stewards and members of the deck crew and the boats were lowered, in some instances, to the water. Many passengers were taken from the lowered lifeboats. There was no panic at any time. The crew went about its duties with fortitude and the passengers, following the seamen's example, were calm and self-possessed. At least one lifeboat of the *Fort Victoria* was smashed when the bow of the *Algonquin* cut into the side. Another boat was suspended over the side of the *Fort Victoria* for thirty minutes before the falls were let go and the lifeboat was rowed to the pilot boat."

The decks of the *New York* and *Sandy Hook* groaned under the weight of the *Fort Victoria's* passengers and crew: some two hundred ninety people in all.

"The excursion which turned into an adventure before it was fairly under way brought forth no great tales of heroism, but at the same time tales of panic were absent. Nearly all the passengers, while admitting that they were 'very much frightened,' praised the crew for their calm and efficiency in handling the lifeboats and their quick removal from the sinking vessel. One or two complained that the boats were improperly manned. . . . A woman, Mrs. Nellie Stringer of Brooklyn, was the only casualty reported. She suffered from nervous shock and was taken to the Staten Island Hospital."

A skeleton crew consisting of Captain Francis and a dozen stalwart officers and men remained aboard the liner as she continued to list more and more to port. The captain sustained the hope that the ship under his command could yet be saved. The *New York* took the *Fort Victoria* in tow and headed back up the channel toward shallow water. Four hours after the collision, however, the valiant liner took her final plunge.

"Captain Francis remained on the bridge of his craft until the last minute. Even when he went over the side he held to a guide rope. A sailor in one of the lifeboats of the sinking ship rowed over to Captain Francis and pulled him in with a boat hook. The twelve other men were picked up later. They had donned lifebelts . . . to be fished out later, none the worse for the cold ducking." The captain and the skeleton crew were then picked up by the tug *Columbine*.

The ship was gone, and with her went the berths and belongings of several hundred passengers and crew. The Bermuda & West Indies Steam Shipping Company (better known as the Furness Bermuda Line) suddenly found itself with people in its charge for which no accommodations were available. Nor did these people have clothing to wear other than what they wore on their backs.

Rescue vessels converged on Pier 18 in order to discharge the survivors. "A restaurant opposite the pier was requisitioned solely for the expected passengers, and piles of clothing for the crew were heaped on the pier. Several big containers of coffee were made ready and automobile buses were stationed outside to whisk the passengers to the [Hotel] McAlpin."

Also waiting for the passengers were more than one hundred fifty "newspapermen and cameramen." Dealing with the media was undoubtedly a worse ordeal than abandoning the sinking ship.

For those who lived through the interviews, "full accommodations for the night and a freshly cooked supper awaited the survivors . . . at the Hotel McAlpin, where a special staff of 200 employees was held in readiness." H.C. Blackiston, a director of the Furness Bermuda Line, said that the loss of the passengers' baggage "was fully protected by insurance."

The next day, the Furness Bermuda Line issued the statement "that passengers who decided to do so could leave for St. George and Hamilton in the Bermudas today on the *Fort St. George*, sister ship of the lost steamship." This offer created quite a stir of activity on board the docked sister, for she was currently undergoing overhaul and was not slated to be ready for service until spring. Overnight, Pier 95 became "a scene of bustling activity as the *Fort St. George* . . . was hurriedly made ready to sail. . . . since 6 P. M. on Wednesday crews from the *Southern Prince* and *Rosalind*, Furness Bermuda Line ships, had been busy scraping paint, putting the staterooms in order and making her ship-shape for the unexpected voyage. Machinists were going over her engines, oil was being pumped into her hold and she was being provisioned. . . .

"Some of the crew who trod her decks yesterday were still wearing *Fort Victoria* ribbons on their caps, only about one-fourth of the *Fort St. George's* own crew having been signed to make this trip. Captain J. W. Findlay was in command of the ship."

Some passengers complained to Furness Bermuda Line officials that "we can't sail, we have no clothing." In response to this, the shipping line "arranged with stores located in the McAlpin to supply the passengers, at the company's expense, with articles of apparel, cosmetics, razors and other necessities."

Such generosity did not replace everyone's losses. Mr. and Mrs. Edward Flegel, who were married on the Sunday prior to departure, were embarking on their honeymoon. "It was to have been the first ocean trip for each and they agreed yesterday that they were through with boats. They said they would take a train as soon as possible for Florida. Their loss, they said, included even the money they had planned to spend in Bermuda."

Ultimately, only fourteen passengers canceled their passage to Bermuda. Sixty-two boarded the hastily refurbished *Fort St. George*, while the remainder took passage on other ships of the Furness Bermuda Line.

The *New York Times* received the following letter to the editor, which it duly published: "The undersigned desire to express their thanks and appreciation to the officers and crews of the pilot boats *New York* and *Sandy Hook* for their gallant care and treatment of the passengers and crew of the ill-fated *Fort Victoria* on the night of Dec. 18, 1929. The chief steward was on the New York, and the ship's surgeon and purser on the Sandy Hook. Every attention was extended and much-needed coffee and sandwiches served immediately after the rescue from the open lifeboats." The letter was signed by Henry D. Thomason (Ship Surgeon), A.F. McAffie (Chief Steward), and James N. Frish (Purser).

The *Algonquin*, whose master was Captain J.W. McKenzie, dropped anchor a short distance away from the sunken liner until a damage assessment could be made. There she floated for more than a day and a half while her one hundred forty passengers paced the fog-shrouded decks in restless boredom. Marine surveyors determined that the *Algonquin* was too badly damaged to proceed. The ship then returned to Pier 38 in order to disembark her passengers. The Clyde-Mallory Line made arrangements for her passengers to depart for Miami on the company liner *Cherokee*, "which goes to Jacksonville, from which point they can journey by rail to Miami. Passengers for Galveston, however, will have to wait for the *Henry R. Mallory*, which is scheduled to sail on Dec. 28."

(n August 10 of the previous year, the *Algonquin* rescued the five-man crew of a foundering schooner in the Florida straits. Six years hence, she assisted in the rescue efforts of her sister ship *Mohawk* (q.v.) after the *Mohawk's* collision with the Norwegian freighter *Talisman* off Sea Girt.)

Once her passengers and freight were discharged, the *Algonquin* steamed under her own power to the Tietjen & Lang dry dock in Hoboken. There she spent the next few weeks undergoing repairs to her damaged bow.

The collision and sinking left a long and churning wake, not the least of which was the loss of most of the mail. Anyone who has ever had a letter go astray can sympathize with the thousands of people who suffered the inconvenience of lost correspondence. The *Fort Victoria* took with her to the bottom 261 sacks "consisting of 15 sacks of letters, 37 sacks of printed matter, 155 sacks of parcels, 52 sacks of mail from foreign countries and 2 sacks of empty equipment." Coast Guard cutter *215* scooped up fourteen of these sacks after the sinking. These sacks had been stowed on deck. "The salvaged mail, consisting of three sacks of printed matter, nine sacks of ordinary parcels and two sacks of registered mail, was taken to the Coast Guard base at Staten Island and turned over to the postmaster at Stapleton, who returned the mail to the Varick Station in New York."

Upon inspection, "there appeared to be little damage other than that occasioned by dampness." Most of this mail was "forwarded to its destination on the *Bermuda* of the Furness Bermuda Line."

There was also the matter of 400 tons of freight in the *Fort Victoria's* cargo holds. This consisted of "everything from a needle to an anchor." In addition to season's greetings, the *Fort Victoria* carried Christmas packages and a large consignment of goods for local stores. The tiny community of Bermuda relied almost entirely on imported items for survival. Shippers worked feverishly "to get substitute cargo aboard other ships heading for the island."

Some four hundred trunks, filled with the "summery apparel" of the passengers, were lost. The Furness Bermuda Line reversed its earlier position with respect to insurance coverage, and argued that "the ship line is not responsible for the baggage of its passengers nor for the freight in its hold." Merchandisers were in the habit of insuring their shipments against loss or damage. More than forty companies carried re-insurance policies on the cargo stowed in the *Fort Victoria's* holds. But the baggage of the passengers was uninsured. Today, most people have homeowners insurance to cover the loss of luggage and personal possessions, but this was generally not the case at the time.

At the time of her loss, the *Fort Victoria* was valued at $1.5 million. The hull was partly insured. Blackiston noted that the liner could not be salvaged, that "the point where the ship went down was too deep for any efforts to raise her to be successful." This statement was not completely accurate. It would have been more precise to state that the ship could not be raised and repaired within the limits of economic feasibility; that total hull salvage and reconditioning of the machinery and appurtenances would cost more than the construction of a new replacement vessel, and would probably take more time. The *Fort Victoria* was abandoned and written off as a total constructive loss. This may have satisfied the owners, if not the underwriters, but it did not completely resolve the situation.

The wreck lay in a precarious position: a hazard to all traffic entering and leaving the most active port in the world - a port that was "already helpless in the grip of the worst fog in years." The wrecking tug *Relief* took soundings around the wreck. The Lighthouse Service marked the site with a buoy. "Steamships approaching the harbor were warned by radioed messages from their lines to proceed cautiously up the channel." It was reported that the depth of water there is from 54 to 60 feet and the difference between high and low tide is about five feet. The vessel is 56 feet beam, so that her starboard side can be seen awash and at low tide her whole length is visible from stem to stern as the swell rolls against it like a miniature reef."

For months, Army engineers worked on designing specifications for removal of the wreck before bidding out the job to private contractors. At first, there was hope that the mail and some of the cargo could be salvaged. But after too much time passed without salvage operations commencing, it was determined that everything would be too water damaged to make piecemeal salvage worthwhile. Army engineers gave up on that idea and decided instead to specify that the hull should be raised without consideration to saving its contents.

"Shipping interests and mariners will be glad to have the dangerous wreck removed from the vicinity of the Ambrose Channel, as it is a menace to navigation. Nearly two months have elapsed since the accident in a heavy harbor fog and pilots of the large passenger liners declare they will be greatly relieved when contracts are let and crews begin pumping out the holds and laying pontoons around the submerged vessel. Such a task will take from three to nine months and will cost at least $150,000, engineers believe. If unforeseen difficulties are encountered the cost might mount to a much higher figure."

This rhetoric was repeated a couple of months later, when the Army engineers were still considering what to do about two wrecks that were blocking traffic in the shipping lanes: the *Fort Victoria* and the former lighthouse tender *Mistletoe* (see *Shipwrecks of New York*). Spring was "a busy time of the year for the engineering department. . . . Projects are being examined which will affect the channels and anchorages of New York Bay, the Hudson River, the East River and Long Island Sound. About $7,000,000 will have been expended by the Federal Government on such projects by the close of the fiscal year June 30."

The *Fort Victoria* was not one of the expenditures for that fiscal year. The summer of 1930 came and went, and still the huge rusting hulk blocked the shipping lanes and caused consternation among mariners and pilots. Not until the first week of October was affirmative action taken. Raising and removing the hull proved impractical. "Removal" became "demolition." Twenty-five tons of dynamite were placed along the submerged hull, all to be detonated in one titanic blast.

Anticipating the event and the attention it would receive, the Coast Guard arranged for a special fleet of cutters to patrol the vicinity of the site. "It is expected dozens of fishing boats will try to get as close as possible to the place of the explosion in order to gather fish killed or stunned by the explosion."

The reaction among anglers was quite the opposite of that expected by Coast Guard intermediaries. Instead of hoping to prey garishly along the sidelines to reap a rich harvest of dead fish, amateur anglers protested in order to have the demolition postponed until the closing of the fishing season, on November 20. With their own best interests at heart, they feared that the gigantic fish kill resulting from the explosion would ruin their sport fishing for the rest of the year - a year in which fish were more plentiful than ever before. Couple this with the fact that the amount of dynamite to be detonated was supposed to be increased threefold - to seventy-five tons - it was certain that fish reserves would be seriously depleted and the sport fishing season terminated early.

The case of the sport fishing folk was pled by John Lynch, the president of the Board of Trade of Staten Island's borough of Great Kills (a name whose ironic implication appears to have been lost among issues considered so serious). The *New York Times* took the torch by printing an editorial on the angler's behalf. Under "Topics of the Times" appeared an editorial entitled "Unreasonable Cruelty to Fish." It stated (with a wry touch of humor):

"No fisherman can read the appeal of the Great Kills (S.I.) Board of Trade without emotion. It seems that some stony-hearted corporation or government official is about to blow up the steamship *Fort Victoria*, which sank in a collision with the *Algonquin* some time ago and now reposes on the sands at the bottom of the sea at the mouth of Ambrose Channel.

"The explosion of seventy-five tons of TNT will kill thousands of fish, which, the board moans, have never been so plentiful. No doubt even those that survive will have their nervous systems shattered, or at least, their dispositions ruined for life. And so much, in the presence of a lure, depends upon the disposition of a fish.

"Really, the aggrieved Staten Islanders should have carried their case to President Hoover instead of Borough President Linch (sic). Mr. Hoover's friendly disposition toward fish is well known. He could call in the head of the Bureau of Fisheries and the head of the Bureau of Navigation - both in his old Department of Commerce - and let them fight it out. Surely he would be able to persuade them at least to postpone the slaughter until after the close of the piscal year on Nov. 20, which is all that the Board of Trade asks."

D-Day was delayed, but only for a couple of weeks. On October 16, more than ten months after the much-loved liner went down, demolition day arrived. Despite a reduction in the size of the charge, "a tremendous eruption of water more than 700 feet in height which spread over an area of the sea 100 by 400 feet, was heaved from the surface of lower New York Bay off Sandy Hook this afternoon, when twenty-four tons of dynamite were set off under the sunken liner *Fort Victoria*, lying alongside Ambrose Channel, in a successful attempt to blast a hole in the bottom of the sea into which the hulk could sink.

"The mammoth charge was detonated shortly after 3 P. M., following a warning to all shipping in the lower bay to keep out of the danger area. The mighty blast, like some great undersea volcanic disturbance, hurled thousands of tons of water into the air, shook the sea and earth for miles around, and tore a hole some forty feet deep in the ocean bed into which the sunken vessel slid. . .

"Recently a contract was let to Charles W. Johnson, Inc., engineers of Lewes, Md., by the Army Engineering Corps for underwater operations to sink the hulk. Bad weather and rough seas repeatedly delayed the laying of the dynamite. The high explosives were put down in four strings, each 420 feet long, parallel with the hull of the vessel. Charges of more than 100 pounds each were set at four feet intervals on the strings.

"Today, with fair weather favoring operations, the last of the dynamite was laid, and warnings sent out to shipping that the explosion would be set off in the early afternoon. Coast Guard cutters patrolled the area within several miles of the sunken vessel, and several larger ships were held outside Ambrose Channel until the blast had been touched off.

"A second after the explosion the great curtain of water shot skyward. The roar of the falling waters could be heard for miles, and after the sea had subsided over the wreck, hundreds of blackfish were found floating on the surface, killed by the heavy concussion. Some crates of provisions also bobbed to the surface from the shaken interior of the hull, and a great film of heavy black oil spread over the sea.

"Engineers who made soundings soon after the explosion reported the liner had sunk about forty feet and were highly satisfied with the operation. A second and smaller explosion will be set tomorrow, weather permitting, to sink the Fort Victoria to a depth of fifty-three feet at low tide, at which depth she will no longer be considered a menace to navigation and will be left to rot in her watery grave."

Still, this was not the end of the demolition derby. An examination by divers found that the wreck had been blown into three sections but was "only partly pushed into its intended grave." Eight months later - on June 18, 1931 - another twenty tons of dynamite were detonated alongside the hull in order to blast it farther down into the bottom. This blast required two weeks of preparation. Divers placed fifty-pound sacks of dynamite at strategic places along what remained of the hull.

"The waters were first cleared of craft for a distance of about two miles radiating from the ship, and after the final sack of dynamite was placed, the charge was exploded, sending a column of water more than 1,000 feet into the air. Residents of Staten Island and New Jersey felt the impact for miles inland and the marine observation building at Navesink Highlands, five miles from the scene, was shaken.

"The explosion sent a quantity of debris and dead fish high into the air and created a high wave of debris-covered water which swept toward a motor launch which had been used in stringing wires attached to the explosives. The result was a race of a half mile between the launch and the wave, which was won by the launch when the wave finally subsided. Fragments of the ship and floating matter were scattered for a great distance. Dead fish which were flung on the waters were gathered up by fishermen who had been held outside the danger zone by the Coast Guard until the work was done."

The *Fort Victoria* no longer presented a hazard to navigation, but the liner was a long way from being forgotten. In human affairs, seldom does the attribute of "accident" serve to appease the financial interests of those afflicted. After an accident - any accident, even one that is called an "act of God" (no one's fault or negligence) - inevitably comes blame and castigation. It is a sad affectation of American culture that acceptance cannot be gained, nor closure achieved, until a person or group of people can be found at fault. So with the steamers *Algonquin* and *Fort Victoria*.

It might seem at first blush that a vessel that was hove to (temporarily stopped dead in the water) could hardly be held accountable for being rammed - any more than a parked car could be held at fault for being hit by a moving vehicle. But suppose that car were stopped in the middle of a highway? Would that not provide grounds for a case of contributory negligence? Surely the *Fort Victoria* was stopped in a highly traveled sea lane, and in a dense fog. Yet the nautical rules of the road permitted her to do so as long as she was tooting her steam whistle and ringing her bell.

As soon as the *Algonquin* was able to dock, her captain and the officers of the watch were ordered by the U.S. Steamboat Inspection Service to give evidence at an official investigation, in order for the inspectors to determine the cause of the collision. Initial findings were unsatisfactory. The *Algonquin's* Captain McKenzie issued a statement in which he claimed that his ship was "proceeding cautiously under very slow speed, stopping at regular intervals, and blowing the usual fog signals. All at once a vessel loomed up and although the captain backed full speed it was impossible for him to clear the other ship." This statement did not constitute evidence.

It should come as no surprise that the Clyde-Mallory Line placed responsibility for the collision on the *Fort Victoria*, on the ground that her "fog signals were not being sounded."

Furness Bermuda Line representative W.J. Love was noncommittal when he heard about McKenzie's accusation. "Very interesting." He then expanded his response by adding that the matter was "purely controversial" and that his company had "no intention of become involved in a controversy." He later amended his statement by saying, "There was no mystery about the sinking of the *Fort Victoria*. It was simply an unfortunate catastrophe that can be blamed on the heavy fog."

Perhaps in a moment of introspection, Clyde-Mallory Line Vice President J.E. Craig backed off his company's hard line by stating that the matter was still under investigation, and that any attempt at that time to affix blame "would be premature."

Hampering the investigation was the fact that the Steamboat Inspection Service had no jurisdiction over the *Fort Victoria* or her captain and crew because the ship flew a foreign flag - she held a British registry. Even though the Furness Bermuda Line operated out of U.S. ports, the company could not be forced to cooperate in the investigation. Nor did they.

On December 26, Captain McKenzie and other officers of the *Algonquin* gave testimony in which they reaffirmed their earlier position that the ship was proceeding slowly and cautiously, and that no one on board had heard any fog signals from the *Fort Victoria*. The investigation was then deferred until other witnesses could be procured, namely the captains of the pilot boats *New York* and *Sandy Hook*: James McCarthy and Frederick Seeth, respectively. They were not available until January 7, 1930. From their testimony it was determined that the *Fort Victoria* had indeed been "blowing her fog signals at frequent intervals when the *Algonquin* suddenly appeared through the fog and crashed into the port side of the *Victoria*, about midships, at nearly right angles."

The *Algonquin* was found to be solely at fault for the collision.

The Clyde-Mallory Line did not concede the investigators' conclusions graciously. The company filed suit against the Furness Bermuda Line. On one hand, the company wanted its liability limited, and in this they were successful. (See *Scotland* for a full explanation of liability limitation.) On the other hand, they claimed that the *Algonquin* "was not liable for loss of the cargo and personal effects of passengers and crew, since the proximate cause of their loss was the negligence of those in charge of *Fort Victoria* in failing to beach her before 4 hours had elapsed after the collision and prior to the sinking. In particular *Algonquin* claimed that the assistance of tug *Columbine* which had answered S.O.S. signals had been improperly refused in order to avoid salvage payments."

The latter point was based upon an Admiralty salvage law, which asserted that any vessel which rendered aid voluntarily to a stricken vessel could receive, as compensation for successful salvage, a sizable percentage of the value of the vessel and cargo that was returned to the stream of commerce.

Perhaps driving the *Algonquin's* offensive was the fact that five hundred eighty-five claimants were seeking compensation for the loss of cargo and baggage.

The case was summed up thus: "The collision occurred at 3:45 p.m. Passengers were gotten off in life boats by 4:48 p.m., but the last life boat was not picked up safely until 5:45 p.m. A skeleton crew of 13-16 then proceeded to make *Fort Victoria* ready for towing to shallow water by pilot boat *New York*. No steam was available and it was dark; it was finally necessary to cut the anchor chain with a hack saw, and towing of *Fort Victoria* did not actually begin until 6:40 p.m. At 7:05 the towing hawser parted; a new hawser was passed and made fast at 7:30 p.m. At 7:50 p.m. *Fort Victoria* turned over and sank."

Algonquin lost the case hands down, but in order to defer payment, her owners kept appealing the court's decision. The case was not settled until April 2, 1934. In its final ruling, the court noted that the "petitioners have taken this appeal from a decree awarding damages to the claimants of the cargo and personal effects on board the *Victoria* on the ground that sufficient time and assistance were available to beach her and save her cargo and that her sinking and damage to the cargo were due to the intervening negligence of those in charge of the *Victoria* in failing to have her towed to a place of safety and that accordingly the collision was not the proximate cause of the loss."

There was no hint of incredibility in the court's written words, yet the absurdity of the *Algonquin's* position cannot be easily ignored. The court went on to note that "to be relieved of liability they must show an intervening act of negligence so extravagant and unusual, and in such disregard of every rule of prudence, as to be beyond the horizon of ordinary foresight." The court found otherwise. The most that the court was willing to allow was that "if, with better judgment, the master had accepted assistance sooner, or had adopted wiser means to get his anchor lifted, or had otherwise expedited towing of his vessel into shallow water, yet it was quite within reasonable expectation that in an emergency there might be delay owing to the exercise of judgment other than the best, which would prevent him from beaching his rapidly leaking vessel until it was too late to save the cargo. . . .

"It is contended by the appellants that the master of the *Victoria* did not get prompt and adequate assistance as he ought, that he was negligent in clearing the anchor chain so that towing operations could be begun and in general was too slow in starting the towing operations, and at fault in employing too short and fragile towing lines. [*Algonquin's* attorneys were clutching at all straws, no matter how slender.] It is to be remembered that it took about an hour to get the passengers off the vessel and another hour to see that the boats in which they had been placed were picked up and the passengers and the crew, except those of the crew who remained on the *Victoria*, were put on boats to take them ashore. We are not satisfied that the *Columbine*, which appellants insist should have been used to tow the *Victoria*, was better for that purpose than the *New York*. It is said she had hawsers more adequate for the purpose than those used, but this fact was never brought to the attention of the master of the *Victoria* and it is by no means certain that long hawsers such as are used for towing on the high seas would have been as good for the waters in which the towing had to be done as the lines actually used. As Judge Coxe held, it was inadvisable to have a long tow line in the darkness and fog. The *Victoria* had no lights and the towing vessel would not have been able to see her tow in the fog and darkness or to steer its course at all if it had been far away from her. A long towing line would certainly have added to the difficulties and uncertainty of the navigation.

"Faults are alleged in respect to the steps taken to free the anchor chain so that the towing might begin. It is said that the master should have used the acety-

Black sea bass.

lene torch of the *Columbine* instead of sawing off a link with a hand saw. But it seems uncertain what, if any, time would have been saved by doing this, for the sawing had begun before the arrival of the *Columbine* and it might reasonably have been thought to take less time to complete it than to get the torch from the *Columbine* and use it.

"The master asked the *Columbine* to stand by and he chose another vessel, equally good, for towing. The *Columbine* did stand by and as a matter of fact furnished the means for enabling the crew to escape from the vessel as she was sinking and likewise saved the life of the master of the *Victoria*, who was the last to leave his ship. It is true that after the *Victoria* had been towed about a mile by the *New York* the cable broke under what was doubtless an uneven strain probably caused in part by the absence of any effective steering apparatus on the part of the *Victoria*. The breaking of a towing line under such circumstances is not unusual and often happens in salvage cases which have come to our attention. The District Judge, in an opinion, held that the master of the *Victoria* did everything that could be expected in the emergency, and we are not disposed to differ with his findings.

"A more detailed discussion of the facts is unnecessary and a more careful scrutiny is useless for the reason that the negligence of the *Algonquin* beyond any question caused the damage and the sinking of the *Victoria*. Whatever errors of judgment the master may have committed, and we are not convinced that there were any, the happenings were those which a vessel wrongfully colliding with another must expect in the situation which she had brought about.

"The decree is affirmed."

The now-defunct Aquarian Dive Club used to dive the *Fort Victoria* in the 1970's and 1980's. The members found an extensive field of debris that gave the appearance of an underwater junk yard in which twisted scrap metal lay heaped upon bent beams and hull plates, interspersed with occasional objects of brass. Since the wreck lay in the shipping lane, their boat was constantly threatened by passing vessels of various sizes - usually many times larger than the *Aquarian*.

Starfish and bergalls.

IOANNIS P. GOULANDRIS

Built: 1910
Previous names: *Maria Stathatos*, *Eggesford*
Gross tonnage: 3,750
Type of vessel: Freighter
Builder: Craig, Taylor & Co., Ltd., Stockton, England
Owner: Goulandris Brothers
Port of registry: Andros, Greece
Cause of sinking: Collision with SS *Intrepido*
Location: 26853.9

Sunk: December 1, 1942
Depth: 200 feet
Dimensions: 362' x 51' x 21'
Power: Coal-fired steam

43577.0

The first ship to boast this odd sounding name was owned by John P. Goulandris, and was sunk during World War One by a German U-boat. She went down in the Bay of Biscay on May 4, 1917.

One war later, another *Ioannis P. Goulandris* met a similar fate indirectly at the hands of a German U-boat because of the U-boat war that Germany was waging against America's eastern seaboard. In this instance, the *Ioannis P. Goulandris* was bound for Searsport, Maine with a cargo of coal from Hampton Roads, Virginia. In response to the U-boat threat, she pulled into the apparent safety of the New York harbor approaches for the night.

Because lighted vessels presented easy nighttime targets to marauding enemy submarines, wartime restrictions contradicted the peacetime nautical rules of the road. Thus the *Ioannis P. Goulandris* was running "blacked out" and was not showing navigation lights. So strict were the blackout rules that portholes were covered to prevent stray light from leaking out, special darkroom bulbs were employed inside exterior door ways, and sailors were not allowed to smoke on deck lest the red glow of a burning butt catch the eye of a German lookout. Of course, plying the shipping lanes at night without showing navigation lights could have deleterious side effects . . .

On December 1, 1942, in the pitch dark at 10:23 p.m., the *Ioannis P. Goulandris* was rammed by the Panamanian freighter *Intrepido*. The *Intrepido* suffered only minor damage, but the Greek freighter began taking on water at an alarming rate. When she radioed for assistance, a plethora of boats responded to her plea.

The Coast Guard dispatched two 83-foot tugs (the *Mahoning* and the *Navesink*), the salvage vessel *Accelerate*, and several motor lifeboats. The *Mahoning's* engine became disabled, and the *Navesink* was turned back by the weather. At the same time, the commercial tug *Joseph H. Moran* intercepted the message, dropped her tow, and proceeded to the scene. But the position was inaccurately given as "off Ambrose Flashing White Buoy." None of the rescue craft could find the site of the collision. By the time the position was corrected to "11

This official U.S. Coast Guard photo was taken six weeks before the *Ioannis P. Goulandris* was lost due to collision.

miles east of Asbury Park," the *Ioannis P. Goulandris* had already slipped beneath the waves.

Fortunately, the entire crew of thirty-one was rescued by the *Intrepido*.

The incident became a mere statistic in the exigencies of war - swept under the rug as it were by another kind of blackout - a news blackout. On March 11, 1942, Secretary of the Navy Frank Knox announced that the news media would no longer be permitted to give the particulars of enemy attacks on Navy or merchant vessels, else Nazi spies and Axis sympathizers could advise German military intelligence on the effectiveness of the U-boat war. Thereafter, newspaper accounts were stiflingly succinct. Gone were the banner headlines and the detailed accounts of sinkings and survivals. The only information that was released by the Navy - and published by the press - were affirmation of a sinking and the size of the vessel in terms of small, medium, or large. In this wise a trenchant, gripping drama was reduced to a single sentence that typically read, for example, "A small merchant vessel was sunk by enemy action in the Atlantic yesterday; the survivors were taken to a U.S. port." Omitted were the name and type of the vessel, tonnage, nationality, location of the attack, and whether or not injuries or fatalities resulted. It was the U-boat war in Cliff Notes!

At the time the *Ioannis P. Goulandris* was sunk, she was involved in litigation concerning cargo that was damaged during a previous voyage. The action taken against the Goulandris Brothers (Basil, Nicholas, and Leonidas - who also owned the General Steam Navigation Company., Ltd., of Greece) was initiated by the American Tobacco Company, R.J. Reynolds Tobacco Company, and Liggett & Myers Tobacco Company "to recover damages to shipments of tobacco moving from Near Eastern ports to ports in the United States."

The Goulandris Brothers declined to reimburse the shippers or to accept responsibility for the damage. The tobacco companies responded by filing suit against the Brothers. Federal Judge D.J. Moscowitz then "arrested" the *Ioannis P. Goulandris* in port. In legal terms, a ship arrest is one in which arrest papers are served upon a vessel by the local marshal, whereupon the vessel is held in custody and is not permitted to depart until the matter has been settled to the satisfaction of the court. However, as a matter of practicality, a vessel may be released from arrest if the owner posts a bond that is sufficient to cover the predicted amount of the award in the event that the plaintiff or plaintiffs prevail.

What transpired in the case of the *Ioannis P. Goulandris* was both creative and unprecedented. Instead of the Goulandris Brothers defending the action on its merits, "the Greek Government made a motion to dismiss the libel upon the ground of sovereign immunity." It seems that "Captain Courbellis, alleged in the papers to be the director of the Mercantile Marine Division of the Greek Consulate General, sent a cablegram to the master of the steamship *Ioannis P. Goulandris* advising him that said vessel had been requisitioned by the Greek Government. Upon receipt of the cablegram the master of the vessel acquiesced in the requisition and made an appropriate entry in the vessel's log to that effect."

The Greek government also notified the U.S. State Department, which then sent a communication to the Attorney General along with enclosures from "the duly accredited Envoy Extraordinary and Minister Plenipotentiary of Greece." These enclosures contained Photostats of the requisition documents (with translations), along with a diplomatic request that read, in part, "The Minister states 'The Government of the Kingdom of Greece, for its public use and in the successful prosecution of the war in which the Government of Greece is now engaged, is in urgent need of this vessel for the transport of materials necessary for the prosecution of the war.'

"The Minister also states that the Greek Government desires that this action against the steamer *Ioannis P. Goulandris* be vacated by the Court as soon as possible and that the vessel be delivered to him as the accredited and recognized representative of the Government of the Kingdom of Greece, or to his duly appointed agents.

"He adds that the *Ioannis P. Goulandris* is engaged upon important public business for the Kingdom of Greece in time of war and that grave damage to the Greek Government will ensue should this attachment be continued and the vessel be detained."

I do not know how the transportation of tobacco could in any way be considered essential to the prosecution of the war. Neither, apparently, did Judge Moscowitz. The judge's written demeanor makes it evident that his suspicious were aroused by the coincidental timing of the vessel's requisition. Either there was collusion between the Goulandris Brothers and a corrupt Greek government, or the Goulandris Brothers had strong political connections and exerted their influence on those in high places.

When "pull" came to "shove," the Goulandris Brothers would have needed connections with the gods on Mount Olympus in order to fob off their legal and moral responsibilities when a certain U.S. district judge was involved, especially one who doubted the veracity of the documents that were submitted to him. Moscowitz continued to exercise his jurisdiction despite increasing pressure from the State Department. He asked for verification of authenticity.

The reply: "While the Department of State obviously was not in a position to pass upon the accuracy of the statements contained in the Greek Minister's note, it felt that, coming as they did from the accredited representative of Greece in the United States, they were entitled to the respectful consideration of the Court."

Moscowitz relied upon relevant case law to assist him in rendering an opinion. In his ruling of June 20, 1941, he noted that the "Department of State in transmitting the communications from the Greek Minister has merely acted as a conduit. The mere fact that the Department of State transmits a claim of immunity of a foreign government is not in and of itself a recognition of a plea of immunity. Had the Department of State accepted as true the statements of the Greek Minister, the Court would accept such action as final and binding upon the Court and would immediately relinquish jurisdiction. The facts here, however, are quite different as has been pointed out. The State Department merely states that the claim of the Greek Minister is 'entitled to the respectful consideration of the Court.' It does not appear therefore that the claim has been 'recognized and allowed' by the State Department. . . . Since it appears that the facts are in issue, a hearing should be had."

Three months later, the case was heard again with respect to the issue noted above. This time a representative of the State Department submitted certified documents from the Greek Minister in which the Greek government's previous position was reaffirmed. Furthermore, the State Department now accepted as true "the statements of fact contained in the Greek Minister's note of May 16, 1941. . . . Motion to reargue is granted and the original motion to dismiss the libel upon the ground of sovereign immunity is granted."

This did not mean that the Goulandris Brothers got away scot-free. It meant only that the *Ioannis P. Goulandris* was released from custody and could not be detained as collateral against adjudicated liability. "The plea of immunity relates to the steamship *Ioannis P. Goulandris* and does not affect the libel *in personam* against Goulandris Brothers."

The court took a dim view of subsequent actions perpetrated by the Goulandris Brothers, noting that they did not "surrender the *Ioannis P. Goulandris* to a trustee nor deposit in Court the value of their interest in the vessel and her pending freight, nor file a stipulation for value therefor." They were ordered to reimburse the tobacco companies for the full amount of their losses. This ruling was sustained upon appeal on May 3, 1943 - five months after the freighter was lost by collision with the *Intrepido*.

At the time of her loss, the *Ioannis P. Goulandris* was not acting in any capacity that could be construed as relevant to Greece's prosecution of the war. She was working as a coastal freighter and was transporting coal from Hampton Roads to northern ports. If a law suit resulted from the ultimate collision, it would not have been heard in the United States because both vessels carried foreign registries.

The *Ioannis P. Goulandris* sank in what is known locally as the Mud Hole: the deep-water trench which connects the Hudson River with the Hudson Canyon. See *Choapa* for more description of this dark river of industrial sludge.

The wreck lies northeast-southwest. Because the hull lists about 20° to port, orientation is somewhat simplified despite normally dark conditions. The starboard rail denotes the high side of the wreck (about 170 feet), the port rail denotes the low side (about 180 feet). If the wreck sat on an even keel it would be difficult to determine one's direction of travel, because one might not be sure whether one was swimming forward along the port rail or aft along the starboard

rail, or vice versa.

Along the bottom of the hull the depth averages 190 feet, but a washout around the sterns goes as deep as 200. In this washout lies the rudder and bronze propeller - a sight well worth seeing. Drop over the taffrail to get there.

The hull is completely intact, as is the midship superstructure and all but the top level of the bridge structure. In 1973, I led the effort to recover the wooden helm and brass stand from the wheel house. The name of the helm's manufacturer (Robert Rogers & Co., Stockton-on-Tees) was stamped on the rudder indicator. This information confirmed the identity of the *Ioannis P. Goulandris*. Previously, this wreck was confused with that of the *Choapa*, which lies only a mile away. Despite the proximity of the two wrecks, the *Ioannis P. Goulandris* has always been strung with less monofilament than the *Choapa*, and visibility, although dark, is typically clearer.

At one time there were two auxiliary steering wheels on the after deck, each about four feet in diameter. In 1985, Bill Nagle, John Moyer, and the author removed one of these wooden wheels by burning off the steel shaft with a Broco torch. Under John Moyer's direction, the other wheel was burned off ten years later by John Chatterton and Danny Crowell. A number of support divers assisted in both operations.

When navigating on the wreck it is best to follow the starboard rail where the working depth is 10 feet shallower than the port rail. Portholes have been recovered from the bridge area where the bulkheads have collapsed. Steve Gatto and the author each found a taffrail log in the silt-filled compartments on the main deck. John Yurga found a sextant. Items of interest have also been found in the midship structure. All the interior compartments are extremely silty, so be careful. The use of a penetration line is advised.

Cod fishing is excellent on the wreck in the winter. The *Ioannis P. Goulandris* is often surrounded by head boats drifting over the wreck. A diver should never carry less than two knives when exploring wrecks in the Mud Hole.

Top two photos: The main bridge helm and bronze stand which were recovered by the author in 1973. These pictures were taken after the lengthy process of preservation and restoration was completed. The name on the rudder indicator led to the identification of the wreck.

Right two photos: One of the pair of stern auxiliary steering helms which the author helped to recover in 1985.

Left photo: The Broco torch in action.

Courtesy of Bill Davis.

LIZZIE D.

Built: 1907
Previous names: None
Gross tonnage: 122
Type of vessel: Tug
Builder: Neafie & Levy Co., Philadelphia, Pennsylvania
Owner: West India Transportation Co.
Port of registry: New York, NY
Cause of sinking: Foundered
Location: 26829.0

Sunk: After October 19, 1922
Depth: 80 feet
Dimensions: 77' x 21' x 10'
Power: Coal-fired steam

43696.3

The precise date of the *Lizzie D.'s* loss is unknown because none of her eight-man crew survived to tell the tale. The steam tug departed Brooklyn on October 19, 1922 and was not seen again until the wreck was discovered fifty-five years later.

The tug's owners claimed that she was on a "cruise of the narrows" (meaning the Verrazano Narrows). But what was meant by "cruise"? Tug boats did not normally go on cruises. Nor does it seem likely that the owners would let her crew take a joy ride around the harbor. Tugs are expensive vessels to operate; they are work boats, not excursion steamers.

The Coast Guard was not notified immediately that the *Lizzie D.* had not returned from her jaunt. In fact, it was not until October 27 that the *Lizzie D.* was mentioned in a Coast Guard dispatch, when the New York division sent a message to headquarters in Washington: "*Manhattan* left 2 pm 26th to search for missing tug *Lizzie D.*"

If anyone truly believed that a tug could be lost in New York harbor for a week without anyone being the wiser, he kept his own counsel. No trace of the

Lizzie D. was found. She was listed as overdue and presumed lost. End of inquiry.

There the matter lay until 1977, when Captain John Larsen went searching for unknown wrecks on his dive charter boat *Deep Adventures*. One of the wrecks he found consisted of an intact steel hull whose upper works had long since rotted away and collapsed. Metal braces that once supported the wooden deck were level with the gunwale. This gave the wreck the appearance of giant bathtub with a metal grille across the top. The depth to the bottom was 80 feet, but the wreck had ten feet of relief.

Larsen brought up a porthole that he found lying loose. Other divers also recovered portholes that day. But the prize artifact was recovered by the *Deep Adventures'* mate, Joanie Fulmer: the ship's bell. The name in bronze identified the wreck as the *Lizzie D.* There is nothing more satisfying to wreck-divers than the discovery of an unknown wreck and its immediate, positive identification.

But this time there was more. Divers dropped between the deck supports into the hull. Sunbeams lanced through the shallow water column and illuminated the interior. In plain view, lying helter-skelter atop each other, were hundreds and hundreds of liquor bottles - many still corked and with their contents preserved: Canadian whiskey, Kentucky bourbon, and gin.

Had the crew been out on a week-long binge? Had the company thrown a party for extraordinary service? Did the men get so drunk that they inadvertently passed out of the harbor and wound up south of Jones's Inlet? None of the above. The cargo was contraband. The *Lizzie D.* was involved in smuggling.

The Volstead Act of 1919 instituted national prohibition and started more than a decade of troubled times in not-too-distant waters. Ordinary citizens were branded as criminals when they exercised their free will to imbibe alcoholic beverages. Thus was born the era of speakeasies, moonshine, the real McCoy, and rum running.

Foreign countries did not recognize the U.S. prohibition against drinking alcohol - for medicinal purposes or otherwise. They found a willing market in American entrepreneurs. Since distributors could not legally deliver their wares to U.S. ports, they were met by local wholesalers in international waters beyond the three-mile territorial limit, where American law did not apply. These clandestine meetings usually occurred in the dead of night - and the less moon, the better.

The Coast Guard had its hands full chasing speedboats laden will illegal liquor. Often they battled it out with deck guns and small arms against violators who were bolstered by the product from their own stock - an uneven battle in which the Coast Guard's fighting spirit clashed with the rum runners' fighting spirits. If the rum runner won by means of escape, a hundred proof cargo found its way to the hands and mouths of willing buyers. If the Coast Guard won by means of capture, the perpetrators were arrested, the boat and its contents were confiscated, and the anonymous investors lost their money and their merchandise.

But the profits were so large that the bootleggers just bought their boats back at auction, then sent them out again to bring home the booze. Sacrificial crews were easily replaced. The truly wise grog dealer prosecuted his business by transporting intoxicants aboard a boat of little value - one whose loss was affordable and could be written off their profits, if not off their taxes. In that case, seizure was only an inconvenience. Apparently the *Lizzie D.* was considered such a craft: old, dilapidated, and expendable.

The *Lizzie D.'s* cargo of social lubricants has been lightered in the decades since her initial discovery. Divers have recovered hundreds, perhaps thousands, of bottles whose contents are now legal and even socially acceptable. (Today's prohibition is against drugs and "controlled substances.")

The easily accessible bottles have long since been removed. Yet down inside the debris and the piles of broken glass, intact bottles yet remain. Dig slowly and carefully, wear quarter-inch gloves or mitts, and gently work your hands through the shards - or else you'll get cut on the sharpened fragments.

For obvious reasons, the *Lizzie D.* is popularly known among divers as the Rum Runner.

This partial name board was recovered by the author. The brass letters are bolted to a steel plate.

MACEDONIA

Built: 1894
Previous names: None
Gross tonnage: 2,268
Type of vessel: Freighter
Builder: Craig, Taylor & Co., Stockton, England
Owner: A.C. deFreitas & Co.
Port of registry: Hamburg, Germany
Cause of sinking: Collision with SS *Hamilton*
Location: 26941.7

Sunk: June 13, 1899
Depth: 60 feet
Dimensions: 280' x 41' x 22'
Power: Coal-fired steam

43645.3

When I first saw this broken-up steel hull in 1976, it had just been discovered by Captain Paul Hepler. The wreck had been flattened by decades of collapse. The only parts that rose higher than a few feet off the bottom were two boilers, an old-fashioned steam engine, a propeller shaft, and an impressive four-bladed iron propeller, each blade of which was seven feet in length.

By studying the engine and boilers and approximating their age, I estimated that the wreck had been built sometime prior to the turn of the century. The degree of collapse and the amount of deterioration led me to believe that the ship had been wrecked around the same time. Based on these conclusions, I conducted a methodical search through the records and chronological shipwreck listings in my research files. The tip that led to my initial identification came from *Perils of the Port of New York*, by Jeanette Edwards Rattray. The chronological list of wrecks at the back of the book gives dates and names which can provide a researcher with a starting point. In this instance, I found a marine casualty that occurred off Sea Bright only a few miles from shore. Once I had a date and the name of a possible suspect, the *New York Times* index revealed the existence of an article about a collision that occurred between Long Branch and the Atlantic Highlands. The location and the condition of the wreck proved a perfect match.

On June 13, 1899, the Old Dominion Line steamer *Hamilton* left New York under the command of Captain Ira Dole. Bound for Norfolk, Virginia were one hundred fifty passengers, fifty of whom where apprentices from the Naval training ship *Essex*. In the dense fog, the *Hamilton* twice ran aground in the Verrazano Narrows before reaching the open sea.

Inbound from Cienfuegos, Cuba was the Ward Line freighter *Macedonia*. Her master was Captain Kuffah. In addition to a crew of twenty-six, the *Macedonia* carried six passengers and 19,400 bags of sugar.

Around 6 p.m., the officers of both vessels were put on their guard by whistles. Captain Dole "said he thought the sound was from the fog whistle of some schooner and that he was clear of her. He gave an answering whistle and ported his helm slightly, intending to get well to starboard of the oncoming vessel, and slowed down. A moment later the black hull of the *Macedonia* loomed up scarcely a ship's length away and heading to port directly across the *Hamilton's* bow. Capt. Dole signaled his engines full speed astern, gave three whistles to show he had given the order, and threw his rudder hard to starboard.

"The *Macedonia* kept on her way, and a moment later the crash came. The bow of the *Hamilton* struck the side of the *Macedonia* a short distance abaft the engine room and at an angle trending toward the stern. The bow of the striking vessel plowed its way into the side of the *Macedonia* almost half way through her, and the air was filled with bits of splintered wood and broken steel and the passengers on the *Hamilton* were thrown into a panic.

"Many women fainted and there were wild rushes for the life preservers. When Capt. Dole saw the grave extent of the collision he started his engines ahead and kept his bow in the hold (sic, should be "hole") of the *Macedonia*, and shouted to her people to climb on board. The *Macedonia's* engines kept going ahead, and in this way for fully four minutes the two vessels circled about, their every movement being attended by the sound of ripping timbers and the crack of breaking iron. The boats of the *Hamilton* were cleared, but not launched, while the *Macedonia* got at least one of her boats into the water and several of the passengers and crew were seen to get into it, while the others braved the storm of flying debris and clambered on to the shattered bow of the *Hamilton*.

"Both vessels were being torn to pieces in the jam, and word was sent to the Captain of the *Hamilton* that his vessel was sinking. . . . He then drew away from the injured vessel and headed his vessel in the direction of the beach. . . . The *Hamilton* was taking in water in torrents through the gaping rent in her bow, and the passengers, believing the vessel was sinking rapidly, were in a state of frenzy.

"The band of passengers from Uncle Sam's navy turned to with a will, and all the pumps were started. It was soon found that the transverse bulkhead prevented the water from getting into the main body of the vessel and precluded danger of her sinking. She was then headed back for Quarantine. . . . Her bow for a distance of fifteen feet above the water line, and extending inboard fully twenty feet, is a mass of twisted and shattered iron and steel. The vessel has a twenty-five foot collision bulkhead, which accounts for her ability to proceed without assistance after the collision."

There was a difference of opinion about the reactions of passengers and crew aboard the *Hamilton*. "The most outspoken of all were the young sailors destined for the Norfolk Navy Yard. They said that many members of the *Hamilton's* crew had acted in a demoralized manner at the time of the accident. They said they rushed wildly about and seemed to have lost their heads."

At least one passenger corroborated these sentiments: "The crew did not man the davits. It was owing to the efforts of some boys from the United Stated training ships that the boats were made ready. Without a word of command the lads set to work at the davits, and practically performed the duties of the crew."

Captain Dole, however, "denies this and said his men were at all times cool and collected. One of the apprentices said he saw one woman running about with three life preservers, and that he saw others who had fainted from fright. Captain Dole was inclined to pooh-pooh the idea of unusual excitement among his passengers."

When a count was taken, it was learned that three passengers and sixteen crew members from the *Macedonia* had made it aboard the *Hamilton*.

While the *Macedonia* lay adrift in the fog, the second mate and five crew members launched a boat and started rowing toward shore a couple of miles distant. On the way they encountered the fishing boat *Conover Gaskins*, whose crew had witnessed the collision. The *Macedonia's* crew told the fishermen that the freighter was in "grave danger" of sinking: an accurate portrayal as she had a twelve-foot hole in her hull.

The *Macedonia's* crew landed at Long Branch. There they "telegraphed the Merritt Wrecking Company to send a tug to the *Macedonia's* assistance."

Meanwhile, the *Conover Gaskins* "put out one of their boats to render assistance to the *Macedonia's* crew and passengers." It was good that fishing boat rescued the people remaining on board, because the *Macedonia* sank before a salvage vessel arrived.

Seaman Edward Wright, "one of the *Macedonia's* crew who came ashore, said that one of the crew was reported drowned, having fallen overboard during the excitement immediately following the collision."

The next day it was reported that "the *Macedonia* lies sunk at a point about two miles off Galilee. Her smokestack, painted cream, with a black top, is about six feet out of the water. Two of her masts can also be seen. The sunken steamer lies in about 45 feet of water in an upright position."

Extrapolating from the report above, if the *Macedonia* were crossing the *Hamilton's* bow from starboard to port, the *Macedonia* would have presented her port side to the *Hamilton*. Yet one official report states that "the *Macedonia* was struck on the starboard side abaft the engine." Today, the hull is so broken apart that it is impossible to determine on which side the *Macedonia* was struck.

The wreck is a popular dive site. Visibility is not the best and the water is generally dark, but the shallow depth makes the wreck an ideal location for beginners with a desire to explore a nineteenth-century steamship close to shore. Fish abound. Lobsters are small. Valves and pipes shine for the brass hounds.

MALTA

Built: 1852

Previous names: *Milford Haven, Queen of the South*

Gross tonnage: 1,611

Type of vessel: Iron-hulled full-rigged ship

Builder: C.J. Mare & Company, London, England

Owner: W.H. Corsar

Port of registry: Liverpool, England

Cause of sinking: Ran aground

Location: Off 9th Avenue in Belmar

Sunk: November 24, 1885

Depth: 20 feet

Dimensions: 243' x 39' x 24'

Power: Sail

One of the worst storms of the decade devastated the coastal states in late November 1885. A furious northeast gale coincided with a spring tide, raising water levels to unprecedented heights. In New York City "the Hudson and the East rivers rose rapidly, and overflowed the streets along their fronts, from the Battery up. Piers were submerged and ferry slips nearly destroyed, while thousands of cellars and basements were flooded." Brighton Beach, near Coney

From *Frank Leslie's Illustrated Newspaper.*

FIRING THE SHOT LINE

From *Frank Leslie's Illustrated Newspaper.*

Island, was cut in two by the sea. Along the New Jersey coast, seaside cottages were literally washed away, bulkheads were uprooted, piers were damaged or demolished, and "miles of railroad track were loosened by the waves, and then lifted by the wind and carried bodily away."

Into this autumn tempest rode the British ship *Malta*, Captain John Moulton commanding. The tall ship was on her way to New York from Antwerp, Belgium with ten thousand empty petroleum barrels and several hundred tons of silver sand. Lost in the storm and unable to maneuver through the driving rain, the iron-hulled windjammer was driven off course by the billowing, wind-swept sea. At half past three on the morning of November 24, she struck the outer shoal off Ocean Beach some two hundred fifty yards from shore, about midway between the Shark River and Spring Lake Life-Saving stations. As the ship thumped and shuddered along the sandy bottom, twenty-four men were suddenly caught in a bitter struggle for life.

The surf was high and dangerous. According to the Life-Saving Service report, "the waves dashed well up on the beach and in places almost covered it. One of the masts went over the side soon after the ship struck. The lower masts were of iron, and as the heavy sea caused the ship to pound violently on the bar the shocks snapped the mainmast in two places, one break occurring fifteen feet above the deck and the other between decks about five feet below the partners. The upper part of the mast, with the topmast, top-gallant mast, and everything attached, fell overboard, while the middle section, twenty feet long, jumped clear of the mast-hole and fell on deck, narrowly missing some of the crew. The upper and lower fore-topsail yards were carried away in the slings at the same time.

"The ship's signal rockets were seen by the patrols of the two stations, and as soon as they could give the alarm the crews hastened to her assistance. Boat service was altogether impracticable in such a sea, and it was only with the greatest difficulty and risk that the Shark River crew crossed the river. They were the first on the ground, but did not take the beach apparatus, as the vessel was within the Spring Lake patrol limits. It would in fact have been next to impossible to ferry the loaded cart over, as the surf was sweeping directly into the river, and to haul it by land would have involved a long and tedious detour of several miles over muddy and almost impassable roads. As it was the boat narrowly escaped upsetting several times in crossing. The ship's mizzenmast fell by the board just as they arrived. The Spring Lake crew came up ten minutes later with their apparatus.

"The ship after striking had thumped along the bar to the southward under the influence of the current and heavy sea, and when the station men arrived was more than a quarter of a mile below the mouth of the river. She had also driven closer in. The two crews fell quickly to work arranging the gear, and in a few minutes everything was in readiness and the gun was fired. The driving rain obscured the vessel almost entirely, and it was impossible to tell where the line had fallen. They had aimed towards the weathermost part of her, the bow, to allow for drift, and the line probably lodged over the head-stays, where it could not be seen in the darkness. After waiting some time, therefore, and finding that the whip was not pulled off, the shot-line was hauled back and thrown to the ship a second time.

"The two keepers, John C. Patterson and Joseph Shibla, judged from the trend of the line that it had again fallen over the ship, and decided to wait for daylight. This was, in fact, their only alternative, although it involved a delay of half or three-quarters of an hour. It was learned afterwards that the firing was heard and understood by the people on board, but they were in so much danger from the broken spars and of being swept overboard that no effort was made to find the line. Two of the masts were gone and the foremast was liable to snap off at any moment.

"As the ship continued to move south the time until daybreak was occupied by the beach men in shifting the gear as she moved and reburying the sand anchor. As soon as it was light enough the men discovered, with the aid of the glasses, that the line had lodged on the end of the flying jib-boom. The people had not yet found it. Keeper Patterson, therefore, waded out into the undertow and shouted to attract their attention, while some of the others held the line up to view. This had the desired effect, as the sailors quickly got the bight of the line in on deck and active operations were commenced.

"It was a long tug to secure the whip, which bowed far to the leeward with the current as the surfmen paid it out from the shore. The tail-block was finally hauled in over the ship's rail and attached to the foremast, and when the hawser followed and was similarly attached, the preparations were complete.

"By this time District Supervisor Havens had arrived from Point Pleasant, in response to a summons by telephone, also Keeper Longstreet and the crew of the Squan Beach Station to the south. A multitude of people had also flocked down from the adjacent villages, and many of them lent willing aid to the station crews. The first man landed in the breeches buoy, at twenty minutes to 8 o'clock, was an East Indian, who had broken his leg two weeks previous, on the passage. He was immediately conveyed in the hand-cart to the cottage of Mr. Davis, and surgical aid called in.

"Shortly afterwards, while the third man was being drawn ashore, a commotion was noticed on the ship's forecastle, and a moment later a man (Karl Edelung) sprang overboard into the surf and struck out for the shore. He was at once swept by the current to the southward, and Superintendent Havens, Keeper Patterson, and several others ran along the beach with a line hoping to reach him. The man was evidently a good swimmer and did bravely until the current carried him from under the lee of the ship and he encountered the full force of the surf, when he was almost immediately overwhelmed and lost. Two or three heavy seas broke over his head in rapid succession when he was yet fifty yards from the shore and seemed to stun him, for the poor fellow threw up his hands and then sank out of sight. It was simply impossible for any one to reach him, he was so far out. The body was not recovered until the following day (25th) near the Bay Head Station, six miles down the coast. It was learned from his shipmates that he had apparently lost his reason through fear, and the commotion observed from the beach was occasioned by the efforts made to restrain him from his rash purpose to attempt to swim ashore. Had he waited his turn with the rest he would have been saved.

"Another of the crew was similarly affected, and when lifted from the breeches-buoy he circled about on the beach, gesticulating wildly, and acted in the most irrational manner. His reason for a time seemed to be completely unbalanced. The effort to save Edelung brought the operations with the breeches-buoy to a temporary standstill, but as soon as it was seen that he was gone, beyond a doubt, the task of rescuing the rest went on.

"It was extremely arduous and trying work, the men being compelled to stand at times waist deep in the water with the rain and spray flying in their faces and almost blinding them. Many of them also had the skin badly worn from their hands by the wet and sand-covered ropes. Moreover, much difficulty was experienced in keeping the hawser taut, on account of the oscillating motion of the vessel and her steady movement to the south. The people, as fast as landed, were conducted to the Davis cottage, where they were immediately supplied with hot coffee and dry clothing. One man, the second mate, narrowly escaped being washed out of the buoy. He left the ship heavily weighted with a bundle of clothing strapped to his shoulders, which almost upset him and nearly cost him his life. The operation of landing the twenty-three men took about two hours, the last one reaching the beach shortly before 10 o'clock. They received the kindest attention from the inhabitants, and on the following day were forwarded to New York, a few remaining to assist the captain. The body of the drowned man was turned over to the coroner and decently interred at Point Pleasant."

After the storm abated there was an attempt to save the stranded vessel. Wreckers installed pumps in an effort to lower the level of the water that had invaded the holds. The hull had been so strained, however, that the sea leaked in through loosened rivets and rents in the plates faster than the pumps could eject it. Salvors did manage to land some four thousand empty barrels on the beach and have them sent to New York by rail.

Salvage operations continued for weeks. By mid December, with winter arriving and conditions worsening, all hope of saving the ship was abandoned.

On December 15, it was reported that the *Malta* "had a large hole in her bottom and the tide ebbed and flowed in her." By that time, some eight thousand barrels had been recovered - a fraction of the total value of her cargo. Salvors recovered less than $3,000 of a cargo estimated to be worth some $28,000.

Furthermore, her underwriters had to write off another $50,000 for the value of the hull. The wreck was then left to rot where she lay, as have so many other unfortunate wrecks. (The two-masted schooner *Peacedale* ran aground near Ocean Grove on the day before the *Malta* came ashore. The *Peacedale* broke up, too.)

Today, not much remains of the *Malta*. Divers who visit her remains are occasionally rewarded by seeing some of her plates protruding from the sand, a grim reminder of heroism that once occurred at this very spot. If the sand is ever washed from the iron hull by a summer hurricane, one might observe a construction design which is inconsistent with that of a sailing ship. This is because the *Malta* began her career as a coal-fired steamer. Her engine was later removed and she was converted to sail.

The *Malta* is just a short swim from the beach. Just in front of the second house south of 9th Avenue, a portion of the wreck sticks out of the water, looking much like a pile (singular for piling, which means piles collectively). The wreck can also be found along an imaginary line extended from the alignment of the two utility poles south of 9th Avenue, and about as far from shore as the end of the jetty to the north. Generally, only ten feet of the wreck is exposed - but you could get lucky and find more.

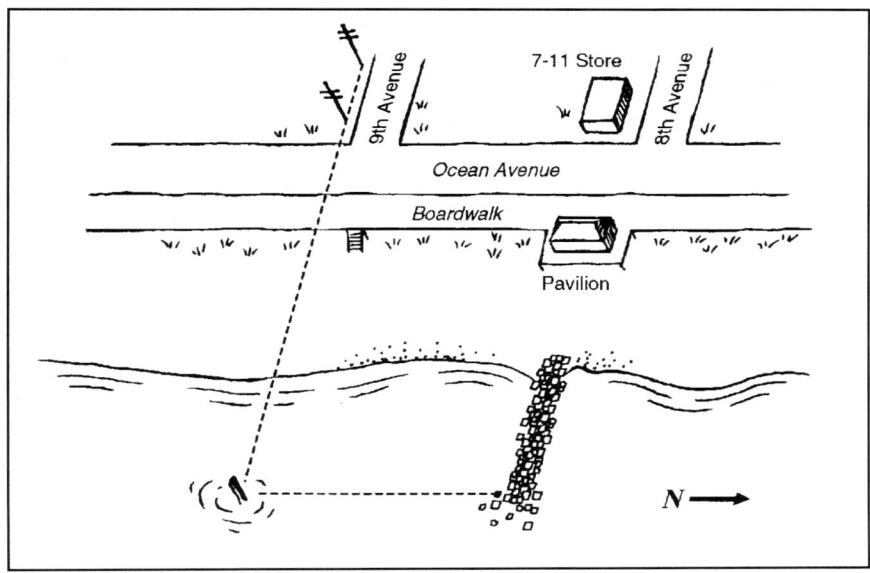

MANASQUAN WRECK

Built: 1816
Previous names: *Amity*
Gross tonnage: 382
Type of vessel: Packet ship
Builder: Forman Cheeseman, New York, NY
Owner: Black Ball Line, New York, NY
Port of registry: New York, NY
Cause of sinking: Ran aground
Location: 1,000 feet north of Manasquan Inlet and 1,000 feet from the beach

Sunk: April 24, 1824
Depth: 30 feet
Dimensions: 106' x 28' x 14'
Power: Sail

The Manasquan Wreck has a long and somewhat sordid history which goes all the way back to the beginning of recreational scuba. Tanks and regulators entered the marketplace in the United States in the mid-1950's. Those who originally ventured into the wild blue deep did so primarily to spear fish. The fact that they dived on shipwrecks had little to do with exploration or a love of history. Shipwrecks were merely places where marine life congregated. A wooden or iron hull offered a substrate on which marine fouling organisms could attach themselves, thus beginning a food chain that climbed the links to the predatory fishes.

A shipwreck is nothing but an underwater junk yard - one which consists of a hull instead of a chassis, ribs or plates instead of fenders, portholes instead of windshields. In other words, refuse. But one person's trash is another person's prize. Treasure is not always measured in terms of gold, silver, and precious stones, but in what is held dear to one's heart. Thus a brass porthole has become an item of desire, and other bits of scrap have assumed an aura of respectability much as old hardware, household commodities, and used furniture have been glamorized. What was once antiquated is now antique, and rubbish has become a relic.

Enter the Manasquan Wreck. Some people were peripherally aware that a wreck existed in the vicinity because, according to charter boat captain John Bogan, in the mid-1940's, a timber from the wreck washed ashore. He said that the timber contained brass bolts (but he may have meant "pins" or "fasteners" instead of "bolts," which by definition are threaded).

In 1955, an angler on a boat snagged his anchor on the bottom. Jack Homer, Edward Patrick, and Robert White were water-skiing nearby when they noticed the angler's dilemma. Homer was a proficient skin diver, so he volunteered to go down and free the anchor. When he did, he found the anchor caught in the low-lying wreckage of an aged wooden ship at a depth of 30 feet. Back on the boat, he observed land ranges so he could relocate the spot.

These three shared information of their find with two friends: John Baker and Robert Franklin. The five men joined forces, purchased some newfangled Aqua-lungs, and proceeded to recover the rich trove of obsolete merchandise that the wreck had to offer: hand-wrought iron cutlery, pocket knives with bone handles, plane blades, iron harness chains, and copper-covered brass pots. The cutlery and pocket knives were still packed in wooden kegs. The pots were nested and fused by encrustation.

For reasons that will soon become apparent, I will call this team of adventurers the Homer Group. They sent some of the salvaged items to the Smithsonian Institution for analysis. The pots were found to have been spun instead of molded, indicating that they originated in Morocco.

In 1956 another team of divers began working the Manasquan Wreck. This team also consisted of five men: John Berringer, Bill Conway, Joseph Magill, Bud Sharp, and William Smith. As a diving platform and salvage vessel they used a 65-foot clam dragger called the *Kingfisher*, which was owned by Berringer and Magill. I will call these men - the Homer Group's rivals - the *Kingfisher* Outfit. Using commercial hard-hat gear, they recovered two tons of sheet lead and three 70-pound tin ingots before the battle for possession of the wreck began. Not to be outdone, the *Kingfisher* Outfit also sent samples of their finds to the Smithsonian Institution.

During that summer there was quite a contretemps over the wreck - literally over the wreck. The Homer Group and the *Kingfisher* Outfit fought verbally over who had more of a right to salvage the wreck: the Homer Group by dint of priority, the Kingfisher Outfit by dint of greater productivity and by non-acceptance of the Homer Group's exclusivity; or dog-eat-dog and may the bigger dog win. Each team continued their work on the site, while fascinated spectators watched the activity from the beach a few hundred feet away.

Once, when both teams tried to work on the wreck simultaneously, hostility raged. The *Kingfisher* Outfit set buoys around the site and began sucking sediment off the wreck with a jet pump, in order to expose cargo that was buried. The ejection pipe spewed muddy water in a thick stream through the air. As the Homer Group approached in a 26-foot boat, the *Kingfisher* Outfit shouted for them to keep away, or they might fill the boat with ejected water and swamp it.

Without inflection and knowledge of the precise wording, this statement could be interpreted in two ways: as a friendly warning intended to save their competitors from harm, or as an open threat about what they would do if their competitors did not leave. The stand-off lasted for four or five hours, during which time both teams "sat and looked at each other."

The upshot of this was that all salvage operations were halted by both teams - not voluntarily, but on the order of Peter Gannon, chief of New Jersey's Bureau of Navigation, Department of Conservation and Economic Development. The State's position was that if there was treasure to be had, the State wanted it, and wanted all of it; and that taxpaying citizens had no right to claim it even though they had worked for it.

As a legal device, Gannon cited the controversial Submerged Lands Act.

According to this Act, passed in 1953, the federal government relinquished all claims to offshore lands in favor of the adjacent State. Gannon asked the State's attorney general to determine if the Act conveyed title to only the land, or if it included abandoned property that was on the land.

The *Kingfisher* Outfit appealed to the Treasury Department. A Treasury Department spokesperson declared that the U.S. could exert a claim only if the ship were a government vessel or carried a government cargo. In the absence of proof of a property interest, the spokesperson also doubted than any other federal agency could claim jurisdiction.

No one could ascertain the identity of the wreck. Based on a study of the items that were recovered so far (such as two-pronged forks, which were long out of use), the date of the vessel's loss was estimated by various experts to be somewhere between 1790 and 1840 - a fairly safe bet with such a wide spread. Records indicated that quite a number of ships stranded on Squan Beach (or Squam Beach, as it was often called in the old days) around that time. Furthermore, Squan Beach was not a pinpoint location but referred to a rather broad area of coast line some twenty miles in length - from what today is known as Seaside Park to the border between Spring Lake and Sea Girt.

Complicating identification was the possibility that two wrecks might be present instead of one. One site yielded tin ingots, and was named the Tin Wreck. The other site lay some four or five hundred feet away and yielded hardware and household items. This second site was variously called the Offshore Wreck, the Barrel Wreck, the Rickel Wreck, and eventually the Manasquan Wreck. Were the Tin Wreck and the Manasquan Wreck two parts of the same wreck, or two disparate wrecks?

Robert Franklin of the Homer Group thought he knew the answer. From some old papers in the Monmouth County Historical Society, he found mention of a sloop called the *Hanna Ann* which went down off Squan Beach on March 24, 1820. The wreck master at the time was John Forman. He compiled a list of the *Hanna Ann's* cargo, which bore "a close resemblance to articles salvaged" from the Manasquan Wreck.

Samples sent to Lloyd's of London received a tentative identification - the *John Minturn*, which was lost in 1846 off Mantoloking: five miles to the south on the other side of Manasquan Inlet, and a few years too late. Equally erroneous was the suggestion that the cargo dated from the era of the Revolutionary War, which was a few years too early.

New Jersey did not express an interest in the wreck's identity, only about possessing its undelivered cargo and relieving the salvors of the efforts of their labor, in order to stuff State coffers with unearned income. The State settled the dispute between the Homer Group and the *Kingfisher* Outfit by bureaucratic fiat: an arbitrary decree which was passed without appeal.

Both the Homer Group and the *Kingfisher* Outfit hired attorneys in order to bring the matter to court. Even though the State assigned itself ownership of the wreck, the two dive teams were the salvors in possession of the recovered items. As such, they were entitled to receive a salvage award for the successful performance of the task. Each also wanted to be named as salvors for future operations.

At an evidentiary hearing, Superior Court Judge Thomas Schettino ruled that the Homer Group held a prior claim to that of the *Kingfisher* Outfit. The judge further determined that the group's priority entitled them to receive a "quite liberal" salvage award, and that they had earned the right to be the State's legal salvors at the sites of the two wrecks. In other words, the State of New Jersey would have to pay the Homer Group a high percentage of the proceeds from the sale of the items that were recovered.

With the legal wrangles behind, salvage began in earnest in 1957. Among the booty that the Homer Group recovered that summer were more tin ingots, rolls of copper wire, a miscellany of iron hardware, broken china, an iron knocker, and 23,000 brass uniform buttons which were marked "London extra rich" on the back. All salvaged items were placed under the jurisdiction of the court, and were turned over to the New Jersey Bureau of Navigation for safe keeping.

An auction was scheduled for Saturday, January 18, 1958. It was held at the Point Pleasant office of the Bureau of Navigation - not inside the building but in an unheated shed. Advertisements lured about one hundred bidders from as far away as Philadelphia, Newark, and Cape May. (Five hundred people had shown up the week before, when the merchandise was spread out for show.)

Perhaps reminiscent of the day the Manasquan Wreck was lost, the weather turned cold and nasty, with wind gusts reaching as high as forty miles per hour. Bidders huddled in hats and overcoats, and perhaps it was the frigid air that prevented them from raising their hands to make a bid. They seemed to be more curious than serious.

The largest sale was a lot of ten tin ingots, which fetched $511. Tin was valued at $1.08 per pound the year before. Then it dropped to just under a dollar. Since each ingot weighed seventy pounds, ten ingots could have been sold for scrap for nearly $700. Someone got a good buy. The ingots were assayed and found to be 99.8% pure - about the same percentage of purity as a bar of Ivory soap.

Copper pots (advertised as kettles) were scooped up by antique lovers for as much as $15. Many, though, were not in good condition - dented, eroded, green with verdigris, and marred by encrustation - and went for as little as $7. The door knocker was sold for $21. The iron hardware fared the worst, for much of it was unrecognizable

Buttons were sold by the bagful - one hundred buttons to the bag. The first bag of buttons brought $15.50, but by the time the last bag was unloaded, only a couple dozen bidders remained, and the highest bid dropped to $3 per bag.

The three hours of bidding could hardly have been called fast and furious, especially as people drifted off the warmer climes during the latter stages of the auction. The grand haul was disappointing. After all that work and legal shenanigans, the entire lot realized $1,648.50, hardly enough to pay for the air. The profits should have been charged a nuisance tax.

This was not the end for the Manasquan Wreck. Stanton Devereux was surf fishing opposite the wreck site when he waded into the surf for a cast and bumped his shin against a "hard rock-like object." He picked up the object, which appeared to be a lump of coal to which pieces of eight were adhered. The object weighed about eight pounds. He took it home and cracked it open with a hammer. What to his wondrous eyes did appear - no, not gold doubloons nor a man on a sleigh and eight flying reindeer - but brass knobs such as those found on old chests of drawers. His daughter's high school chemistry teacher examined the object. He thought the mass of slag had been formed by heat and oxidation. The knobs were sufficiently different from items found on the Manasquan Wreck that many people believed the knobs must have come from a different wreck.

In September 1959, William Baals and his four sons went skin-diving in the vicinity of the Manasquan wreck and found a rusted, barrel-shaped mass which, when broken apart, revealed "silver and pewter tableware, brass hardware items, door knobs, files, eyeglasses, buttons, pewter candleholders, tools, buckles, braces, beaver traps, harness fittings, sledge hammers, and many other home and farm articles, all hand made in England, and placed as belonging to the period from 1750 to 1770, and an assortment of wooden locks." Some of the tableware was stamped "Yates, Ltd."

The depth was given as 50 feet. Another wreck, or another piece of the Manasquan Wreck?

A year later, a forty-foot chunk of wreckage was hauled off the sea bed by Albert Maraziti. He put it on display in a specially-built shed, and professed his belief that it was the remains of a Viking ship. Unlikely. But, could it have been another section of the Manasquan Wreck, separated from the main hull when the ship broke apart in the surf?

After 1960, the Manasquan Wreck faded into relative obscurity. I do not mean to imply that the wreck lay totally forgotten, only that it no longer fired the imagination of the masses. The State lost interest because historic preservation did not bring in the bucks, and the scandal sheets were not willing to waste precious column inches on a story which did not promote sensationalism.

On the contrary, the Manasquan Wreck was very much remembered, but only by a small clique of people. This new group was driven not by the wreck's exploitation potential, the category to which the State and the *Kingfisher* Outfit belonged, but by exploration and discovery for their own sake. This was akin to the force that drove the Homer Group. They were not fortune hunters, but relic seekers: collectors of lost objects which held no monetary worth, but whose value was intrinsic, and based upon the personal satisfaction that was gained by reclaiming a missing piece of history. This new group came to be called "wreck-divers."

Commercial salvage of the Manasquan Wreck came to an end. What took its place was a growing number of divers who were charged by the same excitement and enthusiasm that inspired the Homer Group. From then on, wreck-divers have explored the Manasquan Wreck and have consistently brought back pieces of history that might otherwise have been lost or destroyed by the sea. The most interesting relics recovered were wire-rimmed spectacles which many referred to as Ben Franklin glasses.

As an aspiring novice wreck-diver, I first dived the Manasquan Wreck in the early 1970's. Visibility was never good - arm's length if we were lucky - but then we never timed our dives to coincide with the tides. We usually dived there because the seas were too rough to go anywhere else. Beach wrecks are best dived on calm days during slack tide when the wreck does not lie in the surf zone. Some wrecks lies in the surf zone during high tide, others during low tide.

The Manasquan Wreck lies far enough offshore that tides are generally not a factor: about one thousand feet from the beach, or two city blocks. The site is affected when a deep swell is running or when the waves are high and the troughs are low. During such times, the surge can be tremendous, often sweeping a diver back and forth over the wreck like a horizontal yo-yo. Visibility is best when the cross current is running south. When the current runs north, it sweeps the muddy outflow of the Manasquan River across the wreck. Diving is best after a winter storm sweeps sand and silt from the area, and when northeast currents predominate. Because the depth is 30 feet, bottom time is limited only by a diver's supply of air.

The main mass appears to represent only a portion of a ship. Its approximate dimensions are forty feet by eighty feet. Frames and timbers still exist. Partially buried barrels are evident everywhere. It was common to transport merchandise of all varieties in barrels because old-time stevedores had no mechanical advantage. Barrels could be rolled along the dock and the deck on reinforced bands. The best place to dig or to fan the sand for relics is around the barrel tops and staves.

Some time during the early days of wreck-diving, a belief developed that the Manasquan Wreck was the HMS *Thistle*. Rumor had it that the *Thistle* was a British warship that ran aground in 1813 (this would have been during the War of 1812). The origin of this rumor is obscure. A modicum of truth supports the rumor, but the full truth exposes the rumor and subsequent belief for what they are. Witness this article that appeared in the London *Times* on April 15, 1811:

"*Thistle*, an 8-gun schooner, commanded by Lt George M'Pherson, was wrecked on Manasquan Beach, about thirty miles south of Sandy Hook, near New York. Six of her crew, including four small boys, perished with their vessel." The date of loss was given as March 6. The four boys were probably powder monkeys.

In 1878, Philadelphia publishers Woolman & Ross published a book titled *Historical and Biographical Atlas of the New Jersey Coast*, which was written and compiled by T.T. Price, a medical doctor. This volume lists hundreds of shipwrecks dating back to the Revolutionary War, including this one: "1813. -- --. *Thistle*, English privateer; cast away near Squan Inlet and lost."

Privateering was legalized piracy. A privateer was a person (or a vessel) who was given special permission by a country to raid the ships of another country with which the permitting country was at war. This permission was called a "letter of marque." Among the most famous privateers were Francis Drake and the *Golden Hine*, Jean Lafitte, William Kidd (who later turned to piracy), Edward Teach (better known as Blackbeard the Pirate), and Rafael Semmes and the

Amity Site Plan

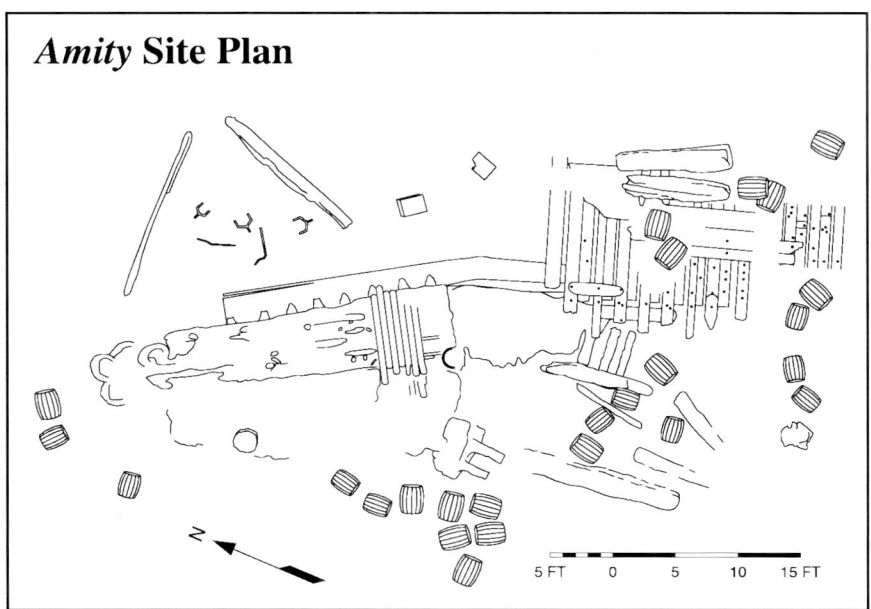

5 FT 0 5 10 15 FT

Site plan courtesy of the New Jersey Historical Divers Association, Inc.

Confederate raider *Alabama*.. Since privateers often had their holds filled with stolen treasure (technically, the spoils of war), a wrecked privateer might contain a valuable cargo.

Now a third *Thistle* enters the picture, this one also British, a schooner that was captured by the American privateer *America* in 1815, while the War of 1812 was still raging. The *Thistle's* cargo consisted of "linens, chintzes, women's shoes, pickles, teas, beads, medicines, wines, hats, muskets, gunpowder, prunes, nests of trunks," and other miscellany. A prize crew was placed aboard to sail the vessel to Salem. On March 19 she was recaptured by the British sloop-of-war *Cossack* off Cape Sable and sent to Halifax, a British port. But the British capture had taken place after the expiration of time established by the peace treaty signed at Ghent on December 24, 1814. The treaty terminated hostilities yet left leeway for word to reach all the theaters of operations. (Remember that this was before telegraph service.) By one of those odd quirks of war, the British then had to return the *Thistle* to the Americans who had stolen her from the British in the first place!

Blend the circumstances of the first *Thistle* with the designation of the second *Thistle* and the cargo of the third *Thistle*, blur the times, stir thoroughly until mixed, and we have the makings of a belief system that has the attraction of an addictive drug.

What is wrong with the hypothesis that the *Thistle* is the Manasquan Wreck - the thistle in the down, so to speak - is that no cannons have ever been found, that neither warships nor privateers were likely to carry trade goods and general merchandise such as those which were recovered, and that the cargo schooner did not sink. Ergo, the Manasquan Wreck is not the *Thistle*, and the wreck of the HMS *Thistle* remains to be located.

John Bandstra reached a conclusion identical to mine, although he went about it in a completely different manner. In fact, Bandstra now takes center stage in the search for the identity of the Manasquan Wreck. Bandstra grew up on rumors of the *Thistle* because his family vacationed at Manasquan. As did most people, he accepted the story without question. But after gaining his majority, he began to look askance at such a notion. Not one to tackle a job by halves, Bandstra went whole hog into research. In 1992, he found that fierce storms had recently cleaned the sand off the wreck all the way down to the clay bottom, exposing portions of wreckage and debris that had never before been seen. This sparked his imagination about the true identity of the Manasquan Wreck, and gave him the impetus to initiate an intense study program. He infected others with his new-found passion for research. This infection led to the formation the New Jersey Historical Divers Association. (See the Introduction for more detail in this regard.)

Bandstra conducted an exhaustive study of the *Thistle* - one to which I cannot do justice - and eventually discounted it as a candidate for the Manasquan Wreck for reasons similar to those given above. It had to be some other ship, not just any ship but one that carried freight. Where to go from there? Bandstra attacked the problem like the avocational archaeologist that he had become.

Quite a few wrecks are known to have gone ashore on Squan Beach at a time when the area was largely uninhabited. The name was applied to quite a bit of territory. I will not go into detail about each and every wreck, nor justify why most of them were excluded. Bandstra has done a thorough job of that already, and published the results of his research in the NJHDA's quarterly journal. Suffice it to say that they did not provide clues to fit the evidence in one form or another. Some of the most likely suspects on Bandstra's list were the *Stafford* (lost in 1802), the *Amity* (lost in 1824), the *Hannah Ann* (lost in 1826), the *Orbit* (lost in 1827), and the *Mobile* (lost in 1828). My own list added the *Sovereign* (lost in 1835). Other wrecks from the mid 1840's and after were easily discounted: items recovered from the Manasquan Wreck were too old to have been found on later vessels.

Bandstra et al conducted a focused, multi-pronged assault on the problem. They prepared a site map of the wreck, recovered sample artifacts for dating, examined artifacts that other divers had previously recovered, conducted historical research in libraries and museums, and even had Weyerhaeuser perform a cell structure analysis on some of the structural members. This latter test proved that the keel, futtocks, and planking were constructed of white oak, not the stronger and more commonly used live oak.

The result of the NJHDA's preliminary investigations was the realization that the dating of the artifacts was the most crucial component in determining the time-frame of the wreck. Knowing when the ship was lost could lead to the identity of the wreck. Thus began the serious detective work. During the next five years, the NJHDA identified fourteen manufacturers' names on artifacts recovered from the Manasquan Wreck. Bandstra estimated that the group contacted some three dozen museums in the United States and England in order to trace these manufacturers, learn their dates of operation, and establish when they manufactured the products found on the wreck.•

If this sounds like exhausting and painstaking leg work, it is. The most telling feature about all the artifacts that could be geographically placed was that they all originated in Liverpool. That fact virtually eliminated two of the best contenders, the *Hannah Ann* and the *Orbit*, because they were coastal ships and not transatlantic freighters. Coincidentally, the tonnage of the *Orbit* was almost identical with that of the *Amity*: 384 for the *Orbit*, 382 for the *Amity*. Except for their cargoes, the remains of these two ships would have been nearly impossible to differentiate.

The major breakthrough occurred when five brand-name artifacts narrowed the time span to a five-year spread from 1820 and 1824. This process of elimination left only one possibility: the *Amity*. NJHDA members then concentrated their efforts on delving into the history of the *Amity*.

In the National Archives in Washington, DC, I found that the original enrollment for the *Amity* still existed. She was registered in New York City on May 4, 1816. The enrollment form was preprinted, then filled out in long hand with an ink quill. Names and other words were written in flowing script, much like calligraphy, and was common at the time. This script is difficult to read today. Photocopying such documents is not permitted, but I transcribed the following particulars. (Words within parentheses were typeset).

"Francis Thompson of the City County + State of New York[,] Merchants (having sworn that) he together with Isaac Wright, William Wright, Benjamin Marshall + Jeremiah Thompson of said City[,] Merchants are the [owners of the] AMITY of New York (whereof) John Stanton (is at present Master) . . . (and that the said ship or vessel was) Built at the City aforesaid in the present year as per certificates of Forman Cheeseman[,] Master Carpenter under whose direction she was built."

Under this paragraph were given the vessel's vital statistics. She grossed 382 and 17/19 tons, and measured 106' 6" in length, 28' 6" in breadth, and 14' 3" in depth. She had two decks, three masts, a square stern with a round tuck, a billet head, and no galleries. (The billet head did not refer to toilet facilities in the crew's quarters; the billet head was the vertical beam or stem post on the prow, and was usually made of hard wood.) The *Amity* was not a prepossessing vessel by modern standards - about the size of an offshore commercial fishing boat - but she was staunch enough to cross the broad Atlantic on a regular basis for eight years.

Small though she was, the *Amity* could carry as much as five hundred tons of cotton and could accommodate "upwards of 200 emigrants," although she rarely carried that many. Her average crossing time was twenty-five days eastbound and forty-three days westbound. The westbound passage took longer because heavy westerly weather was predominant. In January 1919, the *Amity* arrived in New York after "a hard passage of forty-four days." Once she took as long as fifty-eight days. Her swiftest passage was twenty-two days.

Imagine, if you will, being cooped up on a hundred-foot sailboat with two hundred passengers - excluding crew to run the ship and reef the sails - for a month and a half during the worst of winter storms. Those, as they are wont to say, were the good old days. The reality was not so glamorous. People voided in chamber pots then dumped the contents overboard during wind, rain, and snow. The only fresh air was a snow squall in the face. During a summer passage, the heat between decks, where people slept, rose above 100°. Sweat mixed with grime and vomit created an effluvium that was barely breathable.

In 1817, five textile importers decided to pool their resources in order to implement what was then a novel concept in the transatlantic freight and passenger service: they were going to operate a fleet of ships according to a timetable. Scheduled shipping service was unknown in the early 1800's. A ship did not depart until her holds were packed or her accommodations were filled, or nearly so. This played havoc with exporters and passengers. Freight might lie in a ship's hold for days or weeks, and passengers might have to dawdle on the dock for an equal length of time, awaiting that uncertain day of departure.

Take for example these notices from the *New-York Gazette & General Advertiser* for Saturday, April 17, 1819 - an original paper from the author's collection:

"For Liverpool, the ship *Manlius*, D. Tarr, jr master, will be dispatched in a few days."

"For Liverpool, the coppered British ship *Patent*, R. Ward, master, 230 tons; having considerable of her cargo on board, will meet with dispatch. For freight or passage, apply on board."

"For Liverpool, the fine New-York built ship *Ulysses*, --, master, about 380 tons, on her second voyage only; will be ready to commence loading on Monday next, and having most of her heavy freight engaged, will sail from the 1st to the 5th next month."

"For London, the superior coppered and copper fastened New-York built ship *Cincinatus*, A.H. Griswold, master, a regular trader, and intended to sail about the middle of the ensuing month."

What these five men sought to initiate was a packet service - the first of its kind - featuring regularly scheduled departures that people could rely on. These pioneering shipping magnates were Benjamin Marshall, Francis Thompson, Jeremiah Thompson, Isaac Wright and his son William: all part owners of the *Amity* as well as two other ships: the *Courier* and the *Pacific*. At first these ships sailed in succession but not on a fixed schedule. Then, on October 24, they added a fourth ship - the *James Monroe* - and announced their intention to guarantee departure dates.

These men called their company the Black Ball Line. Their ships were distinguished by a large black ball, visible from a distance, that was painted on the mainsail or the foresail. Packet service commenced in January 1818 with the departure of the *James Monroe* from New York and the *Courier* from Liverpool.

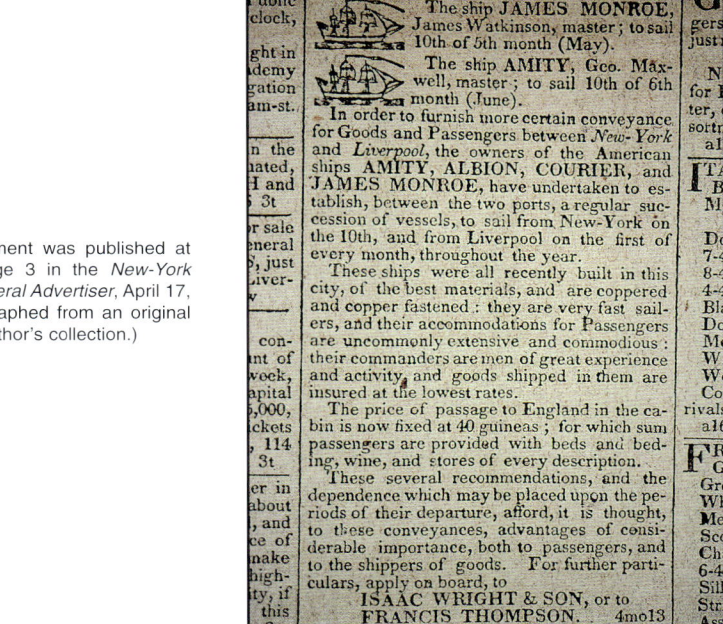

This advertisement was published at the top of page 3 in the *New-York Gazette & General Advertiser*, April 17, 1819. (Photographed from an original paper in the author's collection.)

Thereafter a ship departed at the beginning of every month, the four ships sailing in rotation. These four square-riggers comprised Black Ball's initial core fleet. Of the original four Black Ball liners, the *Pacific* was the oldest. She was replaced in 1819 by the newly built *Albion*.

The Black Ball Line set the trend for sailing packets, and within a few years not only were other transatlantic packet lines edging into the market, but coastal packet lines were being established. The era of certainty and regularity had begun.

Rather than quote again from the *New-York Gazette & General Advertiser,* see the accompanying photograph of the column from that paper in which the schedule of the *Amity* and her running mates was advertised.

Dependability, reliability, and passing accommodations became the watchwords of the day. Once set, the trend to provide faster and better service increased dramatically. And despite the reports of casualties reported in the present volume and elsewhere, transatlantic service was relatively safe. "Only twenty-two out of about six thousand sailing packet transatlantic crossings ended disastrously (to the ship - not necessarily to the passengers)." Another statistic noted that "between 1824 and 1847, only six passengers out of a possible one hundred thousand or more lost their lives in accidents to the New York [transatlantic] ocean packets - something like half a million 'passenger-miles' per death - and the record of coastal packets is equally impressive."

A book such as this, which focuses on casualties, can give the wrong impression that shipping accidents were common and that life in the old days was cheap. Not so. Nor were ships so poorly constructed and maintained that they could be called unseaworthy. Nor were captains untrained and lacking in experience. Nor were crews generally untrustworthy slackers. Accidents occurred at sea just the same as they occur today on the highways - and often no one is to blame.

Most Black Ball ships saw a long and active service. Many, after they were replaced by newer, sleeker, faster, and more commodious ships, continued to ride the waves for years, even decades. The *Pacific* spent seventy-five years at sea. After she left the Black Ball Line she spent sixty-three years in the whaling industry: a true testament of her rugged construction.

In 1822, the Black Ball Line doubled the size of its fleet. With eight ships available the company could offer departures twice a month. The *Amity* continued to hold her own against the incumbents, and there is every likelihood that she would have remained a staunch running mate for many more years had it not been for the accident that caused her premature demise. Her years of usefulness were far from over when she had the great misfortune to lose her way in a fog during her approach to New York harbor.

Hers is a story that is neither dramatic nor fraught with human woe. No storms whipped the sea to a froth, no ice formed on the people in the rigging, no waves smashed her hull to kindling. On April 24, 1824, thirty-seven days out of Liverpool and under the command of Captain William Pease, the *Amity* grounded easily on a sand bar at low tide. The passengers were inconvenienced but were never in any real danger. Once the ship's condition was communicated to New York, two schooners were dispatched to render aid. The passengers were taken off and carried to the city, along with their baggage and the mail. Calm seas and good weather persisted. After a great deal of effort but no risk to life, some of the cargo was lightered. This consisted primarily of dry goods stowed in the upper hold. Then the ship was stripped of her rigging.

The bare hull was left where she lay. When last reported, the *Amity* "had sunk low in the sand and very little cargo has been gotten out. She has hardware in her hold."

The career of the *Amity* was over. Her existence as the Manasquan Wreck began.

Parenthetically, Captain Pease wrecked another Black Ball packet eight months later. On December 24, 1824, he ran the *Nestor* aground at the Fire Island inlet. Again no lives were lost, and again fog was the culprit. But two ships lost was too much for the Black Ball Line to bear with equanimity, so Captain Pease was fired.

No manifest has been found to determine precisely what cargo the *Amity* carried on her final, fateful voyage. So John Bandstra and the NJHDA took a tack that inferred the kind of items she must have transported. They found the auction list from another Black Ball ship, the *Orbit*, which sailed prior to the *Amity* and which arrived in New York before the thick fog descended upon the coast.

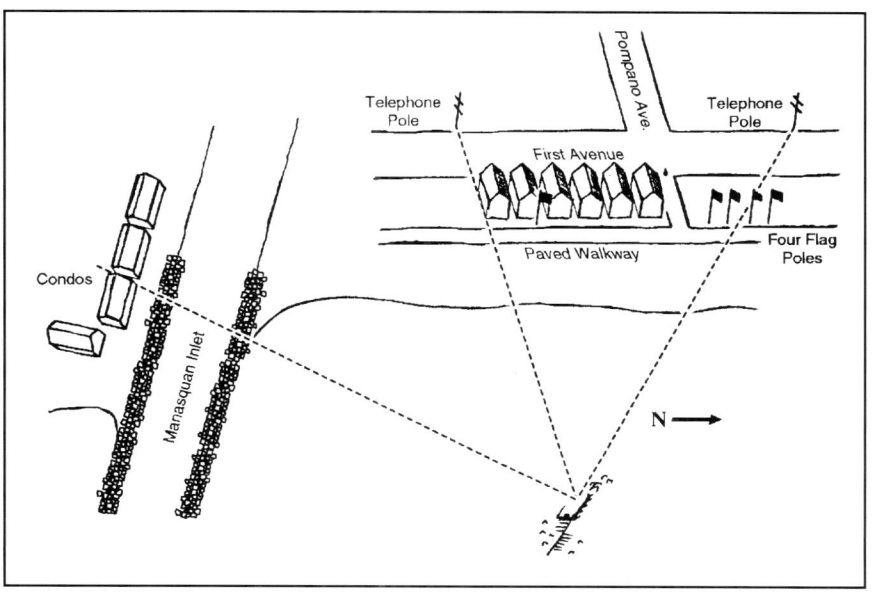

Howard Rothweiler's advice to shore divers is well taken: "This wreck is a long swim from the beach so be prepared and keep your ranges precise." If cross currents are not running fast, gain the beach by way of the Pompano Avenue access, then walk south past six houses. Align the telephone pole on First Avenue with the southeast corner of the sixth house, and swim offshore until you can see a gap between the two eastern condominium units which face the inlet. At this point, look northwest (toward shore) and you will notice four flag poles in a row, and behind them a utility pole. When you align the utility pole with the space between the middle two flag poles, you will be over the wreck's high spot.

Writing in 1997, Bandstra noted that the auction list "was amazingly similar and matched about 45 percent of artifacts recovered from the wreck site from 1955 to our own present day artifact collection. It is important to note that the Squan Beach wreck master, John Forman never recorded removing any of the *Amity's* cargo, so it [is] safe to assume that this wreck site would produce a large quantity of hardware and houseware artifacts, which it has, for over forty years."

Is the Manasquan Wreck truly the *Amity*? Purists would claim that unless an item was recovered from the site on which the name of the ship was spelled, no one could be certain. But those who are experienced at researching shipwrecks know that such a vital clue is usually lacking. Like guilt in a court of law, many wrecks are identified by a preponderance of evidence. If I were a juror hearing Bandstra's evidence, I would find the *Amity* guilty.

Courtesy of the National Archives.

MOHAWK (Revenue Cutter)

Built: 1904
Previous names: None
Gross tonnage: 980
Type of vessel: Revenue Cutter
Builder: Richmond, Virginia
Owner: U.S. Treasury Department (Revenue Cutter Service)
Port of registry: New York, NY
Cause of sinking: Collision with SS *Vennachar*
Location: 26867.6

Sunk: October 1, 1917
Depth: 105 feet
Dimensions: 205' x 32' x 11'
Power: Coal-fired steam

43670.7

    The Revenue Cutter *Mohawk* was the fourth U.S. government vessel to carry the name of the Native American tribe that was part of the Iroquois Confederation. Her primary purpose was to "assist vessels in distress and enforce navigational laws" between Gay Head, Massachusetts and the Delaware Breakwater. In the performance of this duty, she spent six days in 1909 searching the Nantucket Shoals for a derelict, during a gale and heavy seas. She was returning from this task on February 26 when, in order to avoid a big dredger, she ran onto a rock at Hell Gate known as the Little Hogback. Captain Landry ordered full speed astern, but to no avail. The *Mohawk* was stuck fast. As the tide ebbed, the cutter's stern fell, leaving the bow pointing upward toward the New York skyline. Salvage tugs passed hawsers aboard, but they broke with the strain of pulling. It was not until the next day, at high tide, that the *Mohawk* was pulled free from her rocky perch. After temporary patches were placed over holes punctured by the rocks, a small fleet of tugs towed her into dry dock.

After America's entry in the Great War, on April 6, 1917, the *Mohawk* was transferred temporarily to the U.S. Navy, as were all Treasury Department vessels. In her new role as a Naval auxiliary, she patrolled New York harbor and its approaches. Another one of her duties was to ensure that the five interned German merchant ships did not escape from port. She also guarded the Ambrose Channel during convoy operations.

On October 1, 1917, the *Mohawk* was assisting in convoy formation. She was under the command of First Lieutenant Iben Barker. Troop transports and merchant ships were gathering for an escorted Atlantic crossing. Barker reported: "As Headquarters had authorized Cadet Mandeville to stand a regular watch, and as the weather was clear and fine, and all conditions favorable, the other officers were to breakfast."

Unfortunately, Mandeville was not a very observant cadet. At 8:20 a.m., Lieutenant Barker "came on deck and saw a vessel of the convoy a short distance away on our starboard bow, headed at right angles to our course." He hurried to the bridge and took control. He signaled several blasts on the horn, then ordered full speed ahead and the helm thrown hard to starboard.

There was not enough time to avoid the oncoming vessel. The bow of the British ship *Vennachar* cut "into the side amidships, abreast the engine room, between the launch davits, smashing the surf boat, and cutting into the ship's side to such an extent that the use of a collision mat was out of the question."

The *Vennachar* kept her stem in the hole to reduce in inrush of water, but after pirouetting with the *Mohawk* for a moment, she drifted clear. The *Mohawk's* pumps were started, but they could not keep up with the water pouring into the engine room. Barker sounded the general alarm and gave the order to abandon ship. The lifeboats were launched without confusion. Except for September's deck log, most of the ship's papers were saved, including the muster rolls, pay rolls, signal books, and confidential papers.

Barker made a tour of his command, to ensure that no one else was left on board, then put off in the gig. An electrician, who had been reported at his boat, was then discovered emerging from the radio room. He was taken off the sinking ship. Lieutenant Barker reboarded the *Mohawk* for another inspection, and found that the water had by that time risen to the engine room gratings.

The USS *Bridge* arrived at the scene, lowered a boat, and carried an 8-inch towing hawser to the sinking revenue cutter. This hawser was "led through the towing chock and made fast to the forward bitts." The *Bridge* started towing the *Mohawk* toward shallow water.

"A code message was sent to the Convoy Commander, 'Request permission to salve *Mohawk* and join convoy later'. This request was disapproved, but when the reply came, the *Mohawk* was in tow of the *Bridge* and the latter's engines were going ahead one third speed.

"The imperative need of considering all the nation's forces at the present time was appreciated and it was hoped that the *Bridge* could at least reach shallow water with her tow before the latter settled. The Communication Officer was therefore directed to send a second message to the Convoy Commander, 'Have

Mohawk in tow and believe I can save her if granted permission,' but before the message could be completely transmitted it was noticed that the *Mohawk* had begun to sink rapidly and list heavily to port.

"When it was evident that nothing further could be accomplished by towing, the Commanding Officer was forced to cut the tow line and throw both engines full speed ahead to get well clear. With her bow high in the air, the *Mohawk* settled slowly, emitting quantities of smoke; there was no explosion. A boat from the *Bridge* was sent to the spot as soon as safety permitted, and a red anchor buoy secured to a boat anchor was planted directly over the wreck . . . The *Mohawk* sank by the stern almost end on and is lying in fifteen fathoms of water."

The final plunge occurred at 9:35 p.m. Barker: "A considerable disturbance of water was shown near the bow, which was probably caused by air or gases. There was no wreckage visible worth saving."

The collision and sinking was attended by neither injuries nor loss of life. The *Mohawk's* crew, seventy-eight men all told, bobbed around in six lifeboats until they were picked up by the USS *Mohican* and the USS *Sabalo*. Four of the lifeboats were saved as well. The men picked up by the *Sabalo* were later transferred to the *Mohican*, which then transported the survivors to Naval Section Base 6, in Brooklyn.

In addition to the buoy which was planted over the wreck, the *Mohawk's* two mastheads protruded from the water. Thus, there never was any doubt about the wreck's location. Yet salvage was never attempted, nor was the wreck demolished. The buoy was eventually removed, the masts collapsed, and the wreck lay forlorn and forgotten for several generations.

The *Mohawk* was discovered in the early 1970's by a dive club called the Aquarians, the members of whom operated their own boat out of New York. They made positive identification by recovering two artifacts which had the name engraved in bronze: the ship's bell and an engine room gauge panel.

Until recently, most of the wreck's beauty was disguised by sewage. The *Mohawk* lies in an area which, for decades, was a dump site for the City of New York. Instead of having a hard and highly reflective sandy bottom, the wreck was surrounded by sludge and deep mud into which most of its hull plates disappeared. I can remember sticking my arms in the sediment all the way to the shoulders without finding a hard bottom.

For divers, the wreck was dark and foreboding, usually offering visibility

Courtesy of the National Archives   Going, going . . .

ranging from inches to several feet. One swipe of the fins was enough to stir up huge clouds of black silt that completely obscured the vicinity. Only during an incoming tide could one have hoped to find an influx of clean, clear water washing over the wreck, instead of the foul-smelling river water that flowed out.

Conditions on the wreck have improved considerably in recent years. Now one might find visibility in the range of fifty feet. The chance of ear infection - common among divers in the 1970's who were susceptible to such an ailment - is now negligible. These changes have been brought about by the reduction of pollutants and contaminants that are released into the Hudson River, strict regulations against dumping trash and garbage in the ocean too close to shore, reformations in the disposal of industrial waste, improved processes for the treatment of raw sewage, and similar sanitary modifications.

The current condition of the *Mohawk* is a visual validation of the success of these various clean-up protocols: a tribute to the sagacity of environmental protection legislation.

The rounded stern of the wreck is largely intact, tilted 45° to starboard. Most of the decking is gone. One can gain entrance through the large broken section. Take note of the footed bathtubs inside. Caution must be exercised because of the large amount of silt which is trapped inside and which is easily disturbed.

This finely furnished ship has much to divulge, including china dinnerware inscribed "U.S.R.C.S." (United States Revenue Cutter Service). This designation was discontinued in 1915, when the Revenue Cutter Service merged with the Life-Saving Service to form the United States Coast Guard.

The midship section lies open like a flensed whale, exposing the engine and boilers and some of the hull plates that have not fallen outboard into the sand. The sand used to be covered with ooze which had the color and consistency of chocolate pudding. But this muck has been gradually washing out to sea and the sandy bottom is reappearing.

The bow is intact and upright. The hull plates have peeled off to reveal compartments such as the paint locker, the forward storage area, and the crew's quarters (in which personal effects are sometimes found).

In order to avoid confusion with the Clyde liner *Mohawk* (sunk near Manasquan Inlet), the revenue cutter *Mohawk* is often called the RC *Mohawk*, or simply the RC. It is also called the Revenue Cutter. Under any name, the *Mohawk* is a wreck that is well worth diving.

. . . almost gone.   Courtesy of the National Archives.

NEW ERA

Built: 1854   Sunk: November 13, 1854
Previous names: None   Depth: 25 feet
Gross tonnage: 1,328   Dimensions: Unknown
Type of vessel: full-rigged ship   Power: Sail
Builder: Hitchcock & Company, Bath, Maine
Owner: Hitchcock & Company, and Captain Thomas J. Henry
Port of registry: Bath, Maine
Cause of sinking: Ran aground
Location: Off Seventh Avenue in Asbury Park

The early years of immigration to America were fraught with risk.

European emigrants left behind forever their families, friends, possessions, and sometimes their memories and language. They also left behind poverty, political oppression, and religious persecution. The guiding star that led them on their voyage to a new frontier was hope - hope for a better life on the other side of the ocean, hope for a better place in which to rear their children, and hope for that most precious of commodities: freedom.

The transatlantic crossing was not a pleasure cruise. Ships were small, wet, and uncomfortable. They rocked and rolled like wooden corks bobbing in the surf. The bilges were overrun with rats, the food infested with maggots, and the water tainted with moldy scum. Passengers froze in the winter and baked in the summer. The living quarters were so cramped that men, women, and children slept side by side like boards of a cabin floor - grooved together so that if one wanted to turn over, he had to disentangle himself from his neighbor.

The ship reeked with the stench of live goats, pigs, and poultry that were kept for food in pens. The awful odor of animal waste contributed to the effluvium. Sanitation was unknown. There was no water for washing and barely enough for drinking. Toilet facilities did not exist. Ventilation was lacking. And then there was disease.

There was no respite until the destination was reached. Depending upon the vagaries of the wind, a sailing ship took a month or two to cross the Atlantic, sometimes longer. One passage was so protracted that the passengers were reduced to eating rats - uncooked!

Somewhere in mid-Atlantic, an emigrant semantically became an immigrant - that is, if he reached the American shore alive.

One of the many so-called "immigrant ships" to ply the treacherous Atlantic lanes was the *New Era*, a full-rigged ship which was built in Bath, Maine in 1854, the same year in which the ship was lost. In fact, she met her untimely end on her maiden voyage. Under the command of co-owner Captain Thomas Henry, the *New Era* sailed to Bremen to embark her first, and what proved to be her

From *The Wreck of the Ship New Era.*

only, load of emigrants. The captain was assisted by a crew of twenty-nine men: first mate, second mate, physician, steward, cook, carpenter, and twenty-three seamen. Also engaged were twelve cooks whose job was to prepare food for the passengers.

As Captain Henry described it, "We left Bremen on the twenty-eighth of September, last, with three hundred and seventy-four steerage passengers, six second cabin and four cabin passengers on board. Our cargo consisted of six hundred tons of chalk, and twenty thousand cubic feet of merchandise of various kinds. We had a very hard passage, with heavy west winds, and about the twentieth of October, we shipped a sea that swept everything from the decks. The sea struck us fore and aft, and stove in the bulwarks, swept off the passengers' cooking range, killed two or three passengers, and disabled several others. The water passed into the main hatchway. The passengers killed were of the steerage list. The gales continued very heavy, and the sea being so strong it strained the vessel so that she commenced leaking, and when reaching the United States coast, she leaked very badly. The leak was so rapid that it was requisite to keep one pump in operation all the time, prior to arriving here. The last observation I had was 66 degrees longitude west, and 41 degrees, 50 minutes, latitude. This was last Friday; we have had no observation since."

"No observation" meant that the captain had no sure way of knowing his position or establishing the vessel's progress. From that point he was steering by dead reckoning: a method of determining a vessel's location at sea beyond sight of land by correlating the vessel's course, ascertained by compass, and approximate speed, taking into account such variables as drift.

"On Saturday it was thick, the rain falling heavily, and a strong breeze from the south. I then judged the ship to be in 72 degrees, 30 minutes, longitude and 40 degrees, 25 minutes, latitude. On that night we had the wind high from the eastward - changed to southeast about midnight, and commenced blowing very heavily."

Captain Henry calculated that he was nearing land. Every hour he had a seaman take a sounding by casting the lead. The lead is a weight on the end of a knotted line. When the lead hits bottom, the length of the deployed line is a measure of the depth.

"I supposed the ship to be on the Long Island coast, and we carried a heavy press of sail to keep her off that coast. I subsequently found the ship to be more southward and westward than I supposed. At 5:30 o'clock last Monday morning, the lead was thrown, and as nearly as could be ascertained, we were in from thirteen to fifteen fathoms of water. This was about half an hour before the vessel struck. The sea was running very high, and as the vessel went ashore we braced the yards aback to haul her off, but found it was of no use, as she had gone head on, made two or three thumps, swung around, broadside to, and was fast. At this time the sea broke over the ship and she began to go to pieces. We then got all the passengers from the 'between' decks to the main deck, and ordered out the main boat to run a line ashore. The hatches were not closed, and on the contrary I ordered every passenger up to the main deck at the time she struck."

The *New Era* ran aground on Deal Beach, which is now the flourishing summer resort town of Asbury Park. But in 1854 only a handful of people lived there, eking out a livelihood by fishing and farming on what was a "sparsely settled stretch of desolate, bleak and dangerous sandy coast." This time period predated the establishment of the United States Life Saving Service, which a couple of decades later erected boat houses and lookout towers along the inhospitable coast. In the absence of government funded facilities, a volunteer station "was kept up from 1848 to 1857 just above Great Pond, now Deal Lake, by Abner Allen. This was equipped with a surf boat and mortar for throwing a rocket line, but was without either any regular beach patrol or lookout."

The night was dark and the storm was increasing in severity. A driving rain hammered the ground. The wind howled like a thousand wailing banshees. Yet piercing this cacophony created by the elements came the ringing of a ship's bell. The residents were roused from their warm cozy slumber in full comprehension of what the clanging bell signified: ship ashore! They hurriedly donned oilskins and southwesters and charged for the beach. Dimly through the darkness and cloying fog they perceived a ship on the outer bar with all sails set. About daybreak, "a big set of seas lifted the vessel off the outer bar, and threw her fair upon the beach about 150 to 200 yards from shore," and within mortar range.

The northerly set of the current soon turned the *New Era* broadside to the beach, "her head to the south at a place noted for its shifting quicksands, and supposed to be the subterranean outlet for the body of water . . . known as Sunset

Lake. The sea running very high broke over the vessel as high as the first yard arm, and in less than an hour she filled and sank, the roughness of the surf resisting every attempt of the heroic volunteer surfmen to launch their life boat and reach the fated vessel."

Captain Henry's story continues: "The boat reached the shore safe with the line, but the men let go of it. The mate and four or five seamen were in this boat. They let go of the line, went ashore, and stayed a short time on the beach. The other boats were soon after got out, and the balance of the crew deserted, with two of the cabin passengers. There was an exception in the *desertion* of the crew, as two or three of the sailors staid with me, and assisted in saving passengers. *After the crew had taken away the ship's boats*, the people on the beach attempted to launch a surf-boat, but it did not succeed."

Trying hard, however, were Britton White and John Slocum, both volunteers and two of the most experienced surfmen in the area. They made the abortive attempts to launch the surfboat.

Captain Henry: "About noon on Monday, they attempted to shoot the mortar toward us, to give us a line. The first shot went ahead of the ship, the second fell short, and on the third and fourth the wire broke. The next shot made reached the ship, and I got hold of the line, and, with the assistance of the passengers, hauled it aboard. With this line a hawser was hauled on board, and to that they attached a life-boat, and we hauled her out to the ship: the life-boat capsized several times, and when we got her alongside she was full of water. I got into the boat to bale her out, and the passengers rushed into her to such an extent that I had to push off; the line parted, and five of them were drowned, and five, with myself, were saved. There was nothing more to be done, except firing some more shots. When the boat upset I went under her, and could not extricate myself for several minutes. I finally got on the bottom of the boat with the other four persons, and the men on the beach hauled her ashore, bottom upwards. I saved nothing of the papers or manifest."

Captain Henry's version of events, and his own actions, was contradicted by Charles Griffin, a teenage seaman whose graphic statement indicated not only the cowardice of the crew in abandoning the passengers to their fate, but the cowardice of the captain as well:

"She sprung a leak a week or so before she went ashore, and we were compelled to keep both pumps going day and night. For three days previous to our going ashore, we had thick and heavy weather; in fact, during the whole passage we encountered violent head winds. We took soundings at four o'clock on Monday morning and found seventeen fathoms of water; again at five, when we were in fifteen fathoms of water. 5:30 we had shoaled to eleven fathoms. We reported the result of our sounding to the captain, and the second mate came forward and told the watch that from the sand on the lead, we must be near the Jersey shore, and that we must keep a good lookout for land. Two men were placed on the lookout, but the fog was so dense that no object could be discerned more than half a length ahead.

"About ten minutes after six she struck, while going at the rate of six or seven knots per hour, under close reefed topsails, main topmast staysail, fore top-mast staysail, spencer, and spanker. About three o'clock in the morning we had made more sail than we had previously been carrying - had it not been for this we probably should not have been wrecked. Immediately after we grounded, the captain came on deck and gave orders to brace around the yards, which was done, and an effort made to back her off. After several ineffectual attempts we found this impossible, as every sea was driving her further on the beach.

"Orders were then given to clear away the boats. The first boat was manned by the first and second officers and three of the crew, and started for the shore with a line, but in consequence of the line being too short they did not succeed in getting it ashore, as they were compelled to let it go, although the boat reached the beach. The second boat was then lowered and manned for the purpose of try-ing to get another line on shore, but the line became entangled on board the ship, and the boat was obliged to let it go also. Our last boat (the long boat) was cleared away and got over the side, to renew the attempt to get a rope to the beach. That boat was large enough to carry about 25 or 30 persons; five or six of the crew got into her to bale her out. At this time the captain was in the mizzen rigging, on the starboard side, and gave us orders about the boat. Six of the crew were in her baling, when a sea struck her and her painter parted. She was carried away from the ship, and those who were in her were obliged to make for the shore. The ship's surgeon, Dr. Papenhusen, attempted to get into her by lowering himself on a line, but was too late, and the sea washed him off, and he was drowned.

"The captain then descended to the rigging and came forward to the jib-boom. Eight or ten of the passengers, in attempting to follow him, were carried overboard by the waves. When the ship struck she swung around broadside to the beach, her head to the south; the sea broke over her fore and aft, and in less than an hour she filled and sunk. When the ship struck, the passengers were all between decks, in their berths, with the exception of twelve, who were taking their turn at the pumps. The sea broke over us and rushed into the between decks, drowning many of the women in their berths. Those who could do so, rushed upon deck, many of them nearly in a state of nudity, and ran about the deck shrieking in the most painful tones. The houses on deck, the top of the poop cabin, and every place of shelter, were crowded with them. In the forward house were some fifteen or twenty persons, mostly women. These were carried over-board, together with the house in which they sought refuge, by a tremendous sea that nearly cleared our decks. As many persons as were able ascended the rig-ging, and clung to it for safety from the great seas that dashed over us.

"The captain told the people to remain quiet, and they would all get ashore; but they heeded him not, but kept crying for assistance. The captain also shout-ed at the top of his voice for help from shore. The poor people on board were being continually swept off into the sea. The whole of the rigging on the star-board side was filled with them, probably to the number of 200 souls.

"After several ineffectual attempts, the people on shore succeeded in firing a shot over us, and sending a line across our fore royal stay, and a man on the end of the flying jib boom caught it. The captain made it fast by the fore stay, and all of us hauled the life-boat from the shore to the ship. The captain got into the fore chains, and was followed by a part of the crew. The boat having capsized several times in coming to us, was full of water, and the captain ordered some of the crew to get in and bale her out. As soon as they got in he jumped overboard, and scrambled into the boat, leaving five of the crew and his passengers on board. As soon as he got into the boat he cried out to the people on the beach to haul him on shore. When the passengers saw the captain leaving his ship, ten or twelve of them jumped overboard, and four of them got into the boat - the remainder were drowned.

"The coast people hauled the boat toward the shore, but she capsized three times in going, and only the captain, three of the crew and one of the passengers got ashore in safety - the remainder were drowned. On her way to the shore the line connecting the shore and the ship parted, and we were left again to despair. The people on shore again fired lines to us, but only one, the last, was successful; this caught on the foretopsail brace, but beyond our reach. By this time it was nearly dark, and the people on shore had exhausted all their shot, while the sea was running so high that they could do nothing for us with their boats. The few members of the crew remaining on board (five of us) lashed ourselves to the jib boom."

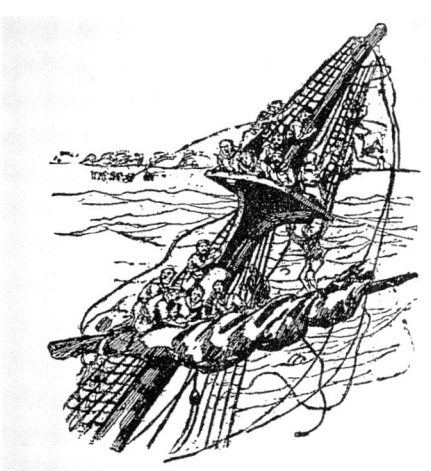

From *The Wreck of the Ship New Era.*

And there they remained, fighting despair, awaiting rescue.

On that first day only one passenger made it to shore alive by her own exertions. This was Mrs. Louisa Heier, a native of Preussenminden, Prussia. A terrible crashing wave broke her hold on the rigging and swept her overboard. She was then tumbled about in the surf and sucked under water. She managed to struggle to the surface several times for a breath of air, only to be pulled back down by the undertow. Finally she struck her head on something hard, held onto it, and found that it was a broken spar from the wreck. She maintained her grip until the spar was dashed upon the beach. The roiling surf tore the clothes off her body. She landed naked but, miraculously, uninjured.

News of the catastrophe spread quickly and, as one chronicler noted, "brought to the shore crowds of men, women and children, who hurried to the scene of the wreck in vehicles of all kinds from far and near, some to aid and assist in the work of rescue, among whom were two local physicians, some from idle or morbid curiosity, others again to capture such of the flotsam and jetsam as might be cast ashore." Such are the vagaries of human nature, from benevolent to base.

A bulletin was sent to New York via telegraph and "was immediately conveyed to Captain Reynolds of the steamer *Achilles*, a vessel employed by the underwriters to render assistance to vessels ashore." The *Achilles* was then lying off Sandy Hook. The message that Captain Reynolds received told him only of the wreck, not of the many people whose loss of life was imminent. Believing this was a salvage job, he prepared to steam to the city for wrecking schooners. Not until after a telegraphic exchange did he learn of the perilous situation of the remaining passengers and crew, which prompted him instead to head south.

Coincidentally, a correspondent for the New York *Herald* happened to be on board the *Achilles* when the fateful message came through. He left this poignant account: "We left the Hook at half past nine, in a dense fog and southerly wind, which raised a very heavy head swell. The fog, however, so increased in density as to render it impossible to discern objects further than the vessel's length, much less to keep sight of the shore at a safe distance, or see objects near it. We, however, kept on, until we must have been within a short distance of where the wreck lay; but as it was impossible to see or do anything, Captain Reynolds after waiting some time, put the vessel's head again to the northward. When opposite the Highlands, the fog suddenly lighted up, so that the land could be distinctly seen, and we again steered to the southward in search of the wreck.

"About eight o'clock we came in sight of her, lying broadside to the beach, heading to the southward, with her fore, main and mizzen topsails close reefed still standing. On reaching her, she proved to be level with the water and full, and the swell breaking in heavy surges across her decks. We had already passed many pieces of the wreck, and half a mile further on we saw the body of a little child, apparently about four or five years old, and in quick succession also that of a man, stripped of clothing, and others with clothes on - four or five bodies in all. As we approached the wreck, so as to get a nearer view, a most harrowing spectacle met the eyes.

"The jib-boom, rigging and top of the ship, fore and aft, were filled with human beings closely packed together, and clinging to each other, and to the ropes while the ship surged to and fro into the rigging and over the ship, drenching and suffocating the passengers, while the poor creatures filled the air with the most soul-harrowing and pitiful outcries for assistance. On the beach were some two hundred persons, gathered in groups, apparently consulting as to how to act, while others sat leisurely upon the gunwale of the boats, which the heavy surf rendered it certain destruction to launch.

"We saw several boats upon the shore, apparently well adapted for the purpose, and a crowd of persons dragging along a life-boat toward the beach, where it was left, and no further attempt was made to launch it. We saw no line from the ship to the shore, and no life-car. From the fact that what appeared to be the ship's boat was lying on the beach, we judged that the officers and crew, or most of them, must have landed or been thrown ashore in her. The tide was now about at its full, the wind had died away, and a slight breeze sprang up from off shore, which greatly increased our hopes that the swell would go down with the tide, and render it possible for the boats to be launched from shore. As to ourselves, we found that we could do nothing.

"The steamer, which is employed expressly by the underwriters to render assistance to vessels ashore, had not the sign of surf-boat on board, nothing but two miserable yawls, both of which would scarcely float the vessel's crew, were she sinking, and one of them could not float herself if put overboard. Not a spar, line or life-preserver - not a piece of cork big enough to float a drowning dog. By 4:30 o'clock the swell had so much subsided that every passenger could have been rescued had there been a surf-boat on board, and there was not a man, from the fireman to the pilot and captain, who would not have rejoiced at the opportunity of snatching the poor sufferers from death had they the means of doing it.

"By whose neglect is it that these steamboats are not provided with surf-boats for such dreadful emergencies as this? Still hoping for a movement toward launching the boats from shore, we continued painful spectators of the scene, ringing our bell to encourage them, and beckoning to them on the shore to launch the boats. When our wheels were put in motion to adjust the position of the steamer, the passengers, apparently fearing we were about to leave them, would rend the air with imploring cries, while other tolled the ship's bell, the sounds of which were borne to us above the wailings of the surf that swept over the ship.

"We were near enough to distinctly see women holding their little ones with one hand, while the other, bleached by the spray, clung with a death grip to the ratlines on which they stood, only one or two in the mizzen rigging having on but a shirt. On the forecastle there stood a few moments ago a group of four clinging to the stay, but they are now gone - a heavy swell has probably swept them away. Men have been seen to fall from the jib-boom into the surf.

"Thus we have looked on, unable to approach the ship. Captain Reynolds twice hailed them on the shore, and asked them to launch the boats, as the surf, to us, seemed to be now sufficiently smooth to do so on the lee side of the ship. Finding that we could do nothing, and as the sun went down, seeing the boats hauled back upon the beach, we left to procure life boats, making signals to the wreck that we would return immediately. Meantime, the *Leviathan* also arrived opposite the wreck, but like ourselves, had no boats to render any assistance.

"On our way up we soon met the *Hector*, having in tow a wrecking schooner, in charge of Captain Bowne, and with him we went back to the wreck. On reaching it, Captain Bowne informed us that although he had boats, he had not two men who could pull an oar, and asking if any on board would go with him in the boat? I replied, 'Here is one,' and Mr. Haskell volunteered to do the same.

"Captain Reynolds then informed Captain Bowne that he could get men to man his life boat by coming alongside of the *Achilles*. We then made preparations to join Captain Bowne, but to our surprise he pulled away from us toward the ship, leaving word for the *Achilles* to return to the city. Thus a large and powerful boat, with plenty of accommodations for the rescue of passengers, was sent to the town, and the *Hector*, a comparatively slow and unsuitable boat, retained."

Griffin's account provides a different point of view of the steamers' attempts at rescue and eventual departure: "About ten o'clock on Monday night, a boat from a steamboat came to us, within hailing distance, and asked how we got along; I replied, we should do very well till morning if the ship held together, but I did not think she would last so long. The captain of the boat told us to hold on and he would soon be off to us with a life-boat and assistance. We got a line ready for lowering ourselves into the boat, and he returned in about half an hour and hailed us again to know how we were. We asked him to come along and take us in, but he waited for fifteen minutes and found it impossible to come, as the sea was so boisterous. About eight o'clock a fire was made up on the shore and kept burning all night, and persons on board were crying and groaning all night, but no earthly assistance could then be afforded to any of us. About twelve o'clock the sea began to break over our place of shelter on the boom, and we got up onto the forestay and into the foretop."

The situation on the *New Era* was desperate. Observed a correspondent on the beach: "The sea is breaking over the wreck, and before dark we could see every available space in the rigging filled with probably some two hundred persons. Not less, probably, than seventy-five have already been washed overboard . . . All the passengers are Dutch or German, and as there is no one here who understands their language, we are not able to obtain from those who reached the shore any information in regard to the condition of things on board, which undoubtedly is bad enough."

Thus the survivors, who had been clinging to the rigging all day, were consigned to spending a desperate night aloft.

Griffin: "All this time the deck was strewn with dead bodies which the sea washed to and fro against the frames and bulwarks and the rolling spars and rubbish, mangled terribly. A cold westerly wind arose about eight o'clock on Monday evening; the night was very bleak, the blast piercingly cold, and many of the emigrants benumbed and frozen, lost their hold and dropped from the shrouds into the sea and were drowned. Others, exhausted, hung by their legs in the rigging, too feeble to longer maintain their hold, and so perished from suffocation. The scene was too awful for further detail.

"Thank God, however, after suffering from cold, hunger, and the buffetings of the waves for nearly twenty-six hours amid horrors at which the soul sickens, we were saved. By seven o'clock on Tuesday the sea had fallen considerably, and three surf-boats put off from the shore to our assistance. Through caution and close watching of the rolling waves they saved all that were on board alive (with the exception of four or five who were drowned in jumping after the boat when they were on their way back to the shore full of people). All were saved before eight o'clock on Tuesday morning."

It was wreck master Edward Wardell who gave the order that, the surf having subsided, it was safe to launch the boats. He and surfmen White and Slocum rowed the first boat to the wreck. All the surfmen exerted Herculean strength of character and physique to bring ashore one hundred fifty-three people: limp and limping immigrants, barely alive, who found the promised land of their dreams.

The strongest survivors left for New York immediately by various routes and conveyances. Others, exhausted, were put up in the homes of local residents. People from neighboring communities brought food and donated clothing to the immigrants who possessed nothing but resolve and the ragged clothes they wore on their backs. During the next day and a half, several survivors succumbed to the hardship of their ordeal. Mrs. Emilia Tautz, who lost both her husband and her brother in the wreck, suffered a miscarriage. Heinrich Weishaus had a broken leg. Doctors attended the weak, the sick, and the injured until they were well enough to travel. The Commissioners of Emigration sent a representative to Deal; his job was not only to lend aid to the living, but to oversee the gruesome task of dealing with the dead.

By Captain Henry's reckoning the *New Era* left Bremen with four hundred twenty-six people on board. It was also noted that between thirty-nine and forty-six emigrants contracted cholera along the way and were buried at sea. This information was imparted almost parenthetically, giving some insight into how people perceived the ravages of fatal illness in the days when death by disease was common. This is not to imply that people felt less of a sense of loss, but that because mortality was a frequent occurrence they viewed such parting philosophically. Thus inured, perhaps people were stronger for their attitude of acceptance, and were able to get on with life more quickly, and with less pain of regret than people seem to experience today.

It was reported at the time that one hundred seventy-one people were safely landed: one hundred forty-three passengers and twenty-eight crew. However, a list of survivors compiled shortly thereafter named one hundred forty-six: one hundred twenty-two passengers and twenty-four crew. The discrepancy of twenty-five was never explained. The list might not have taken into account those who left immediately for New York.

How many people actually died in the wreck is difficult to calculate with precision. The number most likely falls between two hundred twenty-two and two hundred fifty-five - depending upon how many died in the cholera epidemic and how many were swept overboard during the storm at sea. W.M. Wermerkirsch, the representative of the Commissioners of Emigration, noted in an early report that "we have just numbered the last coffin 119, and have thirty more bodies yet to be disposed of." And this before all the bodies were recovered from the wreck or picked up from the beach.

Wrote one correspondent (at 4:00 p.m. on Tuesday): "There is no chance of saving anything from her beyond her rigging. The masts were standing uninjured, and with the exception of the loss of the mizzen-top-gallant, she appeared to have suffered no damage above the bulwarks. The fore, main, and mizzen topsails were still set, as when she went on, treble reefed. The other sails appeared to be loosely clewed up, and rent in many places. In the main shrouds, the body of a female was still visible, nearly nude, her arms and legs thrust through the crossings. The planking of the bulwarks was all torn off, and the sea belched every moment through the frame of the bulwarks, like the smoke from a frigate's guns when firing a broadside.

"Captain Bowne, having kindly invited us to go on board with him, we took a seat in the surf-boat, and were soon rowed through the breakers and alongside the ship's quarter. Watching an opportunity, as a spent wave receded, we leaped into the mizzen rigging. Such a spectacle as the decks of the *New Era* then presented we hope never to be called to witness again. The forecastle was beaten in, and the top of the poop-cabin on the larboard [port] side had a large hole in it that the waves had made. The deck had been swept of everything. The frames of the bulwarks stood above the waves, like the fleshless ribs of a leviathan, while protruding through them were the bodies of men, women and children, all of them naked, or but partially covered with the clothes they had on when asleep in their berths. But the most awful sight of all was directly below our feet. There, between the side of the poop-cabin and the mizzen chains about a score of corpses, all stark, stiff and cold, lay in every conceivable attitude of agony, maimed, crushed and bruised, with eyes washed from their sockets, with teeth set like vices, and every feature fearfully convulsed; there, promiscuously heaped together, were old men whose race had nearly run; young maidens, just blooming into womanhood, and babes whose lives were measured but by weeks. Every age and sex had its representative here, and told in ghastly types how much humanity may suffer. The blood had frozen into blackness beneath their fingernails, and with the half-clenched hand, showed how strong had been the grip upon the rigging - how long and fierce the strife for life; a contest in which they did not yield until the bleak blast had frozen their hearts' blood, and their unconscious hands had loosened their grasp, when their lives went out in the dark night, swallowed up beneath the seething waves that burst madly over the ship. . . .

"And let us here remark, that until we came on board, the sea had been so rough, and the tide too high to venture from the shore, else these remains of the poor strangers would have been taken ashore and prepared for interment. As it was, Captain Bowne ran along the top of the bulwarks to the main rigging, to take down the body of the woman that still remained there. With some difficulty he disentangled her stiffened limbs from the shrouds, and gently lowered her stiffened limbs from the shrouds, and gently lowered her by a rope into the surf boat. . . . The people on shore silently bore off the body of the young girl, that had so long lain stiffening in the rigging, that it might be prepared for Christian burial."

The same correspondent completed his prose with a notion that might have reflected the sentiment of the general populace: "Had the craven crew and paralyzed Captain of the *New Era* but manifested such dauntless bravery as that displayed by the New Jersey coastmen, we should not have had to chronicle such dread result from this last disaster as we do this morning."

Those same self-sacrificing surfmen returned to the wreck to recover bodies. Other bodies were gathered from where they washed up on the beach. Many of the dead could not be identified because their features were almost totally destroyed. Some were identified by papers found on their person. Most were given numbered tags and descriptions in a notebook:

"No. 1. A male child, about one year old. No. 2. A male infant. No. 3. A female, about twenty-five years old. No. 4. The body of a woman, marked E.M.S., had silver rings in her ears. No. 5. A female, of small size, about twenty-five years old. . . . No. 9. A male, marked A.O., died after reaching the shore. . . . No. 14. A male, about fifteen years old, found on his person one $20 gold piece, American, and two $5 pieces. . . . No. 16. A man, about eighteen years old, found on his person pocket book, containing letters, from these it was inferred that the name of the deceased was Samuel Rothschild. . . . No. 38. A male, very much disfigured, about fifteen years old. . . . No. 78. A male, T. Henry Harris, identified. . . . No. 91. A female, disfigured. . . . No. 142. A little boy, apparently ten years of age.

"This closes the list of those buried up to yesterday [Thursday, November 16], although between thirty and forty bodies were then lying near the house of Mr. West, and will probably be interred this [Friday, November 17] morning. Thus far, the sea has thrown up nearly one hundred and eighty of the victims of the fearful calamity of November the thirteenth; and yet, by comparison with the number of passengers, it will be found there are seventy persons missing. Many of these were undoubtedly suffocated in the steerage of the ship, immediately after striking; but as a part were washed off by the action of the waves, it is probable that for weeks to come we shall be reminded of this calamity by the occasional casting up of some lifeless body upon the coast, a sad memento of a terrible episode."

The bodies were "taken to the ten pin alley at Allen's boarding house until an inquest could be held by the Coroner. . . . Each body was placed in a rough wooden box (for which the Coroner charged the county seven dollars) and buried in a common grave in the little Methodist burial ground between Long Branch and Eatontown."

Bodies continued to wash up on the beach for months. The gale of January 22, 1855 must have pounded apart the *New Era's* hull; thirteen more bodies were picked up the following day.

Eventually, Germans living in the area organized the New Era Association. Their primary purpose was to raise enough money to erect a monument on the mass grave in the West Long Branch cemetery, where the victims were buried, so that those who died on foreign soil would not be forgotten. Their goal was achieved. On November 13, 1892 a large granite monument was dedicated with appropriate ceremony. The plot was enclosed with granite posts and iron rails painted white. The Association cared for the site. The monument still stands and the site is still maintained.

After the wilderness of sand dunes and scrub pines known as Deal Beach was transformed to a continuous line of pleasure resorts named Asbury Park, James A. Bradley erected another monument on the boardwalk adjacent to where the *New Era* came ashore. This ornate granite shaft stood twelve feet high and was surrounded by an iron railing. Anchor chains from the wreck were draped around the base of the iron posts. By 1907, this shaft had been washed into the sea by a severe storm and was lost. Still surviving was a wooden pile embedded

Left and right: from *The Wreck of the Ship New Era.*

in the sand on which one of the *New Era's* anchors was hung.

It was suggested by contemporaries that Captain Henry deliberately ran the *New Era* aground in order to collect the insurance money. The hull was insured for $91,000 ($50,000 was subscribed by six Boston companies; $10,000 by the Mutual Insurance Company of Bath, Maine; $25,000 by several other Bath companies; and $6,000 on Wall Street.) Captain Henry was co-owner, along with the builders, Hitchcock & Company, of Bath. The ship was consigned to Charles C. Duncan & Company, of No. 52 South Street, New York City.

It is unlikely that the amount of insurance exceeded the construction costs of the ship. And, since the *New Era* was brand new, she was worth as much as she cost to build. The allegation was most likely made by those who believed that Captain Henry acted dishonorably in leaving the immigrants to their fate. Both allegations may very well have been unjustified.

The *New Era* was lost at a time when immigrants were welcomed to the United States with open arms. Emma Lazarus was then only five years old, and had yet to pen the famous lines of poetry which a generation later graced the base of the Statue of Liberty (on which construction began in 1876). Her sentiments were based upon the current social climate:

"Give me your tired, your poor,
Your huddled masses yearning to breathe free,
The wretched refuse of your teeming shore,
Send these, the homeless, tempest-tost, to me,
I lift my lamp beside the golden door!"

Since then, the American attitude toward immigration has drastically changed. Partly this is the result of overcrowding, competition for jobs, maintenance of the status quo, and a general unwillingness to share the wealth which native born citizens have inherited from previous generations of immigrants: as if those who are heirs by accident of birth want the door of opportunity closed behind them. Today, new immigrants are more often perceived as parasites and interlopers.

To be fair, modern immigrants have done more to engender this negative attitude than those who were born American. Immigrants of the past were infused with a desire to be productive and were eager to work hard in order to improve their lot, whereas the majority of new immigrants do not seem to want to earn a living, but want instead to collect the government dole. When an immigrant's sole purpose in immigrating is to get on federal welfare, native citizens who support the system by means of dedicated labor and industry cannot reasonably be expected to feel sympathy for those who want only to freeload.

Sadly, despite the mighty efforts of the New Era Association a century ago, today the *New Era* is largely unremembered. The fate of some three hundred German immigrants is little more than a footnote in old and musty historical journals. The name may be recalled, but the dread circumstances of death, suffering, and survival have all but been obliterated. The wreck appears to have submerged below the ever-shifting sands of time and the beach.

The aforesaid notwithstanding, local interest in the *New Era* has recently been rejuvenated. This was due to the efforts of two brothers: Richard and Gregory Fernicola. Their long-standing personal interest in the tragedy was suddenly brought to a new height by the Beach Replenishment Project, which would bury any hopes they ever entertained of finding the wreck. The first stage of the state-sponsored project was a survey of the areas to be interred under relocated sand. The Fernicola brothers obtained the results of the side-scan sonar survey, noted the anomalies in the vicinity of where they believed the *New Era* to lie, then began an investigation of the most likely sites.

Their plan was to establish a system of grids on the bottom by dragging a three-hundred-foot rope in circles around predetermined points. They were lucky - the rope snagged on an anchor on the first sweep. Although they found no other wreckage, they believed that the anchor once belonged to the *New Era*. During the next two years they visited the site infrequently. Each time, they cut some netting and fishing line from the exposed portion of the anchor, and they excavated some sand. Eventually, they exposed enough of the anchor to consider raising it. They attempted to recover the anchor in July 1999. With their small boat they were unable to lift the anchor from the water. They managed only to drag it a short distance before being forced to relinquish the iron artifact to the deeps.

The Fernicola brothers issued an appeal for help in the Asbury Park Press. Within days a man stepped forward to answer the call. He was John Masters, owner of Divemasters, Inc. He owned a survey and dive-support vessel called the *Atlantic Surveyor*. The vessel was one hundred ten feet long and was fitted with a large crane that was used to lower survey equipment into the water, but which could also be used for light salvage. This crane had no trouble lifting the fifteen-hundred-pound anchor off the bottom and placing it on the vessel's spacious deck. The anchor, encrusted with barnacles and mussels, was then offloaded onto a truck and taken to where the lengthy process of preservation could begin.

The anchor was originally located some 250 feet off the Seventh Avenue jetty in Asbury Park, in 25 feet of water. The Fernicola brothers hope to have the anchor restored, then placed on public display. They are optimistic that the return of the anchor to human consciousness will increase awareness of the *New Era*, and will give that long ago disaster a more permanent and prominent place in local history.

It has been suggested, and not without good reason, that the awful human drama involving the death of so many German immigrants focused more attention on the need for a government-funded life-saving service than the hugely successful rescues from such wrecks as the *Ayrshire*, *Georgia*, and *Cornelius Grinnell*. If true, then in the greater perspective of humankind, their lives were not lost in vain.

PENTLAND FIRTH

Built: 1934
Previous names: None
Gross tonnage: 485
Type of vessel: Antisubmarine trawler
Builder: Cook, Welton & Gemmell, Ltd., Beverly, England
Owner: British Government
Port of registry: England
Cause of sinking: Collision with USS *Chaffinch*
Location: 26923.0

Sunk: September 19, 1942
Depth: 60-70 feet
Dimensions: 164' x 27' x 15'
Power: Coal-fired steam

43682.4

When the *Pentland Firth* was built, she was considered to be the most modern design in high speed, large capacity, long distance fishing trawlers. The trawl winch had a capacity of 1,200 fathoms (7,200 feet) - nearly a mile and a half. The captain and crew were provided with luxuriously appointed staterooms for the long journeys that were anticipated.

The *St. Nectan* was similar in appearance to the *Pentland Firth*. During the war, these trawlers were fitted with a gun mounted on a raised platform on the bow, and depth-charge racks on the stern. (From the author's collection.)

The Firth Steam Trawling Company, of Hull, Yorkshire, owned the vessel until the outbreak of World War Two. She was purchased in September 1939 by the British Admiralty, then converted for service in antisubmarine warfare. Conversion included removal of the cable drum and trawl net, and the addition of a deck gun and depth-charge racks.

According to the terms of the lend-lease program, the U.S. gave England fifty World-War-One-era flush-deck, four-stack destroyers in return for options on overseas military bases. When the German U-boat campaign pummeled the American east coast after the U.S. entered the war against the Axis powers, the U.S. Navy found itself seriously lacking in coastal protection craft and convoy escorts. England responded to the looming threat by loaning the United States twenty-four armed merchant trawlers and their naval officers and crews.

The HMS *Pentland Firth* nominally retained her classification as a British vessel, and was manned by the Royal Navy, but in February 1942 she was placed under American operational control. She and her British tars performed escort duty until she was run down by the converted mine sweeper USS *Chaffinch*.

By the nature of the *Pentland Firth's* dual control, details of the collision are seriously lacking in official documentation. The British kept no records because the *Pentland Firth* was not their responsibility at the time of her demise. Because the *Pentland Firth* was not commissioned in the U.S. Navy, the Navy kept no record of her daily log. Furthermore, due to the news blackout concerning casualties of war, newspapers did not cover the collision. Worse yet, the Naval Historical Center refrained from mentioning the incident in the history it compiled of the *Chaffinch's* career. And last but not least, the *Chaffinch's* deck log and war diary for the period surrounding her collision with the *Pentland Firth* are mysteriously missing from the National Archives. One afflicted with paranoia might suppose that a cover-up was intended!

Until some lost, misplaced, stolen, or hidden documents come to light, the fate of the poor sailors of the *Pentland Firth* must go unsung.

Initially, a marker buoy was placed over the site. The buoy was removed in 1943 when the wreck was demolished by being wire-dragged to a depth of 50 feet. In 1950, its charted position was changed, with the latest location being 40-25-38 North and 73-51-57 West. The U.S. Coast and Geodetic Survey reported, "There has been extensive dumping by scows and dredges in the immediate vicinity of the reported position of the wreck. Several obstructions were found but it is not known if they result from the dumping or are part of the remains of the wreck."

There are so many rocks and obstructions in the heavily traveled approaches to New York harbor that any one of them could be the remains of this British armed trawler with dual military citizenship. Since the publication of the first edition of this book, several people have attempted to locate the *Pentland Firth's* final resting place. Some of these people have either telephoned or written to let me know what they have found.

Stan Zagleski wrote, "As for the wreck that I call *Pentland Firth*, the exposed wreckage appears to be about 120'-130' in length and about 40' in width.

The highest relief on the site is at the engine which rises to about 53' from a surrounding depth of 64'. The engine and boilers sit near the middle of the site. The wreck sits upright and there are very few recognizable features. Twisted steel plates, I-beams, pipes etc. are scattered about in a haphazard fashion. A 30' section of the port side hull rises vertically about 8' above the sand bottom but otherwise the rest of the wreck is low-lying and averages 2'-4' in height. She has obviously been either wire-swept or blasted at some point in the past. Although I cannot confirm any artifacts that would lead to positive identification, a couple of local divers have told me that divers from a private boat out of New York found and recovered two brass shells from the wreck several years ago.

"The size of the site, the apparent recovery of brass shells, and the fact that it is the only steel wreck that I know of in the area all lead me to conclude that she is indeed the *Pentland Firth*. I both fish and dive on this wreck and my loran numbers [26923.0 / 43682.4] correspond to the highest piece of the wreck."

Another correspondent contacted me via e-mail and signed the message Darren, without a last name, deliverable e-mail address, or return mailing address. According to Darren, the wreck lies in 70 feet of water about three miles east of Sandy Hook. The loran numbers that he provided are 26921.2 / 43682.0. He also noted that "the New York Pilot may get upset with your presence and ask you to leave. Courteously, at first."

Is either one of these sites the wreck of the *Pentland Firth*? Darren was so brief that it is difficult to form an opinion. Zagleski's observations and description, while not conclusive, match what is likely to remain of the long lost trawler. If I were a betting person, I would place my money on Zagleski's position.

PINTA

Built: 1959   Sunk: May 7, 1963
Previous names: None   Depth: 90 feet
Gross tonnage: 500   Dimensions: 194' x 31' x 12'
Type of vessel: Freighter   Power: Diesel engine
Builder: N.V. Bodewes Scheepswerven, Martenschek, Denmark
Owner: Dammers & V.D. Heide's Shipping and Trading Co., Netherlands
Port of registry: Rotterdam, Netherlands
Cause of sinking: Collision with SS *City of Perth*
Location: 26880.5   43563.5

Just as the sun set over a clear blue sky, the Dutch motor vessel *Pinta* was run down by the giant British freighter *City of Perth*, grossing in at 7,547 tons compared to the *Pinta's* puny 500. Both vessels immediately radioed the Coast Guard.

City of Perth: "The *City of Perth* struck *Pinta*, registered Rotterdam. This ship and Dutch ship making water. Require immediate assistance."

Pinta (without the superfluous information provided by the *City of Perth*): "Dutch vessel taking water, requires immediate assistance."

The Coast Guard responded by dispatching five helicopters and two cutters. Nineteen minutes after her first transmission, the *City of Perth* radioed again: "*Pinta* crew abandoning ship and rowing to board me. *Pinta* listing to port."

Half an hour later it was all over for the *Pinta*. Captain Alie Korpelshoed and his crew abandoned ship in textbook fashion. First aboard the lone lifeboat was Mrs. Maria Wallenswinkel-Huiveniers, the ship's stewardess and wife of the first mate. Following her were ten men. Captain Korpelshoed was the last to leave the *Pinta*. A few minutes later they were safely ensconced aboard the *City of Perth*, while the *Pinta* lay on the bottom of the ocean in 90 feet of water.

The *City of Perth* again radioed the Coast Guard, this time stating that no further assistance was needed. Forty-eight minutes had elapsed between collision and disappearance, and, while it was a catastrophe for the *Pinta's* crew and owners, it was hardly an ordeal for the *City of Perth*. Despite a fourteen-foot gash in her bow, the British freighter was in no danger of sinking. She steamed under her own power back to the Todd Shipyard in Brooklyn, the port from which she had departed only a few hours earlier. After landing, the Dutch crew was transported to the Seaman's Church Institute at 25 South Street, where they were put up "pending repatriation." The *City of Perth* was later moved to the Bethlehem Steel Company and was placed in dry dock so that repairs could be effected to her crushed stem. Her intended voyage to Australia was considerably delayed.

The date was May 7, 1963. At this stage in the advance of navigational technology, both ships were equipped with radar. Visibility was fifteen miles at the time of the collision. Clearly, someone was not paying attention. For some reason that was never ascertained, the *Pinta* crossed the bow of the *City of Perth* and was struck broadside. Perhaps both vessels were at fault, or at least contributed to the accident. Were the helmsmen asleep at their wheels? Were the watch officers taking a break? Were the lookouts observing the sunset and dreaming of home? We will never know.

The Coast Guard did not investigate the incident because they had no authority to do so. The collision occurred in international waters (farther than three miles from shore) between two vessels that flew foreign flags. The Coast Guard's sole concern in the matter was the threat to navigation that the sunken *Pinta* might pose. They quickly determined that the steel-hulled obstruction lay deep enough that, despite a least depth of 60 feet that resulted from the breadth of the vessel's beam, traffic could pass safely over the wreck without fear of striking it.

By this time in the world of maritime events, a new element had been added: self-contained underwater breathing apparatus. The acronym SCUBA evolved rapidly into the accepted English word "scuba." Close on the heels of this exciting new activity was an evolutionary branch known as wreck-diving. Within months of the *Pinta's* sinking, local divers descended into the murky depths to explore the sunken wreck.

These wreck-diving pioneers found the *Pinta* lying on its port side almost perfectly intact. The gaping collision hole was pressed against the sand, yet to be obscured by marine encrustation. Identification was easy: just read the name that was painted on the stern. Veteran diver and underwater photographer Mike de

Camp went one better: he took pictures of the name, the propeller, the hull, the wheel house, navigational lights, and the ship's bell before it was recovered by Jack Brewer. De Camp also gave wreck-diving a boost of recognition when he wrote an article about the *Pinta* and published his photographs.

It is interesting to quote sections from that article, published in 1964, and compare his descriptions with the condition of the wreck today. "The bridge and superstructure came into sharp relief, while in the dusky distance and across the sand trailed masts and rigging in a phantom array. Somehow the ship seemed poised and ready for work, yet incredibly off balance."

Thirty-five years later, the bridge and superstructure no longer exist. They have collapsed to form a field of debris that gives the appearance of a junk yard in which rusty metal plates and beams have been pushed into a pile by a bevy of bulldozers. The masts and rigging have sunk into the sand. The integrity of the hull is sound, but it is so thickly encrusted with barnacles and sea anemones that it hardly appears to be the work of man.

De Camp: "The ship could be entered from a number of points. One could swim directly into the engine room by simply going down the stack. Inside were a great array of tools neatly hung and ready for use."

Today, it is difficult to determine where the smokestack once protruded. The engine room is troublesome to reach and dangerous to explore. Thick, clinging silt is too readily stirred into a soupy morass in which the visibility is zero, making the exits difficult to find.

De Camp: "On the bottom side of the bridge lying three feet off the sand a broken glass window gave access to the bridge. Inside the bridge was a big table with drawers which when opened upside down gave forth a shower of flags. Among them was a flag with a big 'D' for the Dovar Line and another long flag

The fish with the fringe beneath its lower lip is a sea raven.

with the word PINTA on it." As already noted, the bridge structure is now an unrecognizable trash heap. Many items that were left behind by the previous generation of divers have long since been consumed by the destructive agents in the sea. Had they been left behind, most of them would no longer exist.

Inside the after portion of the hull, below where the superstructure once stood, are the remains of corridors, compartments, and crew's quarters. Most of the partitions have rotted away and fallen down, leaving mounds of metal and wood that make interior navigation a daunting prospect. *Divers planning to penetrate, beware.*

The holds are choked with a cargo of lumber that was loaded on board in Nicaragua for delivery to New York woodworkers. Because the hatches are large and open, access is easy. One can swim from one hold to another with ample ambient light to show the way. Artificial light is necessary to explore the deep inner recesses, where the lumber is stacked like loose pick-up sticks. Each hewn wooden beam is about one-foot square and twenty feet long. Some of these beams have been recovered and made into mantelpieces and shelving. These beams are constantly shifting. Be careful not to disturb the delicate balance or you might cause a wood slide.

In 1963, Mike de Camp described the wreck as "poised and ready for work." When *Shipwrecks of New Jersey* was first published, in 1987, I noted, "The *Pinta* is a rarity among wrecks, for it still looks like a ship - perhaps lying peacefully on its side, asleep." Today, the hull is collapsing as if a giant foot had stamped on the midship holds. What used to be an easy traverse through the holds has become more difficult. The superstructure has been shorn off as if it had been razed by a vertical wire-drag.

And tomorrow - who knows?

A sea raven in a different color phase.

Courtesy of The Mariners Museum, Newport News, Virginia.

PLINY

Built: 1878
Previous names: None
Gross tonnage: 1,671
Type of vessel: Iron-hulled passenger-freighter
Builder: Barrow Ship Building Co., Barrow
Owner: Liverpool, Brazil & River Plate Steam Navigation Co.
Port of registry: Liverpool, England
Cause of sinking: Ran aground
Location: 26949.2

Sunk: May 13, 1882
Depth: 20 feet
Dimensions: 288' x 33' x 24'
Power: Coal-fired steam

43579.8

    So dramatic a rescue followed the stranding of the *Pliny* that the United States Life-Saving Service published a minute-by-minute account of the event - one which typified with utmost epitome the uncommon valor with which the Life-Saving Service was imbued. I can do no better than to reprint the Service's detailed narrative of the circumstances surrounding this accident. The year was 1882. (Note that the tonnage given in the LSS account is net, or registered, tonnage, not the gross tonnage that is given in the statistical sidebar above.)

    "May 13 - The British steamship *Pliny*, of Liverpool, 1,069 tons register, Robert Mitchell master, stranded on the bar off Deal Beach, New Jersey, shortly after 3 o'clock in the morning, while on a voyage from Rio Janeiro to New York with twenty-five passengers and a valuable cargo of coffee and hides. The bar on which she struck is about one hundred and fifty yards from the beach. There were sixty-one souls on board, all told; the crew numbering thirty-six, including the stewardess. Among the passengers were three women and ten children, one of the latter being an infant two months old.

"Fresh to strong northeasterly gales had prevailed for several days, causing a rough surf upon the shore. The sky was overcast with low and heavy clouds, which rendered the morning a very dark one; the gloom being intensified by drizzling rain, so that the steamer was close to the land before its proximity was known. Her commander had believed himself well to the eastward, off the Long Island coast, and he was therefore heading her on a west-southwest course (dead on to the land) when the lookout descried breakers ahead. The helm was instantly put to starboard, but before she could be brought around she grounded heavily on the sand-bar, broadside to, with her head to the southward. As soon as she struck, the seas commenced breaking against and over her, fore and aft.

"Finding she remained hard and fast, several distress rockets and a 'Holmes' signal were burned to call assistance from the shore. The hatches were soon burst in, and the water poured into the vessel in large volumes, and before long the engines ceased working. The three boats on the port or off-shore side were also washed from their davits and swept away. The passengers, much alarmed, rushed on deck in a state of panic, but the officers reassured them and persuaded them to return to their quarters, there being danger at times of the seas carrying them overboard if they remained on deck. As it was near daybreak the captain felt hopeful that assistance would soon arrive, but to be prepared for the worst he mustered the crew and got the starboard life-boat ready for lowering.

"By the time this was done it was light enough to see a party of men who arrived on the beach abreast of the ship, and, as the captain thought, made signs for the crew not to lower the boat, and then started back from whence they came to the southward. It appears that, the evening before, Surfman Benjamin Van Brunt, of Station No. 6, which, with all other stations in the Fourth District, had been closed for the summer season on April 30, who resides at Whitesville, about two miles inland from Asbury Park, had a social gathering at his house. Among others invited were Joseph S. Knowles, who had served a portion of the 1st season at the station, and Russell White, of Asbury Park. The night being stormy, Van Brunt, Knowles, and White agreed to go to the beach on the lookout for wrecks. Arriving on the beach at about 2 o'clock in the morning, White suggested that they take shelter in his fish hut on the southerly edge of Great Pond, the northern boundary of Asbury Park, and that each in turn keep watch. This being settled, White went out on patrol, lantern in hand, while Van Brunt and Knowles remained inside; the latter busying himself in making a fire in the stove.

"Soon after 3 o'clock White returned and reported seeing a rocket to the northward. His companions hurried out, and the three started up the beach, using a small boat of White's for ferriage across the pond, which was open to the sea. The sight of a second rocket, while crossing in the boat, quickened their movements, and upon reaching the opposite bank they started on a run for the spot indicated by the signals, stopping for a moment at the life-saving station near the pond (No. 6), to leave a hatchet, which one of them carried in anticipation of the necessity of breaking in the doors to get the apparatus out. At the distance of a mile and a quarter from the station they found a large vessel aground on the bar, nearly abreast of what is known as Sickles Pond. The lantern was swung to apprise those on board that their situation was known, and then the three returned in haste towards the station. Mapping out as they went the best course to be pursued, Knowles took the lantern and proceeded in a southwesterly direction to the farm-house of Mr. Hathaway, at Deal, for a span of horses to draw the apparatus, while his companions kept along the beach to the station. Van Brunt attempted to pry open the large boat-room doors, but, failing in this, he suggested to White, after a short parley, that the small door be burst open. It was the best thing to be done, as Keeper Slocum lived two miles away, and to go to him for the keys would involve the loss of too much precious time. Suiting the action to the word, a few vigorous blows on the door gave them access to the living-room, and a moment later the large doors of the boat-room were swung open. Van Brunt's familiarity with the location of everything in the house assisted him, in the dark, to find the signal rockets. But how to fire them was the next question, as neither of the men had a match in his possession. After diligent search, Van Brunt found just one. Without waiting to light the station lamp, in their excitement, they succeeded in firing off two rockets with the match thus found, and then cleared away the apparatus and hauled it out of the house. This was a laborious task for two men, and by the time it was done Knowles arrived with Hathaway's team, which was driven by one of the farm hands. The beach cart containing the Breeches-buoy apparatus was hitched behind the farm wagon and a start made along the country road leading to Elberton and Long Branch.

"Just as they were leaving the station, Cornelius Van Note, one of the old crew, arrived on his way to the beach. He was requested to call Samuel Van Brunt, Benjamin's brother, and when the party reached the road, one of them, Knowles, jumped off at the house of Borden Walcott, another of the regular crew, and notified him. Thus re-enforced, the relief party made all possible haste to the locality of the stranded vessel, where they arrived at about half past 4. It was now light and the scene was a wild one.

"Out on the bar lay a large steamer in the midst of the heaviest breakers, which kept up a tremendous battery against her side, and deluged the deck with foam. Her people could be seen scattered about wherever any shelter was afforded - some on the bridge, to leeward of the chart-room, amidships; some forward under the break of the forecastle; and others aft under the lee of the saloon cabin; but all anxiously peering towards the shore, watching and waiting for help. In the cold gray dawn the sight of those poor people drenched and shivering on the wreck was enough to quicken the pulse of the most callous. The little band on shore seemed nerved to extraordinary exertion, and went to work manfully and earnestly at the task of rescue. The beach opposite the wreck is about fifty yards wide, and back of that rises a steep bluff perhaps twenty or twenty-five feet high. It was on this bluff that the rescuers had called a halt. There were present the two

Van Brunts (Benjamin and Samuel), Van Note, White, Knowles, Walcott, and Mr. Hathaway; the driver, John Smith, having been sent back with his team for the surf-boat.

"Benjamin Van Brunt assumed, for the time, the direction of the operation, and while he and Knowles loaded and prepared the gun, the others planted the sand-anchor, and arranged the lines. Everything being in readiness, Van Brunt handled the lock-string and sent the shot over the vessel with beautiful precision, the line (a No. 9), falling among the assembled people on the bridge, abaft the smoke-stack.

"The steamer's crew, knowing the purpose of the line, ran it in, hand over hand, and on receiving the whip-block it was passed into the fore-rigging and made fast around the foremast, about twenty feet from the deck. Next came the hawser, but owing to the smallness of the party on shore, they were unable to dispose of their force in such a way as would keep the lines asunder while in transit, and the result was that the two parts of the whip became almost inextricably twisted by the action of the current setting strongly to the southward around the hawser, and thus matters came to a temporary standstill. Failing to clear the lines readily, they hauled the boat, which had just arrived, down to the beach, with the intention of launching it. There were scarcely men enough present to man her, and while they were debating what should be done next, Keeper Green, of No. 5 (Long Branch), arrived in his wagon, and also Surfmen John Redmond and John Pierce, of Station No. 7 (Shark River). The two latter had journeyed from the vicinity of their station, several miles distant, having seen the two rockets sent up from No. 6 by Van Brunt and White. From long experience in the service they understood the import of the signals and made all the haste possible on foot, arriving in season to render good service.

"Green, being the only keeper on the ground, assumed command. After consultation it was decided that the surf was still too dangerously high to venture with the boat, although the tide had fallen somewhat. All hands therefore turned again to an effort to clear the entangled lines. After considerable difficulty they succeeded, with the aid of the steamer's crew, in getting the gear into working order and the breeches buoy was sent off. It was then between half past 6 and 7 o'clock. The first to land was a woman, and she was followed by one of the men with a child in his arms, or rather nestled under his coat. Their experience was a rough one from the fact that the hawser had slacked by the vessel working inshore a little. It naturally followed that when midway between the ship and shore, the sag of the line, weighted with its living freight, carried the buoy into the water, and gave the poor baby and the man a ducking. It was only momentary, however, for strong hands and willing hearts soon brought them safely ashore. The hawser was then tautened, and with one or two men to attend the tackle and keep the necessary strain on the large line, the work of rescue went on until all the passengers were landed. As each one came in Mr. Hathaway superintended their dispatch in vehicles to the house of Samuel Hendrickson, which was the nearest place of shelter. Some of them reached the beach in sorry plight, barefooted and almost nude; indeed one woman was so nearly naked that a bystander was called upon for his overcoat to cover her when lifted from the buoy. It was also found necessary to send to the station for blankets to cover others. The children, poor little creatures, were the worst off. Barefooted and thinly clad in garments such as are worn in the tropic climate of Brazil, the searching northeast wind and chilling mist gave them a pinched and woe-begone appearance which excited the active sympathy of the shore folk, who did everything possible for their comfort. The box of clothing placed at Station No. 5, by the Women's National Relief Association, was found very useful at this juncture, as it contained just what was wanted. The residents also contributed freely in the same direction.

"As the work of rescue progressed quite a crowd of people from Asbury Park, Deal, Elberon, and Long Branch had congregated on the scene, so that before long they could be counted by hundreds, many of them assisting energetically in the manipulation of the apparatus. Among the latter were several of the crew of No. 5, who arrived soon after Keeper Green. When the last passenger had been safely landed there was a pause in the operations, owing to the refusal of the officers and some of the crew to leave the ship. With the recession of the tide the surf gradually subsided and the question of using the surf-boat again came up. About this time, say half past 8, John Slocum, keeper of No. 6, arrived. The wreck being within the precincts of his station he took his place at the steering oar, and with a picked crew of men belonging to Nos. 5, 6, and 7, respectively, the boat was taken off in good shape. The ship was upwards of two hundred and

From *Harper's Weekly.*

FIRING LINE OVER THE SHIP.

eighty feet in length and afforded a good lee in approaching her; still, the sea was rough enough to compel the exercise of judgment and skill in making the trip. There were Asher Wardell of No. 5, William Van Brunt and Cornelius Van Note of No. 6, and John Redmond and John Pierce of No. 7, and Benjamin Van Brunt of No. 6, at the stroke. The steamer's crew were brought ashore in four trips, the captain and officers coming last. All hands could have been landed in three trips but for the refusal of the officers to leave her. The boat's crew reported this fact when they landed the third time, and Keeper Green decided to go off and point out the danger of their remaining. This had the desired effect, and the officers were soon afterwards safe on the beach. On one trip a sailor in coming over the ship's side lost his hold and fell into the water between the ship and one of her boats which had been lowered and was lying alongside. The surf-boat, at the time, was alongside the ship's boat. Observing the man fall, Keeper Slocum jumped into the ship's boat from his own, and seized the man by the collar, threw him on his back, deftly rolled him over the gunwale, inboard, and helped him into the surf-boat. But for this feat of skill and strength, which showed true life-saving craft, the an might have drowned, as in a moment more he would have been swept away by the current. It is related, however, that he expostulated at Slocum's rough and ready rescue, when the latter retorted that he could not afford to stand by and see him drown. The fact is, the man was under the influence of liquor, which had been surreptitiously obtained from the spirit room by some of the men while the officers were busily superintending the landing of the passengers. In this connection another incident should be mentioned. When the captain was about to leave the ship he directed the second and fourth officers to make diligent search fore and aft, to be sure they were leaving no one on board. The officers reported all hands out of the ship. With this assurance they shoved off and were taken ashore. This was at ten o'clock. Supposing, of course, that the work of rescue was complete, the beach party naturally turned their attention towards making the visitors cast in their midst as comfortable as possible, the crew of the ship going to Station No. 6. What was the astonishment, then, of the crowd left on the bluff idly watching the wreck, at seeing about 2 o'clock in the afternoon a man moving about the deck, who finally ascended the fore-rigging and made signs of getting into the breeches buoy which hung to the hawser, just as it had been left near the ship, when the crew refused to come ashore in it. Getting responsive signals from the bluff, he clambered into the buoy and in a few minutes was on terra-firma, surrounded by his rescuers, who plied him with questions as to how he came to be left behind. He proved to be the carpenter of the ship. It appeared that while the boat was engaged in landing the ship's company early in the forenoon he had taken his place in it, but changing his mind he managed in the confusion of the moment to climb back on board unnoticed, and go below, out of sight. He claimed that he had been asleep and did not know the rest had gone ashore.

"Most of the passengers and crew were sent by rail to New York late the same day, the latter being taken in charge by the British consul, while the captain and officers remained at Long Branch, at the house of Keeper Green, for several days.

"With the subsidence of the storm on the following day, the mails and some baggage were recovered, but as the ship had then broken in two amidships, all hope of saving her was abandoned. In the operations at this wreck, twenty-one trips were made by the breeches buoy, and thirty-one persons, including ten children, were brought ashore in it, while thirty were landed by the surf-boat; aggregating a total of sixty-one saved.

"The captain was loud in his praise of the rescuing party."

This rescue operation was conducted by men who had already been laid off for the summer. Their humanitarian services were strictly voluntary. No mention was made as to whether they received any pay for their extraordinary efforts.

Northeasterly winds continued throughout the day and night after the *Pliny* came ashore. The "hook" of Sandy Hook was filling up with vessels which were waiting for the storm to abate before setting out to sea. Waves pummeled the *Pliny* unmercifully. Major Wardell, an agent for the Merritt Wrecking Company, examined the wreck with the possibility of salvage in mind.

The stranded steamer broke in two "forward of the machinery, just under the pilot house, and about 100 feet from her bow. The breach has already opened one foot down to the water's edge. The bow and stern have sunk deeper in the sea, leaving her higher out of the water amidship. . . . From the drifting timber and other stuff which was floating in the surf, there was every indication that she was breaking up on her starboard side. . . . The bulkheads and steerage are knocked down, all the joiner work in the cabins is smashed, the doors are torn out, and the furniture all broken up and mixed with baggage, instruments, and the lumber of the shelves and sides of staterooms. The water has swept all over and into every place on deck, and had the Captain and mates not been almost forced to leave the steamer last night they must all have perished. The cabins on deck are started from their fastenings, and will probably go overboard with the next high waves. Even the pilot-house, although perched up high, has not escaped the fury of the waves. It has been swept of everything movable. The wooden decks are badly broken and the iron flooring under them is badly bulged up. A large part, probably 100 feet, of the starboard side is bone, leaving the cargo open to the force of the waves. A large portion, probably one-third, of the cargo has already been swept from the hold, and everything denotes a speedy breaking up of the ship."

By using the lee created by the hull, those of the *Pliny's* crew who remained on site launched boats from the beach and boarded the ship in order to retrieve their personal belongings. In this they were partially successful. "They saved most of the Captain's and surgeon's instruments, together with their baggage and most of that belonging to the passengers that was in the staterooms. As the waves had full swept through the cabins last night it is possible that some of the baggage has been washed away. Most of the passengers' baggage is in the hold and if the vessel does not go to pieces, will be saved when the cargo is discharged. It was harder work to find the sailors' baggage, the cargo having washed into the steerage and covered everything up, but after working a long time most of it was saved and carried ashore in the surf boats. Almost everything movable of any value on the decks was taken ashore before long. All the wood work was swelled, and the drawers and closets had to be cut open with axes. Partitions had to be knocked down so as to clear a way to move the things. . . . At 12:30 the rising sea began to break over the decks and drove the wreckers from their work for the day. From noon to dark the waves dashed over her decks, sweeping all the debris from them, with coffee out of the hold filling the surf as far down as Ocean Grove. The coffee is washing up on the beach tonight. . . . One of the steamer's boats came ashore today in good condition. Three others were washed up during the night, but the latter were badly broken up. . . . Notwithstanding the heavy rain all day there has been a very large number of spectators on the bluff opposite the steamer. They came from this and all the adjoining towns, and some were from New York."

The anticipated break in the weather did not transpire. A temporary lull was followed by a tempest, which brought northeast winds and resultant high waves. "Large quantities of coffee have been washed out of the steamer. The beach for three miles south of the wreck is strewn with it, and large numbers of persons are engaged in gathering it up. Some of them have obtained large quantities of it, and are carrying it away in wagons. The break in the vessel is gradually widening, and as the vessel rocks it opens at least three feet, and the sea dashes through it. The stern is sinking in the sand, and is almost stationary, but the bow still stands high, and rocks with the motion of the waves."

It was estimated that coffee beans could survive one or two days submerged in sea water before being soaked so thoroughly that they could not be washed clean enough for brewing. Longer submersion made the beans usable. Ultimately, the value of the cargo retrieved amounted to only $7,000 - a mere pittance compared to the total worth of 20,000 bags of coffee, 500 hides, and a few bales of wool. The cargo was insured for $250,000 by the Atlantic and Orient Insurance Companies, of New York.

The *Pliny* was worth $200,000 at the time of her loss. Although the records make no mention of hull insurance, it may have been insured by Lloyd's of London.

A British Board of Inquiry found Captain Robert Mitchell guilty of errors in judgment. He was unable to obtain accurate sightings because his approach to New York was attended by heavy weather. As compensation, he hove to several times in order to take soundings. The judges, sitting comfortably in chambers while they took evidence and rendered opinions, believed that Mitchell should have concluded from the depths of the soundings that his vessel was off the Jersey coast and not off the south shore of Long Island. They also believed that the light he mistook for an ordinary light on Long Island must have been one of the lighthouses at Sandy Hook. These opinions were rendered, no doubt, after minute scrutiny of the charts after the fact, and great deliberation based upon events already past. Recapitulation is so much more precise than prediction.

Based on the judges' recommendation, the British Board of Trade suspended Robert Mitchell's master's certificate for six months.

The *Pliny's* hull collapsed and was left to rot. After more than a century of continuous pummeling by the waves, there is not much left that is recognizable as a ship. The wreck is a worthwhile site to see for those who are interested in marine life, and perhaps the occasional item of brass. Mussels and small game fish abound.

The wreck lies off the south end of Deal Casino Beach Club. Align the north gate in the fence and swim east until you see the tip of the jetty in line with the peak of the house with the red tile roof. Descend directly onto the propeller shaft. From this point you can swim north to the stern or south to the machinery and bow. Alternatively, the wreck can be located by walking or swimming to the end of the jetty, which a section of the bow barely grazes. However, unless a significant amount of sand is washed away, exposing wreckage, it will be difficult to follow the track of debris to the main section of the wreck. Another way of finding the site is to look for a surface disturbance, caused by swells when they hit the wreck and surge upward.

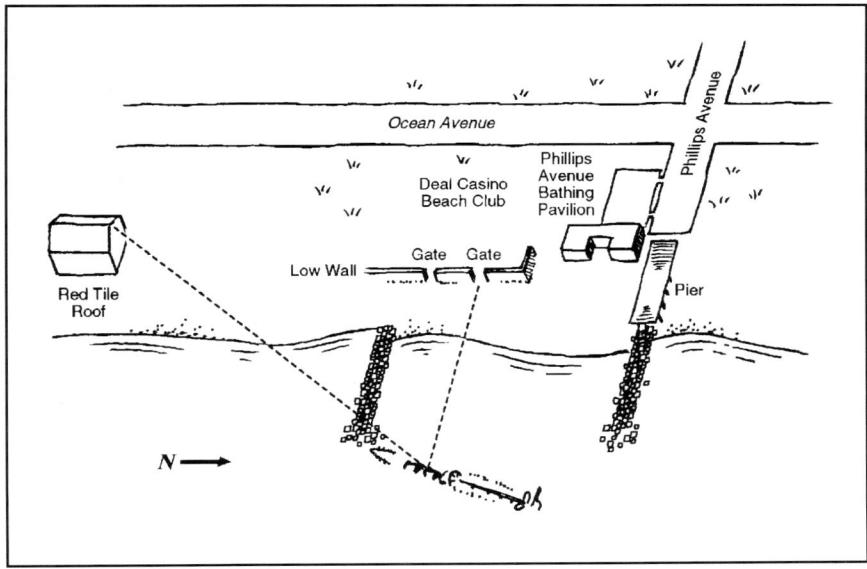

Official U.S. Coast Guard photo.

RELIEF

Built: 1904

Previous names: None

Gross tonnage: 631

Type of vessel: Lightship

Sunk: June 24, 1960

Depth: 110 feet

Dimensions: 129' x 28' x 14'

Power: Diesel engine

Builder: New York Shipbuilding Company, Camden, New Jersey

Owner: United States Lighthouse Board

Port of registry: New York, NY

Cause of sinking: Collision with SS *Green Bay*

Location: 26903.5

43695.9

    Most accidents are said to occur because one is at the wrong place at the wrong time. In the case of the *Relief* lightship, she was right on station where she belonged, guarding the entrance to the Ambrose Channel. The Ambrose Station is generally attended by the eponymous *Ambrose* lightship, but on June 24, 1960, that vessel was docked at the St. George Coast Guard Base on Staten Island for the purpose of annual maintenance.

As the name implies, the *Relief* lightship was not assigned to a regular station, but instead traveled along the coast - an itinerant lightship that went wherever she was needed in order to replace lightships that were damaged, sunk, or undergoing modernization or routine maintenance. She led this peripatetic existence for more than half a century, with no definite place to call her own.

The *Relief* was originally designated as Lightship #83. She was one of five sister ships ordered by the U.S. Department of Commerce & Labor, the others being the *Blunts Reef* (#78), the *Cape Lookout Shoal* (#79), the *Five Fathom Bank* (#80), and the *Heald Banks* (#81). The vessels cost the government $89,000 each in 1904. The *Relief* was equipped with a single 2-cylinder compound engine which, two double-furnace boilers, and was rated at 375 horsepower. This engine was later replaced with a Winton diesel. With a fuel capacity of 15,000 gallons, she could travel 5,150 miles at 8.9 knots.

All five sister ships underwent modifications throughout the years. Gross tonnage fluctuated constantly, recalculated whenever the compartmentation was altered or topside structures were rebuilt. Even the lengths varied slightly, especially when the original pointed stem was lopped off. Radar and sonar units were installed after World War Two. During the war, the *Relief* saw service as an examination ship at Staten Island.

At one time, a lightship marked the entrance to New York harbor by standing station at Sandy Hook. On October 31, 1908, the lightship station was moved farther out to sea, to Ambrose Channel. Transatlantic liners took advantage of this new position to advertise faster crossing times. The run across the ocean became a few miles shorter, making it appear to a gullible public that the ships were proceeding faster.

When lightships were reclassified, the *Relief* received a new designation. No longer Lightship #83, she became WAL-505. (The letters WAL are not an acronym, but simply a designation.) Then came the fateful day when she took the place of the *Ambrose* lightship, and marked her presence with a fog horn and two powerful beacons, shining the way for vessels plying the two-thousand-foot wide channel.

The C-2 cargo carrier *Green Bay* slipped down the harbor from Port Newark through a predawn, pea-soup fog. Loaded with general merchandise, she was on her way to Massawa, Eritrea (an autonomous unit of Ethiopia, bordering the Red Sea in Africa). Despite zero visibility, her radar enabled her to locate the pilot launch. Captain Thomas Mazzella, master, ordered the *Green Bay's* engines stopped. The vessel drifted quietly while the pilot disembarked. The time was four o'clock in the morning.

The lightship was obscured by the same fog that enshrouded the *Green Bay*. The lightship clearly showed up as a blip on the steamship's radar screen. At that time, Captain Mazzella estimated that the lightship was moored a mile and a half away: her fog horn was clearly audible in the silence of the night. The pilot launch shoved off. Captain Mazzella ordered the engines slow ahead, ordered a slight change in course, then walked onto the bridge wing to look for the beacon.

"The lookout on the bow estimated he heard the fog signal from the

Lightship about 3 minutes before collision broad on the starboard bow, then sighted the loom of the light on the same bearing. The bearing then changed slowly to dead ahead. According to the lookout, this information was relayed by telephone to the bridge by the chief mate who was also on the forecastle head, but the chief mate stated that when he first saw the loom of the light about 1 1/2 minutes before collision it was dead ahead and this was the report he made to the bridge. The master, upon receiving the report of the loom dead ahead, went to the wing of the bridge but could see nothing. Moments later the thin loom of the light was visible ahead, whereupon he ordered the rudder hard right to 090° T[rue] to clear the Lightship and the engines full ahead to increase the swing. . . . Within seconds the light ahead became intense and realizing the Lightship was closer than he had originally thought, the master rang up full astern."

Aboard the *Relief,* Boatswain's Mate Bobby Pierce had pilot house duty that morning. This was normally a dull job that did not require much vigilance. He was listening idly to the fog horn of an approaching steamer when he became suspicious of its proximity. Pierce "called the man on watch in the engineroom to come topside and when he arrived on deck," they spotted the freighter's tall stem bearing down on them from only fifty feet away. Pierce vaulted into action and sounded the general alarm. Moments later "the bow of the *Green Bay* struck the lightship on her starboard side just aft of amidships at almost a 90° angle."

Men were tossed out of their bunks as "the *Relief* rolled about 15° to port as a result of the impact, then righted herself as the *Green Bay* backed clear." The engine room flooded and the generator stopped. Light and power were lost.

"All hands were mustered, and left the vessel in a self-inflating rubber raft. By that time the vessel was down by the stern and a few minutes later was observed to go down stern first." So great was the need to abandon ship that the nine men "left behind watches and all personal belongings. Some wore only blue jeans. In the raft, they paddled furiously with their hands, so as not to be drawn into the whirlpool around the sinking ship.

Joseph Tamalonia, chief boatswain's mate and acting officer in charge of the lightship, said that the *Relief* sank ten to twelve minutes after the collision. "She sank stern first. kicked up her nose and went straight down."

"After an hour's groping in the fog-softened beams of searchlights aboard the *Green Bay*, a small boat from the freighter came alongside the raft. Soon the men were transferred to a ninety-five-foot Coast Guard patrol boat and taken to St. George."

The *Green Bay* dropped anchor. An examination established that the freighter suffered only minor damage to her forepeak, and was not leaking. After the steamship's officers and crew were questioned about events leading up to the collision, she was cleared by the Coast Guard and allowed to continue her voyage.

A marker buoy was placed over the site of the wreck. "The Coast Guard Cutter *Yeaton* - also equipped with a flashing light, radio beacon and foghorn - substituted for the lightship. Special radio warnings went out between the time of the crash and the arrival of the cutter," which was 6:15 a.m. Although maintenance was not due to be completed for another two weeks, the *Ambrose* lightship was dispatched that very afternoon to resume her station.

Several days later, Navy diver Richard Barnum was sent down to inspect the damage to the sunken lightship in order to determine if salvage was feasible. During the course of several dives he measured the large gash in the starboard hull: it was twelve feet high, ranging in width from two feet at the second deck to five inches below the first deck. In Barnum's opinion, the hole was "too large to have permitted her crew to have kept her afloat through pumping or through patching with available material."

Barnum's opinion was supported by Commander John Latimer, a naval engineer who studied the evidence and testified at the Marine Board of Investigation that was conducted by the Coast Guard. He thought that "it was doubtful whether the ship's pumps could have coped with the water rushing into the ship. . . . In answer to a question whether the gash could have been closed by damage-control efforts of the crewmen, he said that would have 'depended on their capabilities' and the availability of adequate repair material aboard the ship.

"Referring to earlier testimony about a watertight door between the ship's engine room and machinery room that had been left open, Commander Latimer said the vessel would have sunk whether that door was closed or not." This opinion was based on the fact that the lightship was struck almost precisely on the transverse bulkhead in which the door was located. Water would then have flowed freely through cracks in the crumpled metal when the bulkhead was bent out of line. Contrary to standing orders, the *Relief's* crew commonly left this door open in order to facilitate entry to the compressor room, where the pumps that supplied air for the fog horn were located. These pumps were checked routinely during rounds.

Engineer Eugene Murray said "he had never kept the door between the two compartments tightly closed. He said that during his five months of duty on the lightship the commanding officer had never been aware of this."

Perhaps with too much a touch of the obvious, the Marine Board of Investigation found that "this casualty was caused principally by the *Green Bay* being headed directly toward the Lightship in zero visibility. Contributing to the casualty was the failure of the vessel to fix her position either by radar or radio direction finder bearings before setting her course. Concurring with the Board, the engine order of full ahead under the existing conditions was excessive particularly in view of the fact that the master apparently had no confidence in his radar due to previous erratic operation in addition to the fact that the distance to the Lightship was never established."

Damage to the *Green Bay* was estimated to cost $3,000 to repair. The *Relief* was determined to be unsalvageable in terms of economic feasibility. Replacing the *Relief* "with a new lightship will cost between $1,000,000 and $1,800,000," according to Commander Latimer.

When the wreck was wire-dragged to reduce the hazard to navigation, the masts were raked over the port side and much of the superstructure was demolished. The hull sits upright and is intact except for the gaping collision wound. It can be said truthfully, although with tongue loosely in cheek, that the lightship has more "relief" than most wrecks of similar dimensions. The upper deck stringers are still in reasonably good condition, while the deck planks are nearly all gone. Almost all the interior partitions have collapsed except for those in the engine room. The wreck is entered easily through the missing upper deck, but care should be exercised because the interior silts up quickly.

Members of the Aquarian Dive Club recovered the massive bronze bell. Al Catalfumo led a group of divers who recovered one of the masts, complete with signal light. The wreck continues to yield portholes and other brass trinkets such as keys, door latches, and numerous personal items. It is a wreck well worth exploring.

Although the heyday of lightships is past and they are no longer found in service, several have been purchased by, or donated to, seaside maritime museums. One is located at the South Street Seaport Museum in New York, another at Lewes, Delaware. Others exist. Although they may not be identical sister ships, their hull lines and interior arrangement are similar. Divers who anticipate exploring the remains of the *Relief* are well advised to familiarize themselves with the type by taking a tour of one of these topside vestiges of the past.

Among anglers and divers, the *Relief* is commonly referred to as the Lightship.

The *Blunts Reef*, one of the *Relief's* sister ships, is shown in the original configuration of the class.

RJUKAN

Built: 1856
Previous names: *Endeavor*
Gross tonnage: 960
Type of vessel: Wooden-hulled full-rigged ship
Builder: Robert E. Jackson, Boston, Massachusetts
Owner: Thomas Offenberg & Company, Norway
Port of registry: Skien, Norway
Cause of sinking: Ran aground
Location: Off Newark Avenue in Bradley Beach

Sunk: December 26, 1876
Depth: 20 feet
Dimensions: 184' x 36' x 22'
Power: Sail

The *Rjukan* was a much respected ship in her heyday. She was launched in Boston as the *Endeavor,* and spent nearly all of her two-decade career transporting immigrants from Europe to the New World of promise. For example, on June 15, 1868 she arrived in Quebec after a passage from Norway that required fifty-seven days; three hundred thirty-one passengers were aboard. During another passage eleven children died. In 1873, the *Endeavor* left Langesund (one of Skien's neighboring towns) on a passage that lasted for seven weeks. During that time, five people died and four babies were born.

In 1876, the *Endeavor* was purchased by the Norwegian company of Thomas Offenberg. Her name was changed to *Rjukan* and she was put into freighting service. December 26 of that year found her bound in ballast from London to New York. Captain Theodore Hanson, master, took aboard a pilot from Pilot Boat Number 6 (the *Staten Island*) before proceeding to his ultimate destination. As the ship approached the Jersey shore a strong northeast wind was blowing. Pilot John Philips, now in charge of the *Rjukan's* navigation, did not take into account the severity of the wind. He lost his bearings in the thick fog. The first anyone knew of their proximity to the beach was when the barnacle-encrusted hull grated across the sand. The *Rjukan* was aground.

Odd as it may sound, the *Rjukan* struck the bar stern foremost. The wind quickly blew her bow around until the ship faced south, placing her broadside to the beach. Tremendous waves pummeled her offshore hull like a succession of high-speed battering rams. Within minutes the mainmast snapped off at the deck, followed soon after by the fore and mizzen topmasts. A wild tangle of rigging hung over the ship's side like a giant cat's cradle that had been dropped from the sky, leaving the ship a complete wreck. It was 6:30 in the morning.

The undertaking to rescue the nineteen men on the *Rjukan* was one of the few dark moments in the history of the Life-Saving Service. Some of what was reported by the press was pure fabrication, such as the account of shrieking sailors clinging to the rigging and calling forlornly for help. Other tales of incompetence were exaggerated or distorted or made intentionally sensationalistic in a blatant attempt to rouse the public's anger - and, incidentally, to sell newspapers to the gullible: a practice that is very much alive today.

Chance and the chronology of circumstances conspired to cast the Life-Saving Service in an uneven light. Even the following account - which is better balanced than most - includes some editorializing:

"Last winter the government officials discharged two brothers from Station No. 6, because it was against rules to employ two or more of the same family. These same brothers, Russel and Drummond White, were not only the first to reach the wreck, but voluntarily made the last trip to save the Captain's valuables, when the regular station crew refused - alleging that their business was to save life, not property. It is a sad commentary on the efficiency of our Life Saving Service when the crew, whose house is less than one mile distant, did not get their life-boat to the wreck until three hours after she struck. Had it not been for our brave fishermen some lives might have been sacrificed. . . .

"Edward Ferry first discovered the Norwegian ship *Rjukan*, while on his way to work, on Tuesday morning, a little after six o'clock, and immediately notified Mr. Lewis Rainear, Assistant Superintendent of Ocean Grove, who told him to inform Allen B. Cook, of Asbury Park, who is Wrecking Master in this district. Mr. Cook being seriously ill could not leave the house. Mr. Rainear arrived on the beach a little before seven o'clock, and none of his life saving crew had been there. He then started for the station, and was met half way by one of the crew, who said the vessel had been seen and they wanted to send word to the station below - Abner Allen's - as they were short-handed. (Why short-handed? Don't the government pay for a full crew?) Mr. Rainear replied that word had been sent to Mr. Allen, and the man from No. 7 said that the crew would be on the spot as soon as possible.

"About nine o'clock they came with a wagon load of ropes and the mortar, and then had to send the *same team back after their boat*. Russel White then made up a crew consisting of his brother, Drummond White, John Rogers, Elwood Newman and John Goodman, and went out with an ordinary fisherman's boat and had one load of men landed and were at the vessel getting the second load when the crew from the station arrived. Then the station boat was launched, but was manned, with one or two exceptions, by volunteer fishermen under the control of Russel White. It was nearly ten o'clock [a.m.] when the last boat load landed."

It was noted that when the life-savers - that is, the *paid* life-savers - first arrived with the ropes and mortar, they fired a line across the wreck with the intention of rigging a breeches buoy. Why they chose such an expedience, when it was obvious that a boat could achieve the rescue more effectively, was never adequately explained. According to the press, the life-savers excused their tardiness by claiming that their station apparatus "was not kept in order and in place" and that they had to hunt up the parts." Such a condition was unjustifiable if true - and not likely to be admitted - but the dialogue might have been a case of crass creative reporting.

In retrospect, from the life-savers initial assessment of the situation, it may very well have seemed that the surf was too rough to launch a lifeboat, in which case the breeches buoy would have been their only option to save the *Rjukan's* crew. Yet they stuck doggedly to their breeches buoy mentality despite the efficacy of the volunteer life-savers in reaching the wreck by fishing boat. Did their attitude and actions - or lack thereof - demonstrate poor training, incompetence, cowardice, or fear?

The stranding of the *Rjukan* and the rescue of her crew resulted in two investigations. The Pilot Commissioners investigated the reason for the grounding. Captain Hanson and the first mate testified, not unexpectedly, that John Philips was at fault because the vessel was under his command at the time of the stranding. They relied upon his competence to pilot the ship into the harbor. In his defense, Philips claimed that the mate had given him the wrong soundings. The Board admonished Philips for not taking the soundings himself, regardless of the truth of his claim. His pilot's license was revoked "during the pleasure of the board."

Captain John Merryman, head of the New York Division of the Life-Saving Service, was instructed by the Department in Washington to investigate allegations of inadequacy or want of intrepidity on the part of the local life-saving crew. Captain Hanson was not lacking in praise for the efforts of the life-savers. Drummond White denied statements that were credited to him - to the effect that he claimed sole recognition for effecting the rescue - and testified instead that he had worked in the capacity of a volunteer adjunct. Furthermore, "a large number of affidavits were taken, including those of many residents in the neighborhood of the spot where the wreck occurred, which show that the crew acted with vigilance, promptness, and daring."

If the latter statement sounds pompous and reeks of political whitewash, it may have been an overreaction to protect the fledgling Life-Saving Service from blemish. Contemporaries viewed it otherwise.

One incontrovertible fact is that the *Rjukan's* men were rescued in the nick of time. The wreck soon rolled over onto her beam, and "as the tide rose the sea increased in violence, and each succeeding wave seemed to wrench the ship more. Between four and five o'clock in the afternoon the foremast fell, and was soon followed by the mizzenmast, and then the vessel broke completely in two. The stern remained a while and then sank. The stem was the last portion to disappear. By five o'clock not a vestige of the noble craft was left; the waves broke entirely over the spot where she lay."

Word of the wreck circulated quickly. It was estimated that "not less than five hundred people were standing on the beach opposite the vessel, reminding one of the Ocean Grove surf meetings. During the afternoon the beach was covered with debris of every description - pieces of joiner work, rigging, chests, bedding, tools, clothing, etc.; and a hundred men and boys were watching for valuables or souvenirs."

One correspondent forwent the opportunity to ride the bandwagon of detractors by viewing the wreck in lighter vein. It is worth retelling. "It was really amusing to see the heterogeneous company collected on the beach as the ship

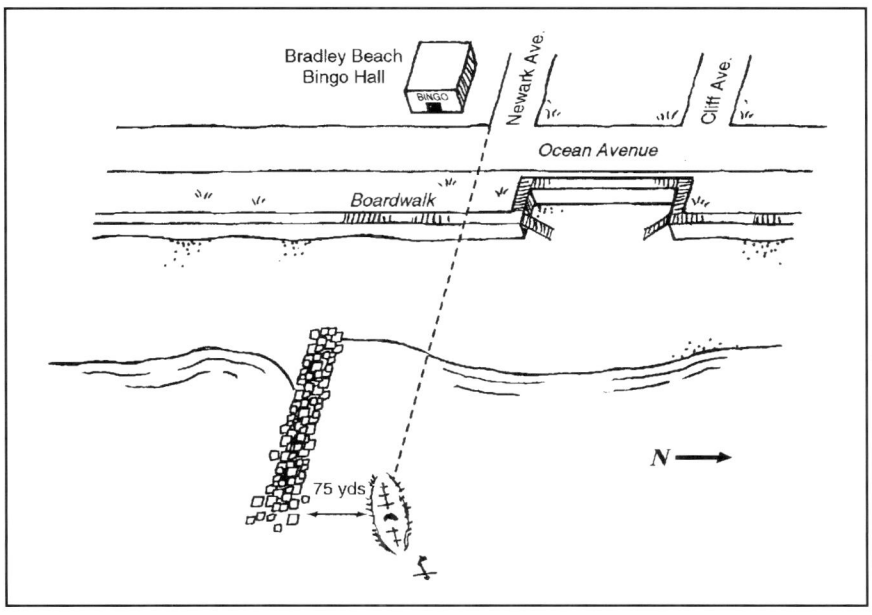

The wreck lies about 75 yards north of the end of the jetty in front of the Bradley Beach Bingo Hall. Swim east from the beach while keeping the south side of Newark Avenue in line until you are just about even with the end of the jetty. You should be right over the wreck. If you descend and do not find the wreck, then surface, swim to the tip of the jetty, descend, and conduct a north-to-south search pattern on the bottom. If the wreck is exposed, you will bump into it. Howard Rothweiler cautions, "Even when there is not much sand on the site it is a very low lying wreck."

went to pieces and drifted ashore. There was Dr. Kinmonth, looking out for a spar to make a flag-pole; Uriah White, ready for something by which he could turn an honest penny; Mrs. Dr. Kinmonth sitting in the wagon raking in the novel scene; Shafto, with a wagon load of ladies looking on; the proprietor of Asbury Park, looking for puncheons [heavy framing timbers] for the new hall; a foreign carpenter, whom Hagerman imported from Philadelphia, who is already looking around among the fair daughters of Shark river to find him a wife; Alderman Griffin, with his usual dignity, advising what should be done; Mr. John Dey, the carpenter, with a piece of the wire rigging to take home as a souvenir; McCabe, the Ocean Grove butcher, with rubber boots big enough for the life-boats; Mrs. Jonathan Cooper and lady friend from Brooklyn, who were astounded to know that a ship could go to pieces in a few hours; the *heartless* reporter of the *Journal*;

Rev. Mr. Harcourt, of Paterson, New Jersey, who was reminded of the 'old ship *Zion*,' whose timber must be sounder than those he looked on or she cannot carry the 'many thousands more,' which the song tells about; Ed. Knight, the ferryman; 'Bumble Bee,' with his round, white head picking up some facts to retail to those who ride with him next summer; Coleman, who was ready to engage in a debate concerning the ill-fated vessel; Newman, the lawyer, who knew all about the maritime laws affecting wrecks.

"In fact, everybody who could go was there. We think the coming ashore of that ship with the unpronounceable name was healthful to the neighborhood. Minds were drawn into new channels of thought - neighbor met neighbor - the talkative told how in 1840, such a ship was wrecked here - and how in 18--, such a bark came on, etc., etc. One man was quite indignant that the three largest wrecks of the past few years should have had such unsalable cargoes, one consisting of salt, another of ice, and this last of ballast only. But, said he, we want a ship laden with India shawls, laces, calico, flour, even - but no more salt, ice or ballast, or wrecks will become a bore. It was as good as a feast, and the dessert is to be served to-day (Saturday), in the shape of an auction of the old material. The city man may talk of the theatre, the city lady tell of the concert, but for a good, square, lively sensation give us a wreck - where no life and but little money is lost."

The last stated sentiment was not quite accurate. The *Rjukan's* hull was worth $25,000.

A week later it was reported that "the wreck of the *Rjukan* was sold at auction on Tuesday for $140. This includes everything that has washed ashore or that is still in the sea. The expense of watching the wreck-stuff has been $100; therefore, the value of the 960 ton ship was just forty dollars." An ignominious end to such a dignified career.

Today, the wreck lies in the surf zone next to a jetty. Generally, little more than the keel and some of the ribs are exposed.

From *Frank Leslie's Illustrated Newspaper.*

RUSLAND

Built: 1872
Previous names: *Kenilworth*
Gross tonnage: 2,538
Type of vessel: Passenger-freighter
Builder: Gourlay, Brothers & Co., Dundee, Scotland
Owner: Red Star Line (Williamston, Milligan, & Co., Managers)
Port of registry: Liverpool, England
Cause of sinking: Ran aground
Location: 26950.2

Sunk: March 17, 1877
Depth: 25 feet
Dimensions: 345' x 37' x 26'
Power: Coal-fired steam

43598.8

(Off the southern end of St. Alphonso's Retreat, in Long Branch)

The *Rusland* left Antwerp, Belgium on March 5, 1877. For eleven days she enjoyed calm seas and pleasant weather - a rare Atlantic crossing. Deep in her holds she carried quite a varied cargo: window and plate glass for a dozen different merchants (of window glass there were 16,617 cases, 1,079 packages, and 7 envelopes; of plate glass there were 197 cases); 536 bales of old paper; 19 crates of paving tiles; 25 casks of minium (now called red lead - a bright red compound of lead and oxygen in powder form, used in paints, glass, pottery, and pipe-joint packing); dyestuffs consisting of 41 casks of bone black, 25 casks and 40 kegs of ultramarine, 4 cases of Prussian blue, 2 cases of colors, and 1 case of aniline; 1 case of stone pots; 12 cases of rolled zinc; 21 bales of greasy wool; 100 packages of iron wire; 28 cases of crystals; 40 casks of wine; 1 barrel of brandy; 1 case of hides; 223 bundles of empty bags; 417 bales of rags; 7 cases of sheet tin; 3 cases of tin leaves; 29 bales of flax; 43 packages of general merchandise for 17 different merchants; 9 cases of glassware; 1 barrel of chicory; 3 casks of sheep roans (sheepskin leather used in bookbinding); and 1 case of church ornaments and chasubles (a chasuble is "a long, sleeveless vestment worn over the alb by the priest at Mass"; an alb is "a long white linen robe with tapered sleeves"). This cargo was valued at $125,000. An unofficial source estimated the value at $200,000.

Also aboard were one hundred ninety-eight people. According to the *Rusland's* master, Captain Jesse De Horsey, these were comprised of thirteen officers, sixty-nine crew members, five saloon passengers, and one hundred eleven passengers in steerage. (The number of steerage passengers was elsewhere given as one hundred thirteen and one hundred twenty.) For years De Horsey had been First Officer on the *Kenilworth*. When the Red Star Line purchased the *Kenilworth* and changed her name to *Rusland*, De Horsey stayed with the ship and was promoted to captain. This was the first voyage of the *Rusland* under her new name, and De Horsey's first command.

The *Rusland* was nearly three hundred miles from Sandy Hook when she encountered the pilot boat *Isaac Webb*. Before the days of the Pilot's Association, pilot boats were privately owned and in stiff competition with each other. It was common practice for pilot boats to patrol far from New York in order to drum up business before someone else got the job. Pilot Benjamin Simonson, of the *Isaac Webb*, was hired and taken aboard.

Captain De Horsey took an accurate noon position with his sextant on Friday, before the fog settled in. With that, his chronometer, and a set of tables, he calculated the ship's position. "The weather was thick on Saturday, with occasional snow squalls, the wind blowing from the east. No canvas was carried. To allow for the effect of the tide and the wind the vessel was steered half a point to windward. I thought she would thus be kept on her true course.

"On 6 o'clock Saturday night we sounded and found 28 fathoms, and from the appearance of the soil brought up by the lead, I concluded that my previous observation was correct. At 8 o'clock another sounding was taken, and 20 fathoms were found, the nature of the bottom again confirming my belief that we were on the right course. Again at 9 o'clock 20 fathoms were found, and sea cakes were brought up. As these cakes have never, to my knowledge, been found west of Fire Island, I concluded that the vessel was off the Long Island coast, and kept a strict watch for the Fire Island and Highland lights. At 10:10, 16 fathoms were found, and the bottom was satisfactory. The pilot and engineer were on the bridge with me, and there was nothing to make us fear disaster.

"Twenty-five minutes later, at 10:30, the lookout cried 'Light on the port bow!' I thought that a mistake had been made by the sailor, as there should have been a light on our starboard bow, but I made out the land, and telegraphed for the vessel to be put about. Before this could be done, however, she struck. Then she slid up the beach. The blow when she struck was so slight that I did not feel it, and turning to the pilot said, 'that was a close shave.' A second after we found the vessel was hard aground."

This was not a good career move for Captain De Horsey. He could not blame Simonson for going astray, for he had not yet turned over control of the ship to the pilot. De Horsey would not have let Simonson take command until the *Sandy*

Hook lightship was sighted.

Captain De Horsey: "As soon as I found there was no immediate danger, I ordered the steerage to be locked, to prevent the people from coming on deck and making trouble." About half the steerage passengers were Italian, the remainder being German and French. Hardly any of them spoke English.

While the steerage passengers were locked below like animals in a cage, the captain treated the saloon passengers differently. Witness this statement made by Mrs. Ferdinand Duysters, who was traveling with her two children, Adrian and Ernest: "I was awakened about 2 o'clock on Sunday morning by Capt. De Horsey, who told me to rise and dress myself and children, as the vessel had struck. He told me, however, not to be alarmed, as there as no further danger to be apprehended, and I would have ample time to dress myself and children comfortably. This was the first intimation I had received of the accident. I dressed myself and children, and wrapped them up warmly, after which we sat down in our state-room, at the Captain's request, to await further directions. I cannot say that I was greatly frightened, although I had considerable apprehension. The hours dragged along wearily until about 4 o'clock, when Capt. De Horsey reappeared and told me to come on deck as, if the vessel should break, it would probably part in the vicinity of my room. I followed his directions and the children behaved nobly, and gave me no trouble. The little girl was somewhat frightened, but my little boy seemed to enjoy the excitement immensely. It was very cold on deck, and the air was full of snow. The officers, and all concerned with the ship, treated us with the greatest kindness, and did all they could to make us comfortable."

Captain Frank Call was a seafaring man, formerly in command of the bark *Union*, which ran between Boston and New York. He was a passenger on the *Rusland*, and asleep at the time that she ran aground. "The stoppage of the steamer roused me, and, hastily dressing, I went on deck. It was snowing hard, and a cold, raw wind was blowing. I made my way to the bridge, where I found the Captain and pilot in consultation. I do not think the pilot had taken formal charge of the steamer at that time. The sailors were shouting wildly, 'Light, ho!' being apparently under the impression that the lights on shore were the lights of sailing vessels in the vicinity of our head. The passengers were not excited, although they looked considerably frightened, and the ship's officers were cool and collected, and assured them that there was no immediate danger."

Captain De Horsey's initial hope that the *Rusland* could be backed off the bar was quickly dashed. The propeller shaft shifted in its housing, the packing gland vibrated loose, and water began seeping into the after compartments. Worse, the raging gale caught the ship's stern and swung it around until the *Rusland* lay broadside to the beach. By an odd coincidence, the *Rusland* happened to have run her nose into the sand only a few feet north of the *Adonis* (q.v.). This wooden-hulled windjammer was cast away in 1859. As the *Rusland* pivoted on her stem, her stern grated over the upthrust timbers of the *Adonis'* ribs. The *Rusland's* iron hull easily crushed to splinters the *Adonis'* wooden frame members. But the *Adonis* carried grindstones in her hold. The *Rusland's*

Shortly after grounding. (Courtesy of The Mariners Museum, Newport News, Virginia.)

plates were punctured by these giant disks of stone. Water then flooded into the hull, sealing her fate.

Still, there was no immediate danger to the passengers and crew. The *Rusland* could not sink since she had already bottomed out. And she had enough freeboard to prevent even the biggest of waves from washing across her decks. But one never knew when a ship might break apart and be pounded to pieces.

Rockets were fired from the *Rusland* in order to attract attention to her plight. It was not long before a life-saver on patrol saw the lights in the sky, and the Long Branch Life Saving Station was soon on the alert. All hands plunged into the squally snowstorm on a defiant mission of mercy. The life-savers

One year after grounding. (Courtesy of Frank Litter.)

dragged the beach apparatus through the wind and snow to a position opposite the stranded steamer. This was no easy task under the prevailing conditions.

The water was too rough to launch a surfboat safely, so the life-savers resorted to another device: the life-car. The life-car worked like a breeches buoy except that the boatlike conveyance was completely enclosed and watertight. It took two shots from the line-throwing gun to get a line to the stranded steamer. Once the line was secured by the *Rusland's* crew, the life-savers set up the life-car so it could hauled through the surf. The time was 4:00 a.m.

Under the cloak of darkness, the passengers commenced disembarking two by two - for the life-car could hold only a pair of people at a time. For the life-savers the operation was strictly by the book. There was no telling how many times they had practiced the life-car maneuver until it was nothing more than routine. But for the passengers who were crammed into a tiny metal boat that was only slightly larger than a coffin, it must have been a frightening experience. Yet there was little to-do or complaint.

By dawn, two and a half hours later, the seas had moderated to the point at which surfboats could be launched in the lee provided by the *Rusland's* hull. Across this protected patch of water the life-savers transported boatload after boatload of passengers. By ten o'clock it was all over except for retrieving the baggage. Hundreds of visitors traveled by wagon from outlying villages to watch the spectacle. If the rescue operation seems too casual, it can be attributed only to the proficiency and expertise of the men of the Life Saving Service.

Not until Captain Jesse De Horsey spoke with the life-savers did he learn that he had not come to grief on the south shore of Long Island. He blamed his faulty navigation on the thick fog that prevented him from taking further star sightings, as well as contrary winds and currents that pushed the *Rusland* farther south and west than he anticipated.

All during the rescue operations, the *Rusland's* crew worked prodigiously to haul the baggage up from the lower deck and stack it on the main deck. The life-savers never slackened their pace. Using the surfboats as lighters, they transported every bit of baggage from the steamer to the beach. This operation lasted until 4:30 in the afternoon. Only then did the *Rusland's* crew pile into the surfboats and let the life-savers row them ashore.

The physical effort must have been daunting to anyone but a dedicated lifesaver. Yet, to a service that was committed to the saving of life under the most horrible of circumstances, the rescue of one hundred ninety-eight people - without the slightest injury - received no more notice than a single-line entry in the Service's annual report.

The Long Branch Life Saving Station swelled with survivors who huddled in the building in order to get out of the weather. The Tower of Babel never suffered so much confusion! However, arrangements were soon made for everyone to be put up at the East End Hotel, and the confusion moved there for the night. The next day, the survivors left for New York by means of the New Jersey Southern Railroad and the ferry *Jesse Hoyt*. They were accompanied all the way by their baggage. At least they did not arrive in America naked and destitute.

"The cabin passengers, at least three of them, were received with demonstrations of joy by anxious friends, but there were none but curious, ordinary sightseers in waiting for the 113 steerage passengers, who were taken to the Castle Garden." This was the time of the great western expansion. The steerage passengers were on their way west.

The Coast Wrecking Company sent the salvage vessel *Relief* in hopes that the *Rusland* could be pulled off the bar. During a lull in the storm, wreckers managed to get a salvage pump aboard the steamer, but were unable to offload any cargo because the weather again turned foul. "The steamer still crushes out the timbers of the old ship *Adonis*, and the shore is strewn with fragments for miles." The Western Union Telegraph Company strung a special line "from the shore opposite the wreck to connect with their lines for the agents of the steamer, in order that they may telegraph direct to the steamer from their offices in New York and Philadelphia."

The *Relief* anchored half a mile offshore of the *Rusland*, waiting for better weather. Lighters arrived from New York. The *Rusland's* starboard side was pummeled by the waves. Seas "broke over her nearly from stem to stern in a cloud of spray." The ship assumed a slight starboard list.

Two days after stranding, it was reported that the bow was elevated "high in the air, while her stern is above the water not more than three feet, the line of descent to the stern being very steep." A photograph taken shortly afterward confirms this description. It was widely surmised that the bow was being held up on the *Adonis*. This observation is at variance with the present-day position of the wrecks relative to each other. Today, the stern of the *Rusland*, including the propeller on its shaft, rests on the wreckage of the *Adonis*.

By the time the storm blew itself out, the steamer had dug itself so deep into the sand that extrication seemed improbable. Salvors boarded the ship and found that the starboard rail had been carried away by the pounding sea. "Where the water has broken over the side of the vessel it has frozen so that to-day the wreck has glistened brightly in the sun. As the hull settled down it filled with water, and the furniture of the saloon is now floating about, while the engine room is flooded to the bases of the cylinders." The engine also rose "considerably," indicating that the vessel's bottom under the engine was resting on a hummock of sand while the ends of the hull were sagging.

On April 4, it was reported that a moderate wind and a smooth sea were facilitating the discharge of cargo into four lighters that were in attendance. On April 9, the hull broke in two and began to break up in heavy weather. By April 17, the after bulkhead in number two hold was gone, but the work of discharging cargo continued. By April 24, divers were required to recover cargo that lay under water in the lower holds. Work progressed favorably enough during the following week to fill three schooners with salvaged cargo.

The hull proved to be a total constructive loss. The *Rusland* was valued at $300,000 and was fully insured overseas. On May 2, an auction was held at Robinson's Stores, in Brooklyn. Some five hundred people attended. At this auction the broken hull fetched only $9,100, the highest bidder being George

163

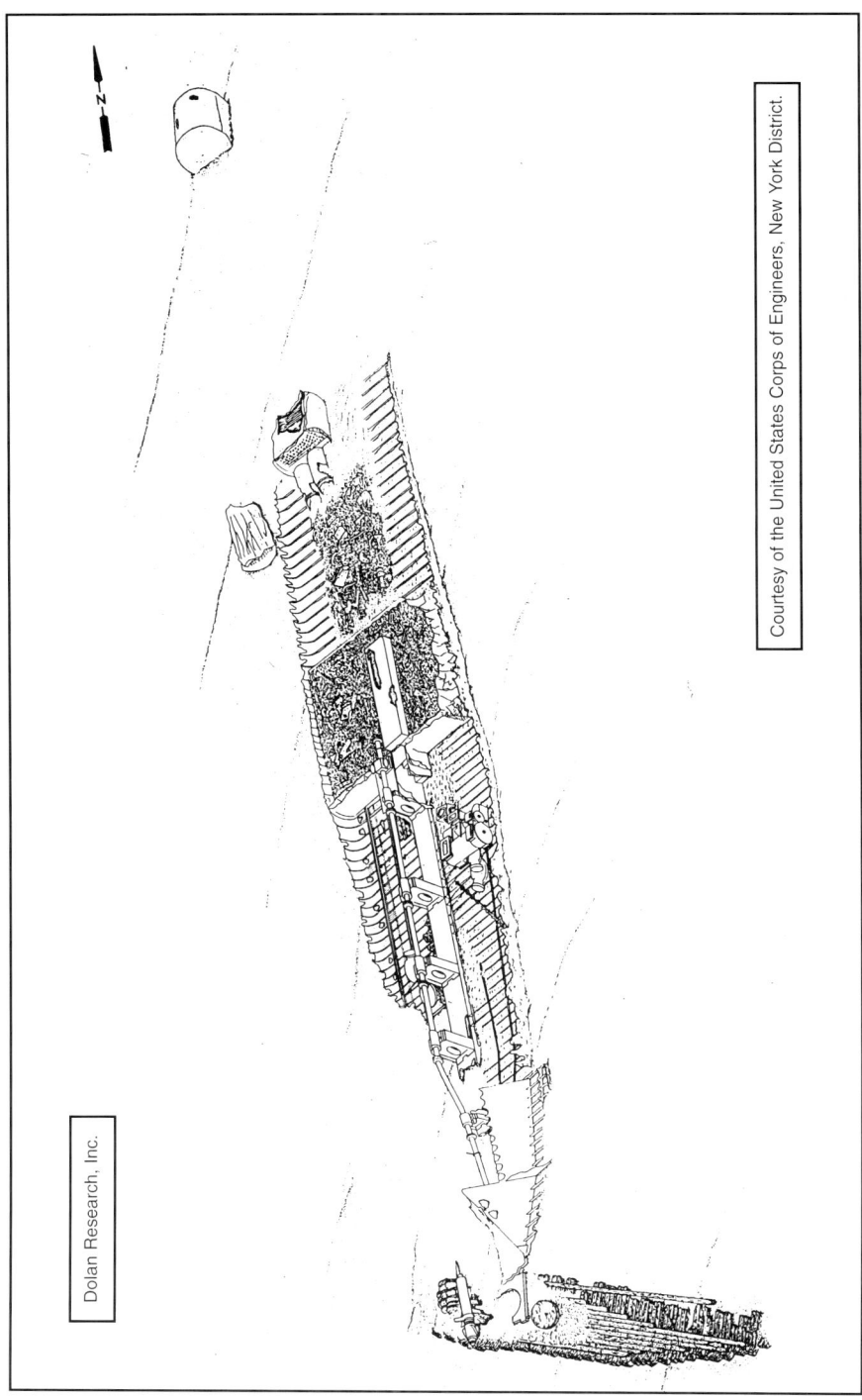

Dolan Research, Inc.

Courtesy of the United States Corps of Engineers, New York District.

Townsend of Boston. The purchase price did not include any of the cargo that remained within. The rest of the recovered property included thirty tons of chain, sails, cordage, lifeboats, and "miscellaneous stuff. . . . The boats were sold at $45 each, and the life raft, Nonpareil, brought $50. John H. Draper & Co., the auctioneers, considered the sale altogether a very good one."

A local newspaper reported that "the shore is strewn with pieces of the old *Adonis* which the steamer is breaking up. Hundreds have visited the wreck, and Pach, of New York, and Hill, of Elizabeth, have been engaged in taking photographic views of her."

The hull of the *Rusland* was broken down before the Beach Replenishment Project covered the wreck with sand. A fair amount of structure remained above the stratified clay bottom. The boiler tubes, engine area, and propeller shaft were exposed and contiguous, and stuck up several feet above the natural level of the sea bed. Many of the frames were exposed. Of the original four-bladed propeller, there remains only the hub and a single blade, pointing down.

During an official survey prior to the Beach Replenishment Project, Dan Lieb found several more propeller blades which he concluded must have been spares. He also found in the engine area what might be either the engine bedplates or the base structure of the engine. The engine itself appeared to have been salvaged long ago by parties unknown.

Due to the proximity of the beach, any slight wave action stirs up the sand and bottom sediment and reduces visibility. Ten to fifteen feet of visibility is not uncommon during spells of good weather. Before the *Rusland* was covered with sand, the wreck was fished and dived by boat, and was also reachable by divers willing to swim to the wreck from shore - a distance of about two hundred feet. The experience was rewarding for spearfishers, with tautog and black sea bass being the prime targets. Small lobsters could be found foraging at night.

As with the *Adonis*, exposed structure offered numerous hiding places for small bottom dwellers, and provided a substrate for sessile marine organisms such as barnacles, anemones, and seaweed. Winter storms stripped the wreck naked, but as the summer season progressed, marine growth reattached itself, attracted other denizens, and the wreck became alive. These combined sites constituted one of the most popular beach dives along the entire Jersey shore.

The *Rusland* and the *Adonis* are known collectively as the Dual Wrecks. Considering the way the two wrecks fought each other when the *Rusland* came ashore, they might just as well be called the Duel Wrecks.

The Dual Wrecks lie off the southern end of St. Alphonso's Retreat. The retreat resides on private property but the beach is public. If the residents of St. Alphonso's deny permission to access the beach from the grounds, you will have to gain the beach elsewhere and carry your gear along the water's edge to the entry point, or enter the water upcurrent and drift along with the current.

Who knows how much time must pass before nature becomes offended by man's effrontery and the artificial deposition of sand, and wipes the wreck clean?

For a sketch and description of land ranges, see page 15 under *Adonis*.

SANDY HOOK

Built: 1902
Previous names: *Privateer*
Gross tonnage: 361
Type of vessel: Pilot boat
Builder: Crescent Shipyard, Elizabeth, New Jersey
Owner: New York & Sandy Hook Pilots Association
Port of registry: New York, NY
Cause of sinking: Collision with MV *Oslofjord*
Location: 26908.3

Sunk: April 27, 1939
Depth: 80 feet
Dimensions: 168' x 34' x 23'
Power: Coal-fired steam

43700.4

In the old days, before the New York and New Jersey pilots formed an association existed, private pilots beat out their competitors by sailing far out into the ocean, sometimes more than one hundred miles, in order to be the first to pick up an inbound vessel. Life is simpler now, both for the pilots and the ships that employ them. Modern day pilots are unionized, and must pass stringent tests in order to prove their skill in local pilotage.

Today, pilot boats prowl close to the approaches to New York harbor. They communicate with vessel masters not by signal flags or semaphore, but by radio. They are always prepared to transfer pilots to inbound vessels, and retrieve them from outbound vessels. These transfers and retrievals are tricky maneuvers for everyone involved. The vessel must first reduce speed and maintain a steady course. The pilot boat operator must then match the vessel's speed, press the side of his boat against the moving hull, and hold it there. A Jacob's ladder is lowered from the vessel's deck above or from a hatch in the vertical hull. If a pilot is transferring from the pilot boat to the vessel, he must grab or leap for the ladder - often holding a briefcase or suitcase in one hand - then ascend the dangling rungs. If a pilot is being retrieved, he must descend the swaying ladder until he is a step or two above the pilot boat's deck, then jump for it when a wave lifts the pilot boat within reach. A misstep would plunge the pilot into the water and probably to his death in the vessel's suction or churning propeller. These transfers must be done day and night and in all kinds of weather, no matter how severe.

Not only are these operations dangerous for the pilots, but they are dangerous for the pilot boats as well. There is always the risk of collision in the heavily trafficked sea lanes. A number of pilot boats have been lost in this manner throughout the years. Here is a sampling of pilot boat casualties. In 1901 the *James Gordon Bennett* was run down by the *Arlene*. In 1906 the *Hermit* was sunk by the *Monterey*. In 1912 the *Ambrose May* was fatally struck by the *Delaware*. In 1914 the *New Jersey* was hit by the *Manchoneal*. In 1962 the *Cape May* was lost off Cape Henlopen. And there were others.

In the strictest sense of the term, the *Sandy Hook* was not actually a pilot boat, but rather a pilot hotel. The *Sandy Hook's* primary functions were to house and feed pilots who were coming or going, and maneuver close enough to inbound and outbound vessels so her yawls did not have to travel long distances. Thus, she did not transfer pilots or retrieve them. Those jobs were delegated to the yawls which were carried on the *Sandy Hook's* after deck.

The *Sandy Hook* was a fishing vessel prior to her acquisition by the Pilots Association, in 1914. As the *Privateer,* she had operated as a head boat since practically the turn of the century. After refitting and renaming her, the Pilots Association gave her a numerical designation: Pilot Boat Number 2. After a quarter of a century of faithful service, on April 27, 1939, the *Sandy Hook* joined the ranks of those boats that had carried their last pilot.

Her nemesis was the Norwegian liner *Oslofjord*, a giant motor vessel grossing 18,672 tons - the newest and largest liner in the Norwegian merchant marine. Among her 681 passengers were the crown prince and princess of Norway. Prince Olaf and Princess Martha were on their way to a dedication ceremony of their country's exhibit at the New York World's Fair, after which they planned to visit in the United States for two and a half months. An elaborate reception had been arranged for their arrival. From the reception they were to be whisked away to city hall to meet with Mayor Fiorello La Guardia.

At six o'clock in the morning, the harbor was shrouded in dense fog, visibility stretching only a couple of hundred feet. The *Oslofjord* reduced speed not only because of the fog but because she needed to pick up a pilot. She proceeded cautiously at three-and-a-half knots - barely enough to maintain steerage way against the ebbing tide. She sounded single whistle blasts at regular intervals in order to announce her invisible presence to nearby vessels in the fog.

For the *Sandy Hook* it was a busy morning. Ship-to-shore radio kept her apprised of vessels requiring the services of a pilot. By six o'clock she had already placed five pilots aboard inbound vessels. She knew the *Oslofjord* needed a pilot, heard her signals, and was maneuvering to find the liner in the cloak of fog. In addition to tooting her fog horn, the *Sandy Hook* also sounded her pilot signal - one long, two short, and one long. Aboard the pilot boat were thirty men: Captain William Baeszler, seventeen crew members, and twelve pilots. Several of the crew members were apprentice pilots. Navigating the *Sandy Hook* were Goetz, the mate, and Sullivan, the pilot.

The *Oslofjord* entered a clearing in which the visibility extended for as much as three quarters of a mile. She increased speed to eight or nine knots for about nine minutes. The pilot boat's whistle was distinctly heard in the vicinity of the *Ambrose* lightship. Then the fog closed in and Captain Ole Bull ordered all engines stopped. For several minutes the *Oslofjord* drifted forward by means of her momentum.

Then came the toots of a tug and tow - one long and two short. The tug was towing three dump scows on hawsers, outbound to the dumping grounds. Captain Bull ordered a slight change in course: 28° to starboard. The tug and the liner then passed port to port. As the tug came abreast of the *Oslofjord*, Captain Ulrich, master of the tug, blew the dumping signal of four blasts. (This was when it was permissible to dump trash and garbage that close to the harbor.) The time was 6:18 a.m.

Captain Bull judged that by 6:19, the *Oslofjord's* headway was down to about one knot - this in light of the fact that the engines had been stopped for about nine minutes. He ordered the engines started at dead slow. He could not see the pilot boat but he could hear her whistle blasts to starboard, then drawing aft. He thought the pilot boat would round the liner's stern in the usual way in order to put the pilot aboard on the port side. According to subsequent court records, "at 6:22 the bearing of the whistles of the pilot boat appeared to change, and no longer were drawing aft. The engines of the *Oslofjord* were then stopped.

"The engines remained stopped for about a minute, or until 6:23, when the cut water and masts of the *Sandy Hook* were seen on the starboard bow 'heading right across or toward' the *Oslofjord*. The *Oslofjord* was then making 2 to 2 1/2 knots. Captain Bull at once jumped for the telegraph, and placed the engines full speed astern. The *Oslofjord* was equipped with a new device which only required the slight turning of a wheel to put the engines in reverse at full speed; and Captain Bull said it only took 3 or 4 seconds to start the full speed revolutions. The engines continued at full speed astern for about twenty seconds before the collision; the speed at the time of contact was stated to be one or one and a half knots."

The pilot boat was proceeding at three and a half knots when Goetz and

Sullivan thought they heard the *Oslofjord* give two blasts on her whistle - the signal that the liner was stopping. What they probably heard was half of the tug's dumping signal of four toots. For several minutes the pilot boat proceeded toward the *Oslofjord* on a reciprocal course. Neither vessel was visible to the other. Goetz and Sullivan interpreted the position of the *Oslofjord* by the regular blasts of her fog signal. Instead of rounding the liner's stern and coming up her port side, the usual procedure, and in the belief that the *Oslofjord* had stopped in mid-channel, the pilot boat turned ahead of the liner and crossed her bow.

But the *Oslofjord* had not stopped. Much to the horror of Goetz and Sullivan, the liner was moving forward slowly. Goetz spun the wheel and increased engine speed in order to turn away from the *Oslofjord* and surge across her bow - a maneuver which he failed to accomplish. The liner's stem cut into the pilot boat's port side amidship.

The impact was not severe, but it was hard enough to catapult one pilot overboard and knock down one of the *Sandy Hook's* masts. The pilot boat had been sorely struck. Captain Bull tried to keep the *Oslofjord's* bow in the hole in the side of the *Sandy Hook* in an attempt to reduce the flooding, but the pilot boat drifted away. She was then steered toward shore in hopes of running her aground before she sank. The badly crippled boat remained afloat for half an hour, perhaps for forty minutes, before succumbing to the inevitable. During that time, her yawls were launched and most of her men abandoned ship. Some were picked up by a lifeboat from the *Oslofjord* (which was not badly damaged), others by the pilot boat *New York*. James Petersen, the man who was thrown into the water, was picked up by an inbound ship - none the worse for his dunking.

The captain and six men stayed on board the pilot boat until she was about to sink from under them. They got away in a yawl, and were soon taken aboard the *New York*.

When all was said and done, not a life was lost nor had injuries been sustained. But the royal party was inconvenienced by showing up late for their regal party.

The *Sandy Hook* was found to be at fault for the collision.

The *Oslofjord* survived the *Sandy Hook* by a year and a half. On December 1, 1940, she struck a German mine in the North Sea, broke in two, and sank.

In 1950, the wreck was wire-dragged to a least depth of 68 feet, in the course of which "a piece of iron pipe guard railing was brought up on the ground wire which was fouled on the wreck."

Today, the mud bottom reflects very little light, so it is usually a dark dive. The sediment stirs up easily and visibility is poor. Large pieces of wreckage lay scattered over the bottom. On good days one can see intact sections, and enter portions of the wreck. Brass trinkets are the reward for those who are willing to sift patiently through the wreckage.

The *Sandy Hook* is generally called the Pilot Boat.

From *Harper's Weekly.*

SCOTLAND

Built: 1865
Previous names: None
Gross tonnage: 3,695
Type of vessel: Iron-hulled screw steamer
Builder: Palmer Brothers & Company, Jarrow-on-Tyne
Owner: National Steam Navigation Company, Liverpool
Port of registry: Liverpool, England
Cause of sinking: Collision with *Kate Dyer*
Location: On the Outer Middle Bar off Sandy Hook, inshore of the old *Scotland* lightship

Sunk: December 1, 1866
Depth: 22 feet
Dimensions: 430' x 38' x 33'
Power: Coal-fired steam

The *Kate Dyer* was a wooden-hulled, full-rigged ship whose gross tonnage was calculated at 1,275 tons. She went to sea at a time when many sailing vessels were private enterprises. The master was often the sole owner, or at the very least a part owner. If a vessel was owned by more than one person, the ownership was divided into fractional shares: sixteenths, thirty-seconds, even sixty-fourths.

Joseph Dyer spent his life in the shipping business. He worked his way up from the bottom as an apprentice, and eventually became a master, a builder, and an owner. Throughout his long career he held ownership interests in more than a dozen ocean-going vessels. He built the *Kate Dyer* at Cape Elizabeth, a coastal community in Maine that is situated southeast of Portland. "I built her for myself, and of the best materials I could find in the country. She was as good a ship as I could build." Her keel was laid in 1855, and she was launched and went to sea in 1856.

In the partnership that was formed to operate the *Kate Dyer*, Joseph Dyer owned 9/16, Samuel Shaw owned 4/16, James Phillips owned 2/16, and William Leavitt owned 1/16. From her first year to her penultimate, the ship's master was Ansel S. Dyer, Joseph's brother. For the first seven years he ran the ship between New Orleans and Le Havre, France. He then made two voyages to the Chincha Islands, off the western coast of South America and south of Lima, Peru.

In 1865, the *Kate Dyer* was thoroughly overhauled. Her bottom was newly coppered and she was fitted with new spars, new sails, and a new mizzenmast. On April 1, Ansel S. Dyer relinquished command to part-owner William Leavitt. Leavitt then ran the ship "around the horn" from Boston to San Francisco. From there he proceeded north to Puget Sound, thence south to Callao, the port facility that serves Lima, the capital city which is eight miles inland.

The *Kate Dyer* was chartered to the Peruvian government. She proceeded to the desolate Chincha Islands, a couple hundred miles away, where she onloaded 1,665 tons of guano in bulk. "In bulk" meant that the guano was stowed loose, not in bags, although several thousand canvas sacks were used for dunnage. That's a lot of guano by any means of measurement! The guano was shoveled onto launches, brought to the ship at anchor, then shoveled aboard by hand. It was backbreaking work for the local laborers, and a foul, excremental exercise for all concerned.

How long did it take to load all this guano? According to the contract, "Ten working days for each one hundred register tons to be allowed to the charterers for loading the ship at the Islands; nevertheless, in no case shall the charterers have less than thirty days nor more than eighty working days in all."

After months of manual labor in loading the ship, the Kate Dyer returned to Callao for inspection prior to obtaining final clearance, to receive some $6,000 in Peruvian currency "in case needed," and to embark a couple of passengers. *Then* she began the three-month passage to New York.

Today, people look back upon the glorious days of sail as if following the sea were a glamorous occupation. Marine artists who strive to capture the majesty of tall ships - gracefully breasting the bounding main with the unseen wind billowing canvas - overlook the finer details of reality. The life of a seaman was one of harshness, discomfort, drudgery, ceaseless toil, loneliness, boredom, and sometimes death. It was anything but glamorous - no more than driving an eighteen wheeler can be considered glamorous. It is a job, and a tough one at that.

Conditions aboard the *Kate Dyer* were no different. Not because the officers treated the men badly - there were no complaints in that regard. No, it was simply because the sea was a cruel, often ruthless, and unsympathetic mistress. Yet the men aboard the *Kate Dyer* knew no other life. Seaman Robert Fiske stated it simply, yet eloquently, "I have no occupation. I always followed the sea."

Of the *Kate Dyer's* twenty-four crew members, most had started serving their time before the mast at an age when today's youths graduate grade school.

They worked as cabin boys from age 13, and if they survived long enough they became able bodied seamen before their teenage years were over. Many were illiterate, placing their mark on their shipping articles with an X. But a man did not need a formal education or know how to read in order to be proficient at his job. Instead, he had to "learn the ropes" in the original and precise meaning of the phrase. He had to furl the sails in the worst of storms, climb the ratlines in crashing seas, holystone the decks in calmer weather. There was always, always something to do: for twelve hours a day, seven days a week, months at a time, in rotating watches of four hour shifts. Off time was spent lying exhausted in a bunk in the cramped crew's quarters in the forecastle, or possibly playing games.

When the *Kate Dyer* approached Long Island - on December 1, 1866 - she had been at sea for eighty-four days without ever touching land. New York harbor bristled only a few hours away. Around two o'clock in the afternoon she picked up a pilot from the *Charles H. Marshall*, Pilot Boat Number 3. At that time, she lay hove to about ten miles west of the Shinnecock lighthouse. Pilot Michael Collins took command of the ship for the remaining sixty miles of a journey that was more than 12,000 miles in length.

Collins put the ship on a western tack. For five and a half hours the *Kate Dyer* proceeded close hauled toward her final destination. When darkness fell, lanterns were placed in the mizzen rigging: a red light on the port side, a green light on the starboard. No masthead light was displayed, for sailing ships did not display such a light.

Captain Leavitt retired to his cabin. After so many months away from home he was eager for local news. Collins had given him the latest newspapers, so Leavitt settled down, lit a candle, and by its feeble glow soon became engrossed in current events.

Hugging the wheel was able seaman Patrick Cassidy, still a young man but with twenty-three years at sea. Collins paced the deck in an effort to keep warm on what he described as a bitter cold night. At 7:30, third mate Frederick Williams tossed the log over the taffrail. As he pulled in the device he counted seven and one half knots. Able seaman John McGowan was busy working the bilge pump amidships. A steady stream of dirty water was drawn up from the bottom of the ship and ejected over the side. Keeping his eye on the helmsman was 21-year-old Ansel L. Dyer: the son of Joseph Dyer, the nephew of Ansel S. Dyer, and the second officer of the *Kate Dyer*. The ship was very much a family affair.

The night was dark but starlit. The lookout on the forecastle called out that a light was visible ahead. The light was white: a masthead light, designating the vessel as a steamship. Collins thought the light must be that of a tug come to offer the windjammer a tow into port. He estimated her distance at about five miles, and closing. The ship was then some ten miles south of Fire Island light. Collins and Dyer continued to observe the approaching steamer from the starboard rail. They expected the towboat to slew around and speak them (in the nautical usage of the time).

Suddenly a red light appeared. With the port light visible, the steamship must have executed a turn in an attempt to cross the ship's bow! A huge iron hull loomed higher than the *Kate Dyer's* deck.

When the approaching vessel was fifty feet away, Collins shouted, "Where the hell are you going with that steamer?" An instant later he turned and bellowed orders. "Hard up the helm and let go the spanker sheet."

There was no time to carry out either order, for two to three seconds later the steamer's port bow struck the *Kate Dyer's* starboard bow forward of the rigging. The ship's entire forward compartment was crushed in. Her foremast sheared off at the deck and fell across the forecastle. The top rigging of the mainmast broke off at the cap. The windjammer rebounded half her length from the force of the collision, and was spun around abruptly so that her head pointed in the same direction as the steamer, which then passed along her side. The *Kate Dyer's* lookout was heard to groan.

According to Collins, it was "like shoving your hand through a sheet of paper. The steamer never stopped until she got to the leeward. She went right through the ship."

The vessel which struck the *Kate Dyer* such a telling blow was the British screw steamer *Scotland*. She was 430 feet in length and grossed 3,695 tons. Her propeller was turned by a 500 horsepower engine. She left pier 47 in the North River about the same time that the *Kate Dyer* picked up her pilot off Shinnecock. Her "crew consisted of upward of 100 persons." In addition to a large general cargo, she carried "over 100 steerage passengers and about a dozen cabin passengers." She was bound for Liverpool after a short stop at Queensland.

The *Scotland* was built at a time in the evolution of steam propulsion when confidence in its reliability was lacking - and with just cause. Machinery had a nasty habit of breaking down. More then one steamship suffered mechanical malfunctions which left the vessel stranded at sea. As a consequence, early steamers - whether propelled by screw or paddle wheels - were also fitted with sails. In order to save on coal as well as to increase speed and efficiency, these steamers often proceeded with their engines chugging and all sails set. This expedient necessitated the employment of two full crews: engineers for the engines and sailors for the sails.

At 7:15 in the evening on December 1, 1866, the *Scotland* was proceeding east at a speed of ten to eleven knots. In order to assist the engine in maintaining this pace, all the sails were set on the fore and main masts, braced forward on the port tack. Captain William Hall was the *Scotland's* master, but he was in his cabin at the time. Second officer Thomas Daunt was on watch. Daunt was an experienced mariner in his own right, and had been a master on other vessels. At the con (in charge of steering) was John Gibson Watson, the fourth officer, although the man who actually had his hands on the helm was the acting quartermaster, John McGinnis. The helm was located all the way aft, right over the rudder head. There were two wheels on the same barrel, one forward and one abaft the rudder head.

Chief engineer George Taylor was not on watch in the engine room. William Lindsay, third engineer, had the watch.

The *Scotland's* lookout was the first to spot a ship's green light in the distance. The watch officers judged that the ship was yet five or six miles away. McGinnis received an order for hard astarboard. He knew exactly what to do: he pushed the top spoke of the wheel to starboard (right), an action which caused the steamer to veer to port (left). This may confuse modern readers who are used to turning the steering wheel of a vehicle counterclockwise in order to obtain the same result. But in those days, the steering linkage was reversed in order to simulate the action of a tiller.

About twenty minutes, later McGinnis received an order for hard aport. The steamer responded sluggishly to the wheel due to the disposition of the wind. For ten minutes the *Scotland* veered slightly to the right. When the ship's green light was judged only two miles away, Daunt saw sails over the steamer's port bow. About three minutes later he signaled the engine room to stand by, which Lindsay did. A minute later Lindsay heard the order to stop, and a minute after that came to order to reverse the engine. Engine room personnel were frantically shunting steam by spinning the hand wheels of a multitude of giant valves.

Captain Hall overheard Daunt's shouted orders. He came up on deck and saw a ship off the *Scotland's* port bow, "the whole of her starboard side."

The *Kate Dyer's* cathead struck the steamer's iron hull about fifty feet abaft the stem, in the middle of the top-gallant forecastle. The blunt end of the cathead punched a perfectly square hole through an iron plate five or six feet above the waterline. Another hole was made in the steamer's bow either at the waterline or just below it. The ship then bounced away amid a crash of falling spars. The time was 7:45.

On the *Scotland's* forecastle, seaman Alexander McClennan was helping to lash down the anchors when he realized what was happening. He ducked under the windlass in order to save his life from falling masts and rigging - from his own vessel as well as from the other. Seaman Richard Crichton noted, "As we struck the ship we glided right past her and took her forestay away."

Some of the *Kate Dyer's* rigging became entangled in the steamer's figure-head and was torn off when the ship ricocheted like a struck billiard ball. The *Scotland*, with her forward momentum partially arrested and her engine going in reverse, glided to a halt about a quarter mile away. The steamer's trim shifted down by the head because the forward compartment immediately filled with water. Soon the forward hold was also flooded.

The situation was far worse on the *Kate Dyer*. Alerted by the shouting that something was amiss, Captain Leavitt laid down his paper, put on his hat, and prepared to go up on the deck - but the shock of the collision forced him to steady himself against the jamb. The men topside were knocked about by the sudden stop. The lookout's legs were crushed by falling spars. The two passengers and half the crew were asleep at the moment of impact, but were jostled awake. The crew members who survived the smashing of the forecastle struggled through the wreckage in the darkness to find their way on deck.

There was no doubt about it: the *Kate Dyer* was going down, and fast. Michael Collins gave the order to clear away the boats. All able hands leaped to obey - from seaman right on up to the captain. One boat was stove in during the launching. The other barely got away because the oarlocks were missing, and because the ship was making sternway as she came to in the wind.

According to Michael Collins, "The water was right up to the mainmast before I left the ship" in the boat. Six men got away in the ship's boat: Captain Leavitt, Michael Collins, Patrick Cassidy, seaman George Gates, and the two passengers, who were berthed aft.

Ansel Dyer jumped into the water and "was picked up by the *Kate Dyer's* boat, the one the captain was in."

John McGowan, an ordinary seaman still in his teens, lent a hand with the boats but, upon hearing that the lookout was trapped on the bow, ran forward to see if he could help. The lookout was not trapped, but both legs were broken and he could not move. The ship lurched suddenly. It was going down by the head. A wave of water broke over the bow, washing the lookout as far as the main rigging and chasing McGowan to the stern. By then, the boat was gone so he leaped overboard.

It was all over in ten minutes. The *Kate Dyer* nose-dived to the bottom, her after sails still gathering wind. When she came to rest her mizzen-royal-yard protruded from the water.

John Butler was "knocked clean over the stern." As seaman Thomas Tracey related, "I stood by the ship until she went down. I didn't jump, I was washed off her rail as far aft as I could get." According to John Jenkins, "I went right aft and stepped on deck to see the water, and jumped overboard, me and the mate and two boys together."

Charles Bailey went over the side and swam to a nearby boat. This was a boat from the *Scotland*, manned by three crew members and a passenger. The steamer's boat picked up Jenkins too, but the mate and two cabin boys were never seen again. Thomas Tracey spent ten minutes treading water before he was rescued by the *Scotland's* boat. Also saved in this manner were John McGowan, Robert Fiske, and John Butler. Third mate Frederick Williams was swimming toward the steamer when he intersected her boat and was plucked from the frigid sea.

Thus seven men were saved by the quick launching of the *Scotland's* boat. Another seven men were aboard the *Kate Dyer's* boat, which was rowed to the steamer and picked up. A second boat from the *Scotland* looked for more survivors in the darkness, but found none. Missing were thirteen men and boys - if they escaped from the forecastle, they either drowned or died of hypothermia. Frederick Williams was not exaggerating when he said, "I was almost out of my senses when I got on board the *Scotland*, with the cold."

By now the reader must be wondering why this chapter is entitled *Scotland* instead of *Kate Dyer*. The sailing ship is the one that sank, and with nearly half her complement. There is more to this collision than has so far been related, although the rest may seem anticlimactic by comparison.

The *Scotland* was sorely damaged. Two compartments were flooded and she continued to take on water. Captain Hall, now in command, had no choice but to turn the ship around and head back toward safe harbor. She never made it. The

Scotland was very close to foundering when she reached the harbor approaches. Rather than have the steamer sink in the channel, Captain Hall drove her onto the Outer Middle Bar, off the Highlands.

Working to free a brig that had grounded on nearby Romer Shoal was Israel J. Merritt, superintendent of the Coast Wrecking Company. "I knew the steamship *Scotland*; I saw her on west side of channel, close by channel, south of Sandy Hook. I should judge about two to two and a half miles from Jersey shore. . . . It was Sunday when I saw her. . . . about nine o'clock in the morning. My attention was drawn to a steamer being pretty low in the water, and west of the channel and apparently on the shoals."

Merritt mustered his salvage crew and diver. On board the steamer *Amanda Wynants*, with the wrecking schooner *Meta* in tow, he proceeded to the *Scotland* and offered assistance. Captain Hall refused, saying that he "would not accept, until he had heard from his agent, to whom he had sent in New York." Merritt tried to reason with the captain, not because he needed the job but because the weather was turning bad and, unless his crew started right away, they might not be able to lighter the ship in time to pull her off the bar before the storm. Merritt argued "that it being Sunday, it would perhaps be pretty hard to find his agents." Captain Hall was adamant.

"He spoke about salvage, and I told him I would leave the compensation to the New York Underwriters or his own agent. I also told him, if that was not satisfactory, I would make a contract for any price that he might name - as low as $100. . . . He refused. I then recommended him to send the passengers ashore; that I would take them to New York free of charge; that I was going to New York. He asked me what salvage I would charge for the baggage. I answered, none of his business. I thought it was an insult, and I answered him that way. I said then, that if there were any passengers who wanted to get to New York, that they better get on board the boat, for I was going."

Most went. Some, including the *Kate Dyer's* survivors, went by pilot boat. The *Scotland's* crew remained aboard. At that time, the *Scotland* "was not aground the whole length of her keel. Her stern was in motion, very slight, because there was no sea on, to speak of, and her bow was fast."

Around three o'clock Monday morning, when Merritt was fast asleep, a messenger from the steamer's agent beat on the door of his house. He delivered an urgent request to render all assistance possible to the *Scotland*. "I was from that time until about 10 or 11 o'clock getting steam pumps, cables, &c., getting ready to start, getting my gear on my vessels. Arrived at the ship between 4 and 5 o'clock in the evening. Hauled alongside and commenced putting my pumps and boilers on board. At that time the water was perfectly smooth and had been from the morning before. At about 7 o'clock that evening, while putting up our gear, the wind came in S.E. and commenced blowing strong. Hauled the schooner to the forward gangway and commenced discharging cargo. At about 9 o'clock began to rain a little. About 12 it was blowing a fresh gale or a pretty strong breeze. Captain and his crew left the ship in a tug. My schooner and steamer left just after. I remained on board with two surf boats' crews and 2 surf boats. About 3 o'clock in the morning of Tuesday, the sea was going all over the ship, with the exception of some dry places where we stayed - blowing heavy - a bad sea. At daylight we left the ship with our boats and men and headed for Sandy Hook. The weather was very thick and the steamer was completely buried with water then all over. We had a pretty hard time getting away from her."

Merritt's outfit did not have time to get the boilers and steam pumps going. In the few hours available, they managed to save only a cargo of cheese. They returned two days later, after the storm blew itself out. By then the hull had ruptured and the ship could no longer be saved. Merritt was contracted to salvage whatever possible. His men stripped the ship of "anchors, chains, rigging and cabin furniture," which he delivered to the *Scotland's* agent, Mr. Hurst. The value of all the items recovered totaled less than $5,000.

And there she lay - a hulk.

The wreck of the *Scotland* now presented a hazard to navigation, "directly in the track of vessels entering the port of New York from the south and east." So important to the safety of commerce was the clearing of the shipping lane that within ten days of the collision and subsequent grounding, the Committee on Appropriations of the United States Congress was petitioned to have the wreck removed. The primary petitioners were the marine underwriters of the City of New York, and fifty Sandy Hook pilots. The House of Representatives gave the matter immediate attention.

A fortnight after the collision, the Coast Wrecking Company was engaged to conduct a survey of the sunken ship. Merritt reported that "she is imbedded in the sand about fifteen (15) feet, and parted amidships about five (5) feet; her decks are about even with the water. After careful estimate, I believe that it will require about $150,000, in addition to what may be realized from the saving of the wreck, to complete the removal of the said wreck, and make the channel free from all obstructions as before, and I will agree to remove the wreck for the above sum, completing the work to the entire satisfaction of any properly appointed party, or forfeit all pay."

Merritt's offer of forfeiture has become a standard clause in the salvage business - that of "no cure, no pay."

Merritt wasted no time in presenting his bid to the Quartermaster General. The QM believed that a solicitation for competitive bids could lower the cost to $100,000, but, in petitioning Congress for the appropriation of funds, thought it better to request the higher amount. The big wheels of government turn with agonizing sloth. Not until over a year later - in January 1868 - did a Congressional resolution allocate the money, and at last give Merritt the job.

During that time the wreck lay exposed - visible during the day, but cloaked by darkness at the night. Underwriters and pilots continued to press for protective legislation for more than a year. Finally, in direct response to the hazard posed by the *Scotland*, on March 2, 1868, a joint resolution was passed which authorized the Light-house Board "to place a light-vessel, or other suitable warning of danger, on or over any wreck or temporary obstruction to the entrance of any harbor, or in the channel or fairway of any bay or sound," when, in the

Board's judgment, it was deemed necessary. On April 15, relief lightship No. 20 was placed on station by the wreck in order to ward off ships which might blunder into the wreck at night. It was called the *Wreck of Scotland light-vessel*. This was done merely as a short-term expedient until the giant ship could be demolished.

John Newton was the engineer in charge of destroying the wreck, although the Coast Wrecking Company supplied the divers and performed the actual work. Newton was a lieutenant colonel and brevet major general in the U.S. Engineers Office.

The fine art of underwater demolition was then in its infancy. Destruction of the wreck began in 1868 and continued into the following year. Initial attempts to break up the hull failed miserably. How the feat was finally accomplished was recorded by Thomas Scott. In 1869, Scott entered the employ of the Coast Wrecking Company as a young diver. Hard-hat dress being the fashion of the time, he and his fellow divers crawled all over the wreck - dragging their hoses behind them - and set some thirty charges at strategic locations: under the lower deck, in the forecastle, and around the boilers and engine. Each charge was actually a wine cask which was filled with gun powder, sealed, and connected to a battery in a rowboat by means of a rubber-coated copper conductor. The connection to the battery was triggered remotely through another wire leading to the salvage vessel moored a safe distance away. The rowboat disappeared in one titanic explosion as all thirty charges detonated simultaneously. The *Scotland* "was split like a melon dashed on a sidewalk."

Parenthetically, after working as a diver for more than three decades, Scott established his own wrecking company, in 1903. He maintained offices in Connecticut, and to a certain extent was his previous employer's competitor. By that time, Merritt had merged with the Chapman Derrick and Wrecking Company. In 1922, Scott's company merged with the other two, and he became a partner in Merritt, Chapman & Scott.

Newton wrote to U.S. Navy Rear-Admiral Charles Boggs, the Third District light-house inspector, "I have the pleasure of informing you that the wreck of the steamer *Scotland* has been removed to the depth of 22 1/2 feet at mean low water, and that, in fact, there is more water upon the wreck than upon the shoals in the neighborhood thereof." By "removed," Boggs meant "blasted flat." He did not mean that the metal plates and demolished machinery were hoisted up and carried away for disposal. The hazard to navigation was removed, not the hull and equipment.

Boggs reported the same to the chairman of the Light-house Board, Rear-Admiral W.B. Shubrick. In his annual report, dated September 30, 1870, Boggs made the following recommendation: "The work of removing the wreck having been successfully accomplished, there is no longer any necessity for maintaining a light-vessel in this place for the object for which the station was established."

Notice to Mariners No. 112, dated November 2, 1870, repeated Rear-Admiral Newton's words practically verbatim: "Official information having been received that the '*Wreck of the Scotland*' has been removed, and that there is a depth of 22 1/2 feet water at mean low tide where the wreck was, which is a greater depth than in places in the immediate neighborhood of the wreck, the *light-vessel placed to mark that obstruction* will be removed on the 5th day of December next, and that light-station will be from that date abolished." This was by order of the Light-house Board.

This should have been the end of a long and harrowing episode in the annals of a navigational obstruction. Instead, there rose an anguished tide of protest. It seems that in the two and a half years since the *Wreck of Scotland light-vessel* had been placed on site, mariners had come to rely upon it as an essential navigational aid. Letters poured in to the Light-house Board from many prominent quarters, pleading for its retention.

Dozens of shipping companies joined in the objection and sent a petition to Admiral Shubrick, beseeching, "This light is of such great benefit to the masters and pilots of the ships entering and leaving this port, that its removal would prove a serious injury to navigation."

The Cromwell Steamship Line sent an individual protest to the Secretary of the Treasury, stressing the lightship's importance. "Its existence there has proved of invaluable assistance to vessels approaching Sandy Hook, particularly from the southward, as it most clearly indicates the entrance to the channel used by such steamers or vessels. It is now principally relied on by such, and its removal would cause great inconvenience and probable loss to vessels not informed of its removal. It has fully proved its great usefulness, and commanders of steam and sail vessels are united in considering it a most valuable and necessary aid in approaching New York Harbor at night."

Russell Sturgis, owner of the Black Star Line and president of the Board of Pilot Commissioners for twenty-six years, emphasized that "this light-vessel marks the northern end of a dangerous shoal called the Outer Middle, and also is a true guide to the passage over the bar, crossing the mouth of our harbor; and is also a safe guide into the Lower Bay, and, in fact, is far more indispensable than the regular floating-light, lying four miles farther off."

George Elder, Vice-President of the Old Dominion Steamship Company, went so far as to offer to "furnish your [the Treasury] Department, from the shipping interest of New York, with good and ample bonds to cover any expense the Government may be called upon to cover the cost of maintaining her [the lightship] until Congress may make the necessary appropriation."

These strong and sundry protestations did not fall upon deaf ears. Shubrick was sensitive to the needs of the protesters, but he would have been derelict in his duty had he not cautioned George Boutwell, Secretary of the Treasury, that "as that vessel is now required to be kept in readiness to replace the *Sandy Hook* or any other light-vessel in the vicinity which may, by stress of weather or other cause, be driven from her station, it will be necessary for Congress to authorize the permanent establishment of a suitable light-vessel near the place where the wreck of the *Scotland* was until recently removed, for the building of which $50,000 will be required. It may not be out of place to add that the vessel now on the Sandy Hook light-station has not been away from her moorings for repairs during the last eight years, owing to the fact that the position could not be safely left without a vessel, and until the wreck of the *Scotland* was removed there was no vessel available as a relief for the Sandy Hook station."

The Treasury Department, to which the Light-house Board was subordinate, was powerless to comply with the objectors' reasoned request. Wrote Thornton Jenkins, Naval Secretary, "It rests with Congress and not with the Department to determine whether or not the 'Wreck of the *Scotland*' light-vessel can be permanently kept at her station." He ordered Shubrick to "have the words 'Wreck of the *Scotland*' painted out, and to hold the vessel in readiness to take the place of the *Sandy Hook* light-vessel, in case of accident to the latter."

Shubrick did as he was commanded, but also wrote a long letter to Boutwell in which he advocated the cause of the petitioners to establish a permanent lightship on the *Scotland* station. He sent copies of the protest letters and petitions. He noted that "prior to the sinking of the English steamer *Scotland*, the only light-vessel authorized by law to mark the approach to the outer bar of the entrance to New York Bay, was the one shown on the chart herewith transmitted, known as the *Sandy Hook* light-vessel. It appears to this board that this is a mere question of law. Prior to the passage of the joint resolution of March 2, 1868, which authorizes the temporary establishment of lights, under certain prescribed circumstances, no light could be established in the absence of a specific appropriation or joint resolution authorizing its establishment." He noted that it was up to Congress to give "special authority to make it a permanent aid to navigation. The probable annual expense, including wear and tear, of this vessel is not much under $10,000."

Light-vessel No. 20 was duly removed from her station as prescribed by law. On December 14, Boggs reported that she was "securely moored in Mulford Basin, Stapleton, Staten Island. The crew were discharged on the 9th instant; the former keeper (Mr. Evan Davis) remains in her as ship-keeper, at second mate's wages; a cook is also retained. The vessel is in excellent condition, clean and neat, ready at any moment to go on station as a relief vessel."

Boutwell also championed the petitioners' cause. He forwarded copies of all petitions, correspondence, suggestions, and professional advices to the House of Representatives. Congress suffered from a rare attack of reason and rationality, and soon voted to approve the construction and permanent establishment of a light-vessel near the previous location of the wreck. It was appropriately named the *Scotland* lightship.

A more favorable location was found in which to moor the new light vessel, in slightly deeper water offshore. Undoubtedly, during more than a century of operation, it has been moved from time to time as the channel has been broadened or deepened or otherwise reconstructed. Anyone seeking to locate the wreck of the *Scotland* should obtain a contemporary chart and look inshore of the lightship's location. According to a 1965 chart, the *Scotland* lightship was then located at 73-54-12 N / 40-26-10 W, in 55-60 feet of water.

Lightships are no longer in operation in the United States. They have all been replaced by lighted buoys or towers. The entrance to New York harbor is now marked by the automated Ambrose light tower.

In addition to being responsible for the establishment of the *Scotland* light-ship, which served as a beacon of safety for more than a century, the steamer *Scotland* left another legacy in her wake: a blight on maritime law.

The four men who owned shares in the *Kate Dyer* filed suit against the National Steam Navigation Company to make good on their loss. Since the company that owned the *Scotland* was headquartered in England, beyond the juris-diction of U.S. courts, it declined to appear at any New York proceeding. The federal court took a dim view of this conduct. To force compliance with the court's order to appear, the judge sent a U.S. marshal to seize the company's steamer *Denmark* when it next docked in New York. The ship was arrested, and was not permitted to depart until the company put up a bond of good faith.

Representatives for the British company appeared under protest. This pat-tern of behavior set the tone for the defense that was to last through twenty years of bitter litigation, which did not end until an opinion was handed down by the highest court in the land.

Joining the plaintiffs in presenting a united front against the National Steam Navigation Company were Henry Rollins and the Republic of Peru. Rollins "had in his possession in his trunk and his own property five thousand dollars in American gold coin, together with nautical instruments, charts and wearing apparel, and two revolvers and two spy glasses of the value of about nine thou-sand dollars." The Peruvian government lost a load of guano estimated to be worth $135,000.

Dyer et al lost a ship, freight costs, and personal possessions valued at $120,000. This amount included the belongings of the surviving crew members, who escaped with only their lives and with the clothes they wore on their backs.

Litigation went through the full gamut of delays, depositions, delays, live testimony, delays, trials, delays, and appeals. The multitude of delays was the result of tactics practiced by the defendants. To make a long and tedious story short, on March 17, 1869, the Honorable Charles L. Benedict, District Judge for the Eastern District of New York, found the *Scotland* solely at fault for the colli-sion. In his summation of events, he noted the steamer did not take immediate evasive action, nor did she reduce speed until a collision was inevitable.

"This failure to sooner notice the ship, and take steps to avoid, may have arisen from absence of an attentive lookout or from a failure on the part of the officer of the deck to observe the reports of the lookout, if any such there were, and in this connection the omission to produce either of the men claimed to have been upon the lookout is very noticeable, while the statement of one of the crew of the steamer who was upon the forecastle and is called by the libellants, that the first report of the ship's light from the forecastle received no attention, tends to increase the significance of the omission. The statement of this witness is, moreover, strengthened by the circumstance that, although the deposition con-taining the statement was taken in December, 1866, and the witness then named several others of the crew who were on the forecastle with him, none of those witnesses are called to contradict him."

The judge also noted that, despite the defendant's lawyer's attempt to blame the ship for causing the collision by changing course, "no witness produced on behalf of the steamer testifies that he saw any change whatever in the ship's course . . . My conclusion . . . is that the collision cannot be attributed to the fault of the ship in not holding her course." He awarded damages in the amount of $255,000.

Judge Benedict was wise in other regards, for he properly characterized the attitude of the defense by noting that his decision "will, without doubt, be re-examined in the Appellate Court." By this he meant that the National Steam Navigation Company would appeal his decision, which it did.

The Appellate Court re-examined, and found no flaw in Judge Benedict's argument or in his interpretation of the facts. The National Steam Navigation Company then appealed to the Supreme Court. The Supreme Court reiterated the findings of fact and law, established the rules of proceeding, and remanded the case back to the lower court with an order for the National Steam Navigation Company to make restitution for the losses of the claimants.

Subsequently, a commissioner was assigned to oversee the ascertainment of damages. The defense admitted no rough estimates. The process of evaluation was resumed from scratch, with the single exception that the *Kate Dyer's* crew men were not recalled to state the worth of their lost clothing and personal possessions. The par value of every other item was computed to the penny and one-quarter rial (the basic currency denomination of Peru). Attorneys for the defense met any rounding off with numerous and unjustified objections.

Others who testified previously or who gave depositions were recalled: Joseph Dyer, William Leavitt, and agents and representatives of the Republic of Peru.

Joseph Dyer re-attested to the amount of money paid for the *Kate Dyer's* upkeep and refurbishing (over $40,000), and to her fair market value at the time of her loss. A surveyor and a ship owner were sworn in to give their expert opinion on the ship's resale value. They not only corroborated Dyer's appraisal of her condition, but judged that his estimate of $56,000 to $60,000 was too low - one thought it could have sold for $63,000, the other for $70,000. William Leavitt re-itemized the ship's paraphernalia and navigational instruments, as well as the personal items necessary for a ship's master to own.

With respect to the guano, the defense adopted an obstructionist policy of challenging the precision of every calculation, including the cost and amount of twine used in sewing the dunnage sacks, and the percentage of ammonia found in Chincha Islands guano! Representatives of the Republic of Peru were forced to give a detailed account of the country's guano shipping practices, the method of excavation (it was dug by hand), the politics of exportation, the system used to arrive at the product's fair market value, and numerous similar irrelevancies. They were also obligated to calculate and deduct ordinary costs that were unincurred by dint of the guano failing to reach its destination: freight charges, import duties, discharging costs, weighing, storage, agents selling commissions, and so on. The defense nit-picked about the difference between how much money

Peruvian guano brought in 1864 and how much it might have brought in 1866, had it been delivered and sold, as well as how those figures related to its current market value. Since the supply of guano from the Chincha Islands - prized as a fertilizer because of its high ammonia content - had since been exhausted, the latter calculation could not be made. No more Chincha Islands guano was to be had, so American farmers were guano out of luck.

So long did this phase of the case continue that not until April 23, 1873 was Captain Henry Rollins recalled in order to re-substantiate the number of $20 gold pieces he had stowed in a bag in his trunk. He re-confirmed that he lost 250 double eagles. (A gold dollar was then worth $1.38 in U.S. currency.) In addition, he lost all his clothing, personal belongings, and navigational instruments (he was a ship's master).

Every penny that was claimed was challenged by the defense, repetitively ad nauseam. If the word "shyster" did not exist at the time, the attorneys for the National Steam Navigation Company invented it by their conduct. They managed to retard the progress of the case so much that the commissioner died before he concluded his assessment of damages. The duty then fell upon Judge Benedict. This was to the defense's advantage, for whereas the commissioner had assigned interest at the rate of 7%, Benedict reduced the interest to 6%.

Worse yet, defense attorneys claimed that the steamship company was not responsible for full indemnity for the loss of the cargo. Not content with subtracting the various unincurred charges, they insisted that the value placed upon the guano was based on its selling price, not on what it cost to extract it from the ground, where it had no value whatsoever. The failure of the goods to reach the market reduced the valuation by the amount of profit that would have been made upon its sale. By extrapolation, the owners of the *Kate Dyer* could not demand payment for their six-months effort at sea because of their nonperformance in delivering the goods. Defense attorneys claimed that no profit should accrue to any of the claimants for their efforts; only the losses actually incurred - that is, the value which the guano possessed when it lay on the ground undisturbed.

Judge Benedict did not buy into this torturous twist of illogic. He found for the claimants, but at a slightly reduced amount. The interest totaled nearly half again the award for actual damages. He filed his final decree on July 17, 1874. The National Steam Navigation Company wasted little time in filing an appeal - not on fault for the collision, for that action had already been settled by the Supreme Court - but on entirely different grounds.

Defense attorney's had been holding an ace up their collective sleeve - and they had waited eight years to show their hand. The ace was called "limitation of liability." This mischievous device was an Act passed by Congress on March 3, 1851 (9 U.S. Stat. at Large, 635). It has come to be known as the Limitation Act. This Act stipulates that in cases of collision, the liability incurred by the vessel that is found responsible for the collision, is limited by the value of that vessel after the collision. For example, if a vessel is worth $300,000, and sustains $200,000 worth of damage as a result of a collision that it caused, the owner of said vessel would not be legally obligated to pay more than $100,000 to any and all claimants.

Since the *Scotland* became a total constructive loss, its value after the collision was, in simplified terms, zero. To this figure was added the value of the items recovered from the wreck (excluding cargo): anchors, chain, rigging, and furnishings. Thus, the National Steam Navigation Company sought to limit its liability to the owners of the *Kate Dyer*, to the officers and crew members, to the passengers, and to the Republic of Peru, to less than $5,000.

Until then, the Limitation Act had never been tested. It took twelve more years for the United States courts to adjudicate the case of the *Scotland* versus the *Kate Dyer*. In order to hasten the conclusion of this gross miscarriage of justice, I will distill 450 pages of published court documents and touch upon the highlights of the complex legal deliberations that ensued.

Judge Benedict denied the validity of the defendant's claim because the issue was not raised and tested during the course of litigation, but was brought in as an afterthought - after all other legal recourse had been exhausted. Clutching at straws, as it were.

The Appellate Court agreed that the steamship company had waived its rights under the Act of 1851 by waiting for so many years before initiating such proceedings. It also found that in order to validate the Limitation Act in the first place, it was incumbent upon the defendant to surrender the salvaged items to the court, not only to establish the company's intention and responsibility, but, should the claimants prevail, so the items could be sold and the proceeds distributed accordingly. This opinion was filed on June 12, 1878.

The case was again taken to the Supreme Court, this time on the grounds of liability limitation. Two other issues were presented to the Justices: could the *Scotland*, being a vessel of foreign registry whose owner's home forum did not have a limitation law, use the Act against an American owned vessel; and could the insurance money collected by the steamship company be construed as part of the vessel's value for the purpose of establishing the limit of liability?

On June 5, 1883, the Supreme Court issued an interlocutory decree in which it ruled that the Limitation Act *could* be invoked by a foreign entity because the forum of litigation was the United States, in which the Act was a law of the land. It also ruled that the $300,000 paid to the National Steam Navigation Company by its underwriters did not constitute part of the vessel's value at the time of loss, because the insurance money did not accrue to the company until after the loss. It further ruled that the Company was liable for only $4,927.85 - the amount of money received for the items recovered from the wreck after the ship was run aground. This paltry award had to be split among all the claimants - and without the addition of any interest or penalties.

Not until 1886 - twenty years after the case was initiated - did the Supreme Court issue its final decree that affirmed the prior rulings. By that time, the National Steam Navigation Company - operating under the name of National Steamship Company and called the National Line - possessed an entire fleet of passenger-carrying steamships (more than a dozen), and had a thriving business transporting immigrants to the land of legal opportunity. Also by that time, many of the original claimants were dead. In retrospect, perhaps more guano was shoveled in this case than ever existed on the Chincha Islands.

It is worthwhile to note in passing that these two exasperating decades of judicial manipulations concerned loss of property. Not a single word was mentioned about restitution for the families of the sailors who lost their lives in the collision.

In summation, the *Scotland* was responsible for sinking a ship, killing thirteen people, losing a cargo, letting the government pay for the removal of the wreck, and abusing the legal system so as to avoid paying damages and to escape its moral obligations. Then her owners collected the insurance money and kept it! Not only did the *Scotland* establish the legality of the Limitation Act, but she was cited as a precedent in subsequent maritime collision cases. Limitation of liability continues to exert a malignant force in maritime law today. It is interesting to speculate if the congressmen of 1851 proposed and passed such an Act because of their own shipping interests.

The wreck of the *Scotland* may be largely forgotten today, but her long-lasting legal legacy lives on in infamy.

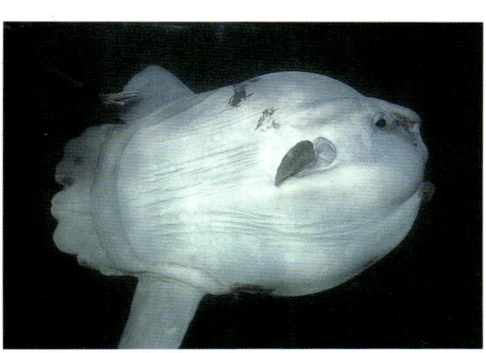

Courtesy of Skyfotos Ltd.

STOLT DAGALI

Built: 1955
Previous names: *Dagali*
Gross tonnage: 12,723
Type of vessel: M tanker
Builder: Burmeister & Wain, Copenhagen, Denmark
Owner: A/S Ocean (John P. Pedersen & Son, Managers)
Port of registry: Oslo, Norway
Cause of sinking: Collision with SS *Shalom*
Location: 26787.6

Sunk: November 26, 1964
Depth: 130 feet
Dimensions: 582' x 70' x 30'
Power: Oil engine (diesel)

43484.4

The 616 passengers and 450 crew members of the Israeli luxury liner *Shalom* had much to be thankful for on that cold, Thanksgiving Day morning: they all survived. At 2 a.m. most of them were asleep, dreaming of the forth-coming Caribbean cruise, and did not even feel the rending impact of the liner's stem as it sliced into the bowels of the *Stolt Dagali*. Nor were many awakened by the crash.

Not so lucky were some of the forty-three people aboard the Norwegian tanker. The *Stolt Dagali* left Philadelphia on November 25, 1964, with a load of edible oils and fats, and industrial solvents. She was on her way to Newark, New Jersey, in heavy rain and dense fog.

Both ships were equipped with radar, and had their units switched on. Yet they still managed to find each other in the dark.

Said a *Shalom* passenger who wished to remain anonymous, "There was this terrific bang. I went to the porthole and I saw half of this ship beginning to slide away. It had a greenish striped stack." Celia Pearlman was taking a bath at the moment of impact: "There was this terrific crash and this can of hair spray flew over my head." She got out of the tub and picked up the can. Louis Ganz gath-ered Crackerjacks that spilled from an opened box. Aside from these comical interludes, the only injury occurred when crew member Marge Tostalisco was struck by a watertight door which bruised her ribs. Bleeding internally, she was later evacuated by helicopter and flown to Walston Hospital at Fort Dix.

The *Shalom's* sharp stem cut into the *Stolt Dagali's* port after tanks like a knife into butter. The charging liner then drove completely through the tanker on a diagonal from fore to aft, slicing the *Stolt Dagali* neatly in two. The forward section - comprising of about three-quarters of the tanker's length - remained afloat, buoyed by watertight cargo compartments. The stern section, containing the engine room and crew's quarters, sank almost immediately, dragged down by the weight of the machinery and the water that flooded the huge engine room.

Gone in an instant were the lives of eighteen men and one woman. One seaman was fortunate enough to have been sleeping in a cabin which lay precisely where the ship was torn asunder; he awoke in the sea! One can only imagine the shock and disorientation he must have experienced when his pleasant, placid dreams turned into a stark and horrible nightmare as he was rudely thrown out of his dry, warm bunk into a bath of frigid water. Others were not so lucky: torn and twisted bodies littered the surface of the sea for miles - a ghastly human flotsam.

Despite the loss of her propulsion machinery and her primary generators, auxiliary generators provided emergency electricity, enabling the tanker to transmit a radio distress signal. "SOS. This is *Stolt Dagali*. Collided with unknown ship. Sinking repeat sinking." This and other messages from the *Shalom* fomented a flurry of activity. Nearby vessels altered course in order to converge on the site of the collision. The Coast Guard dispatched seven cutters and patrol boats, as well as a helicopter from the Floyd Bennett field in Brooklyn. A navy helicopter departed from Lakehurst, New Jersey.

Notwithstanding the rapid deployment of multiple rescue craft, the actual rescue of beleaguered personnel was initially delayed because the position that was given by the *Shalom* was fifteen to twenty miles north of the spot where the two ships had come together. First to arrive on the scene was the *Santa Paula*, a Grace Line cruise ship returning from the Caribbean under the command of Captain Theodore Thomson. "We had to circle around a wide area until we saw the *Shalom* standing still with her lights lit. Her bow was badly damaged. Then we saw the remains of the tanker, the bow section with some sort of a light lit, and we could see ten men aboard it." Captain Thomson positioned the *Santa Paula* so as to provide a wind break for the *Stolt Dagali's* bow section.

The Coast Guard requested the *Shalom* to continue sending radio signals so that rescue craft could home in on her position. This proved to be an effective means of location. The *Stolt Dagali* soon reported, "Coast Guard helicopter and plane circling around us but has not sighted us." Visibility was half a mile. The *Stolt Dagali* also revised her original estimation of her condition: "Now not sinking immediately." Captain Kristian Bendiksen, master of the *Stolt Dagali*, was more concerned about the crew members on the separated stern section (which no one at the time knew had already sunk). Working on the premise that the stern was still afloat, he radioed, "My whole stern has disappeared." Then, "thirty-three persons on after missing section."

Magnesium flares dropped by aircraft illuminated the area and presented an eerie sight for the crews. Navy helicopter pilot Lieutenant George Gilpin spotted a lifeboat, awash, with nine people aboard. "They were in all states of dress. Some just in their skivvies. They were elated when they saw us."

With his helicopter hovering above the sinking lifeboat, Gilpin lowered a cable to which was attached a "horsecollar ring, a large padded life ring." One at a time, he hauled men up into the belly of the chopper. He managed to recover four shivering seamen before a Coast Guard cutter arrived, threw a net over the side, and scooped up the remaining five.

Two merchant ships arrived and stood by in case they were needed. These were the *Reza Shah* and the *American Manufacturer*.

As a result of the collision the *Shalom* suffered a deep forty-foot gash in her bow. Captain Avner Freudenberg, master, soon determined that although there was some flooding in the forward compartments, his ship was not in immediate danger of sinking. He gave the order to man and launch a lifeboat in order to search for survivors from the vessel through which the *Shalom* had driven. Thirty knot winds and twenty foot seas hampered small boat operations. Nevertheless, the *Shalom's* lifeboat succeeded in plucking five of the *Stolt Dagali's* crew members from the water.

Captain Bendiksen was the last man to leave the *Stolt Dagali's* bow section. He heaped praise on his Coast Guard rescuers. "It was the best thing I saw in my life. The planes and the ships were there even though the sea was very rough and the fog very heavy." The survivors were taken to the Naval Air Hospital in Lakehurst, where they were treated for exposure and given heavy woolen shirts and denim pants. They were later transported to the Norwegian Seaman's House in Brooklyn.

With her bow low in the water, the *Shalom* returned to her berth at a speed of four knots. She was escorted by the Coast Guard cutter *Spencer* until they reached the safety of New York harbor. Captain Freudenberg was fearful that the *Shalom's* collision bulkhead might collapse if he proceeded any faster. A pair of tugs accompanied the liner after the *Spencer* turned back to sea.

After daybreak, the Coast Guard stepped up search and rescue operations, which continued all day. Five helicopters combed the sea in strictly regulated patterns. Initially the flight crews were looking for survivors, but when it became apparent that the stern section had sunk and that no one else could possibly be alive, the mission became a body recovery operation. Thirteen bodies were picked up - by cutter and by helicopter - and were taken to Point Pleasant Hospital, where they were identified.

By sunset, the *Stolt Dagali's* forward section had drifted fifteen to twenty miles north of the collision site. Throughout the day, the tug *Cynthia Moran* circled the *Stolt Dagali's* floating bow, trying unsuccessfully to get a tow line aboard. As one reporter described it, "The tanker was cut diagonally across, the cut angling from the starboard afterdeck slightly forward to the port side. The amputated end hung low in the water, rising and falling feebly. Each time it slapped downward, geysers shot upward. Nothing moved on the green deck, except the flooding sea. No flag flew."

After dark, the Coast Guard cutter *Spencer* patrolled around the aimless tanker in order to warn passing merchant ships of the menace to navigation. Searchlight beams stabbed at the deserted decks and superstructure, illuminating the floating wreck for all to see. Not until the following day was the *Cynthia Moran* able to take the *Stolt Dagali* in tow. The salvage tug *Curb*, of Merritt-Chapman & Scott, provided escort. By that time, the sea was calm and the weather clear.

The ship's stability was so precarious that the Army Corps of Engineers withheld permission for the tug and tow to enter New York harbor. They were afraid that the tanker might sink and block the channel. The wallowing forward section was towed as far as Gravesend Bay, then moored.

The Zim Line, owner of the *Shalom*, was forced to return $300,000 to passengers whose vacations had been cut short. Meanwhile, the six-month-old $20-million-dollar luxury liner was undergoing inspection. "Using searchlights, surveyors entered the damaged area to photograph and measure it. At the same time, they investigated to determine if any of the hull's steel plates had been loosened by the impact of the collision. Divers were sent down to inspect the underwater portions to determine if there was any damage there."

On November 29, the *Shalom* was moved into the graving dock at the Todd Shipyard in Brooklyn. The Zim Line then entertained bids for repair of its famous flagship. The *Shalom* was soon moved to the Newport News Ship Building and Dry Dock Company, in Newport News, Virginia. Repairs took over a month and cost more than half a million dollars. The following two cruises had to be canceled.

The *Shalom's* damaged bow. (Official U.S. Coast Guard photo.)

The *Shalom* resumed her cruise schedule on January 5, 1965. Captain Avner Freudenberg was still in command. It is interesting to note that the *Shalom* was unique in that, except for special winter cruises, the Israeli liner's kitchens provided only kosher cuisine. "Shalom" is Hebrew for "peace".

Divers were called in to inspect the hull of the still-floating section of the *Stolt Dagali*. They determined that it was in no danger of sinking. Since a tanker is essentially a collection of watertight tanks that are held together by a hull, most of the tanks remained intact and their cargo unharmed. The *Stolt Dagali* was known as a parcel tanker, one that "specialized in carrying different types of liquid cargoes in specially coated tanks." The forward tanks - those in front of the midship superstructure - were filled with propylene tetramer (a solvent),

The section of the *Stolt Dagali* that was towed to port. (Official U.S. Coast Guard photo.)

methanol (a wood alcohol), and heptane (a petroleum derivative). Marine inspectors hypothesized that had the *Stolt Dagali* been struck by the *Shalom* in the tanks containing these volatile and inflammable liquids, sparks created by steel grating on ruptured steel may have ignited the spilling cargo and caused both vessels to burst into flame.

By offloading some the cargo into small tank vessels, the *Stolt Dagali's* draft was reduced from forty feet to twenty-seven feet. "She was then moved three miles north to an anchorage off Bay Ridge, where she is to remain until five more tanks can be pumped out." After further lightering, the *Stolt Dagali* was moved to Pier 16 on Staten Island, where the rest of her cargo was removed and the truncated ship was laid up. On January 26, 1965, the forward section was moved to a dry dock at the Hoboken yard of the Bethlehem Steel Corporation.

In March 1965, the 440-foot-long forward section again went to sea. Not under her own power, of course, since her propulsion plant lay at the bottom of the ocean. Instead, she was towed across the broad Atlantic by a German tug that was bound for Goteborg, Sweden. The *Stolt Dagali's* forward section had been sold to C.T. Gogstad and Company of Oslo, Norway. That company's ship, the 18,880-ton Norwegian tanker *C.T. Gogstad* had broken in two after stranding off the Baltic coast of Sweden, a few weeks following the collision between the *Shalom* and the *Stolt Dagali*. The forward section of the *C.T. Gogstad* was pummeled to pieces, but the stern section with the propulsion plant was salvaged. The company was planning a marriage between the *Stolt Dagali's* bow and the *C.T. Gogstad's* stern - cargo tanks and engine - "till death do us part."

In May 1965 it was reported that "because of the similarity in vital statistics - only a one-foot difference in extreme width - ship-construction surgeons at the Eriksberg Shipyard at Goteborg were able to 'stitch' the two vessels together. Cargo tanks, cargo pipe lines and other gear - such as heating coils - were replaced, and the 'new' tanker is now being completed for service." The actual "stitching" took only one month to complete.

The new tank ship, grossing more than 19,000 tons, "will be operated on long-term charter in world-wide service by Parcel Tankers, Inc., the world's leading operator of highly specialized tank ships that move valuable high-grade liquid cargoes in quantities of up to 1,000 tons." She was christened the *Stolt Lady*.

There was rampant speculation about the cause of the collision. After a press conference at which a Zim Line spokesperson declined to permit Captain Freudenberg to answer penetrating questions, one reporter noted wryly that the captain stressed the fact that his radar unit was switched on, but "he did not say whether it was being watched." Neither captain would admit as to whether fog horns had been blown or whistle signals exchanged. Nor would either one comment about the speed of his vessel at the time of the collision. Another searing concern was the *Shalom's* erroneous position report - had the bridge watch been so lax in navigation that they did not know the ship's location within fifteen to twenty miles?

All these issues and more would have been addressed at a Coast Guard inquiry, but the Coast Guard lacked jurisdiction. The collision occurred in international waters between two vessels flying the flags of foreign nations. Claims, suits, and countersuits were the province of insurance companies and the governments of the countries in which the vessels were registered. As expected, the owners of each ship alleged that the collision was solely the fault of the other ship. Accusations came fast and furious as attorneys for each side issued prepared statements which bolstered their client's position.

The Zim Line statement declared that the *Shalom* had not encountered fog until ninety seconds prior to the collision, until which time she experienced perfectly clear air. The opposition scoffed that the statement was "a futile attempt to justify the *Shalom's* admitted speed of more than 20 knots in dense fog." Ironically, the *Shalom* contended that the *Stolt Dagali's* speed of fifteen knots was excessive under the circumstances. The *Stolt Dagali's* representatives countered by contending that the tanker had reduced speed some twenty minutes prior to the collision, then had come to a dead stop at the approach of the *Shalom*.

The *Shalom's* second mate, Yehoshua Welt, later testified that the radar scope was cluttered with interference mixed with sea return (the reflection of radar signals from wave tops). He said he tried unsuccessfully for five minutes to clear up the interference by adjusting the radar set's controls. "It cleared a bit, but I couldn't get a perfect picture." Thus, he was not able to spot the radar blip that represented the *Stolt Dagali* until the two ships were less than two miles apart.

Weakening the case for the *Shalom* was the fact that the lookout was given permission to take a coffee break in the crew's mess shortly before the collision occurred. He returned to the bridge "just as the collision was happening."

The aforementioned notwithstanding, the Zim Line offered to reimburse the families of the *Stolt Dagali's* dead to the tune of $450,000 - this professedly because the company's investigation showed that "under Norwegian law, the *Stolt Dagali* is not liable to its crew members. . . . realizing that although recoveries cannot recompense the loss, but that recoveries by the families of the deceased may avoid hardship."

The *Stolt Dagali's* owners, A/S Ocean, stole a march on the Zim Line by having authorities in Goteborg, Sweden detain the Zim Line freighter *Nahariya* when she docked. The *Nahariya* was held for ransom until the Zim Line put up

$1.5 million as bail. Attorneys representing the *Stolt Dagali's* interests claimed that the Zim Line's gracious offer to compensate families for their losses constituted an admission of guilt. A/S Ocean then filed a suit against the Zim Line in Sweden.

On January 3, 1965, an Israeli inquiry predictably absolved the *Shalom* of all blame for the collision, and found her captain and crew innocent of charges of negligence. The *Shalom* subsequently filed a damage suit against A/S Ocean for $2.3 million in the United States District Court for the Southern District of New York. "The damage sought consisted of $1.9 million for the repair of the liner and the loss of profits while it was in a shipyard and $450,000 to meet the claims of the representatives of the crewmen who lost their lives." (One of the lost crew members was a woman.)

Ordinarily, litigation between shipping companies was heard by the courts of the countries in which the interested companies were headquartered or maintained offices. However, in this case, or cases, two suits were filed in the United States: one a personal injury suit against both ship owners (the shotgun approach) by a passenger on the *Shalom*, and another co-filed by the Pacific Vegetable Oil Corporation and the Bunge Corporation, both of which sustained cargo losses and which filed libels against the Zim Line for reimbursement of their losses. Six months later, after the latter two companies paved the way through litigation, two other companies jumped on the bandwagon and filed suits against the Zim Line. These were the Cargill Company and the Unifood Company. Three months after that, Klockner and Company grabbed the bandwagon's tailgate and hitched its own suit for a free ride. All the food company suits were consolidated as a single libellant.

What followed was an extremely complicated proceeding, one with as many tangles as a dropped cat's-cradle As Federal Court Judge David Edelstein summarized it, "Many of the problems in this case arise because there are two main suits in two jurisdictions between the same parties to the same collision."

He went on to note that there was a "substantial difference in American admiralty law and the Brussels Collision Convention which is applied in Sweden. Counsel for all of the parties chose forums and maneuvered in a manner which best served their respective tactical positions. No element of fault or wrongdoing can fairly be attributed to any of the parties by reason of their choice of forums."

This statement underscores the evil essence of jurisprudence - that which is generally overlooked or ignored in the pious pursuit of moral judgment. Law suits are seldom filed in order to obtain justice; they are more often filed in order to obtain a legal opinion which is advantageous to the filing party.

Subsequent testimony contradicted earlier statements. Captain Bendiksen testified that he spotted the *Shalom* on radar at a distance of five miles, but took no immediate action because he was waiting to see how the *Shalom* intended to maneuver. For a long time, it seemed as if the *Shalom* did not intend to respond to the situation at all. When the liner was only half a mile away, a lookout on the *Stolt Dagali* heard a whistle signaling a turn to starboard, signifying that the

Shalom intended to pass astern of the tanker. Bendiksen then ordered full speed ahead in order to charge in front of the liner's bow and increase the distance between the two ships. He was found at fault for failing to take radar fixes to determine the *Shalom's* speed and direction of travel when he had ample time and opportunity to do so.

Despite Captain Bendiksen's admission, the Zim Line sought to prove that the *Stolt Dagali* had been proceeding at excessive speed in fog prior to the collision. The company hired divers to photograph or recover the tanker's engine room telegraph and tachometer, expecting to find the telegraph needle showing full speed ahead and the tachometer registering one hundred rpm's.

Initially, the Zim Line divers were unable to settle the dispute because they claimed that a hole had been torched in the sunken tanker's hull and the instruments removed. "The prevalent opinion among well-informed shipping men is that a scavenging diver took the instruments for the brass value. However, some concede that the diver might have been hired by someone with an interest in the outcome of the damage suits. Waterfront experts point out that it is not unusual for independent divers to strip wrecks of brass, copper or silver, which is melted down and sold."

In fact, on December 1, 1964 (only five days after the sinking), a group of wreck-divers located the *Stolt Dagali's* sunken stern by following the oil slick. The first two down were Michael de Camp and Robin Palmer, followed shortly by James Caldwell, Jack Brewer, Jack Brown, and Russell Koch. They told newspaper reporters that they had entered the engine room and some of the passageways, "but did not find any of the six missing bodies." De Camp took photographs of the wreck, Brewer shot movie film. It is unlikely that they would have made their actions public had they done anything illegal. Nor in the course of a single dive would they have had sufficient time to remove the instruments from the bowels of the engine room, even if they knew where to look for them.

It then developed that the diver later hired by the Zim Line to photograph or recover the instruments was the same James Caldwell mentioned in the previous paragraph. It was Caldwell's opinion that some other diver had entered the engineering quarters, and that "a room he saw in these quarters had been stripped clean of everything including furniture." Caldwell said, "It looked like a professional job by hard hat divers."

A/S Ocean claimed innocence, and noted that the very facts that the Zim Line wanted to prove had already been admitted, and that any evidence produced by the navigational instruments would merely bolster the *Stolt Dagali's* case by verifying Captain Bendiksen's belated attempt to take evasive action.

Caldwell eventually found the navigational instruments intact and bolted down precisely where they belonged. His photographs showed that in her final moments afloat, the *Stolt Dagali's* engine was set for full speed ahead. Zim Line attorneys showed the photographs to A/S Ocean attorneys, who shrugged at the confirmation of Captain Bendiksen's testimony. This part of the controversy eventually petered out. Perhaps it was never anything more than the lawyers' smoke and mirrors - or a legal red herring - intended to distract opposing counsel from more pertinent facts in the case.

The Zim Line finally agreed to settle the claims against it, at least as much as 90 percent of the losses. But it did not offer to settle until after it had forced its opponents' attorneys to expend 3,208 hours in preparing their case. These hours amounted to more than $125,000 in chargeable time. That did not include expenses for pretrial discovery, such as travel and lodging costs for the *Stolt Dagali's* crew, who were brought to the United States to be deposed in New York, where the first case originated. Only after causing this great expense did the Zim Line offer to discontinue the suit "without prejudice."

A ruling without prejudice meant that the Zim Line could sue again. As the judge noted, "The danger of harassment and 'repeated and vexatious suits' is thereby usually inherent." Furthermore, the Zim Line did not believe that it should have to pay its opponents' costs. Judge Edelstein denied the motion to discontinue "where the trial date had been fixed and postponed repeatedly at the behest of the libellant, all parties were in court ready to proceed, extensive pretrial investigation and depositions had been taken, over 200 exhibits had been marked in evidence, expert opinion on foreign law had been obtained, and documents had been translated. Proceedings had progressed too far to allow libellant to dismiss without prejudice and with the payment only of statutory costs."

In Sweden, on the other hand, the Zim Line was being forced to defend itself against A/S Ocean. After further convoluted legal logic, the judge permitted the Zim Line to discontinue the case in New York as long as it agreed to several stipulations: that no other claims be filed except for the case that was pending in Sweden, that the depositions and documents already marked in evidence be introduced as evidence in the case that was pending in Sweden, and that Zim pay $2,485.05 in court costs. Reimbursement for attorneys' fees and evidenciary costs was disallowed because it would have cost A/S Ocean an equivalent amount to prosecute the case that it initiated in Sweden when it arrested the *Nahariya*.

Eventually, the Zim Line paid 90 percent of the claims. A/S Ocean paid 10 percent of the claims for contributory negligence.

The *Stolt Dagali's* sunken stern quickly became a main attraction for wreck-divers. Mike de Camp and his wreck-diving friends made several return trips after their initial exploration. On one of these trips, de Camp peered into a port-hole and saw the body of the stewardess pinned to the overhead by the buoyancy of her life vest. He reported this gruesome find to the Norwegian embassy. The Norwegians were extremely thankful for the information, so much so that they asked if it was possible to recover the body, and to look for others that might still be trapped inside. De Camp said it was possible.

He then organized a body recovery operation. The group worked in turns to open the jammed door to the laundry room with a crowbar, then to drag the body through the passageways to a door leading outside the wreck. This difficult chore took place nearly a month after the sinking, by which time the body was not a pretty sight. The feet and face were gone, and loose flesh sloughed off against the divers' wetsuits as they squeezed the body through the doorway, brought it to the surface, and placed in a body bag provided by the Norwegian embassy. An undertaker took charge of the body at the dock. No other bodies were located.

The *Stolt Dagali* is no longer a tomb. Her engine has been forever silenced, her drive train has been stilled. But three and a half decades of marine growth have converted the wreck to a high-profile reef that is magnificently encrusted with large sea anemones and other marine fouling organisms, providing a substrate that attracts large numbers of pelagic fish (those that live at the top of the food chain).

The stern section is one-hundred-forty feet long. Lying on its starboard side at a depth of 130 feet, it rises as high as 65 feet from the surface. The 'S' painted on the stack, once photographed by Mike de Camp, was no longer visible when I first dived the wreck in the 1970's. This was because of marine encrustation. Swimming into the stack was like entering the maw of a huge, dark cavern. Now the stack is gone.

The wreck offers the ultimate in penetration diving, with doorways leading to large, wide corridors, and ample light piercing two deck levels through double rows of portholes. Inside, the partitions have given way, leaving unblocked long passageways full of debris, broken furniture, ship's appurtenances, and personal effects. Divers should be aware, however, that the right-angle list is quite disorienting: the decks and overheads are vertical, the bulkheads are horizontal, and the stairwells on their sides. The stairs are now collapsed. Beware that large cavities in the decks make it possible to switch levels unknowingly, especially during a silt-out.

One can enter the engine room through the gaping skylight, then descend past ghostly catwalks and railings all the way down to the massive rocker arms and the bedplates below. The room is as large as a small house. Although comforting ambient light fills the vast central portion, and all but the darkest of corners filled with piping and machinery, one can easily get disoriented in the compartment's immensity by straying into the shadows and cubbyholes.

Safer to explore is the chief engineer's office, which occupies the superstructure house, because the roof has rusted away. An outside companionway goes completely around the perimeter, with the portion on the sand appearing like a long black tunnel. Doorways and rust holes permit access to the interior from inside the companionway.

Large lobsters are found on the bottom, under the giant propeller, in the scattered wreckage, and also inside. But one should be careful picking up crustaceans from the deep interior, because rusting metal and rotting wood has left thick layers of silt which is easily disturbed. The act of grabbing a bug and stuffing it into a bag often causes one to muck up the companionways with horrifying, and possibly disastrous, results.

Alan Ferry found this out when he got turned around in a room, could not relocate the door, and was forced to doff his tanks and drop his weight belt in order to squeeze through a porthole and make a fast, free ascent to the surface. Others might not be so bold and clearheaded - or so lucky.

A great deal of the wreck's exterior has changed since the original publication of *Shipwrecks of New Jersey*. The superstructure is still largely intact, and the hull has so far retained most of its integrity. But the steel plates are pock-marked with giant rust holes, as if basketballs were thrown completely through the metal. In places, jagged perforations are stitched together to form large, amorphous openings, some big enough to swim through. Alan Ferry take note.

Additional deterioration has occurred inside, where the steel plates that form the partitions are thinner than the steel plates of which the hull and bulkheads are made. These interior changes are subtle, however, rather than massive: rust holes, fallen partitions, and the like. Continue to exercise caution.

For the underwater photographer the *Stolt Dagali* is a dream site. Ambient light visibility often ranges between fifty and one hundred feet, sometimes more. The intact hull offers a great silhouette for available light photos because the wreck reaches so close to the surface and because it lies in a commonly clean area. The outer hull is painted with large sea anemones which, when feeding, extend a multitude of tentacles and give the appearance of a flowing flower garden. This is a perfect setting for macro and close-up photography.

Cod and pollock are often found swimming around the wreck. Large tautog and black sea bass are the delight of spearfishing advocates. Ling live on the bottom and inside. Lobsters live everywhere. Bottom dwellers may be found in the debris field formed by machinery that has fallen off the upper deck.

Relic hunters still bring out mementos: portholes, brass engine parts and accessories, personal belongings, galley dinnerware stenciled with the shipping line's flag and crest, and other odds and ends. And, because the high side of the wreck is so shallow, even the novice wreck-diver can see how a shipwreck *should* look.

The *Stolt Dagali* is a wreck for everyone.

Courtesy of Skyfotos Ltd.

Sister ship *SC-144*, photographed circa 1918. (Courtesy of the Naval Photographic Center.)

SUB CHASER 60

Built: 1917
Previous names: None
Displacement tonnage: 77
Type of vessel: Submarine chaser
Builder: New York Navy Yard, New York, NY
Owner: United States Government
Port of registry: New York, NY
Cause of sinking: Collision with MV *Fred W. Weller*
Location: 40-22-26 N

Sunk: October 1, 1918
Depth: 45 feet
Dimensions: 110' x 14' x 5'
Power: Three 220-HP gasoline engines

73-56-34 W

The exact whereabouts of this submarine chaser are unknown. It is possible that the remnants of the vessel's wooden hull have been engulfed by shifting sand. A wreck symbol was placed on the chart in the position reported above, along with a notation that the obstruction was cleared to a least depth of 45 feet. Whatever clearing method was used probably destroyed much of the wreck, and teredos undoubtedly got most of the rest. Nevertheless, the spot may yet be marked by the engines and metal machinery, the 3-inch deck gun, the two Colt machine guns, the Y-gun, and the depth charges in their racks. The SC 60 was one of more than three hundred such vessels constructed between 1917 and 1919.

Very little fuss was made over the casualty, in either official reports or the newspapers, despite the loss of two of the sub chaser's crew. Against the intensity of warfare on the western front in Europe, where thousands of men died daily, the loss of two low-ranking seamen paled into relative insignificance.

On October 1, 1918, the *SC 60* departed New York harbor on routine patrol and proceeded south. Because German U-boats were running rampant along the eastern seaboard, a restriction against the display of navigational lights was in effect, this to make it difficult for enemy marauders to find merchant ship targets at night. Since the primary purpose of submarine chasers was to spot and destroy lurking submarines, they were doubly charged to proceed under this restriction.

In the darkness and heavy downpour, the sub chaser showed such a small and vague silhouette that the American tanker *Fred W. Weller* did not see her until it was too late to avoid a collision. The contest between the two vessels was uneven: in one corner stood a 77-ton wooden-hulled submarine chaser, in the other corner stood a 10,627-ton 500-foot-long steel-hulled twin-screw motor vessel. The time was 2 a.m. According to one account, the collision occurred "about six miles southeast of Seabright, near the Shrewsbury rocks." Another account gave the location as five miles south of the Ambrose Channel lightship and two miles north of the Shrewsbury Rock gas buoy.

Due to the proximity to shore, "Coast Guard men from stations 99 at Seabright, 100 at Monmouth Beach and 101 at Long Branch went to the rescue at 3 o'clock. There was a heavy surf with a stiff northerly gale at the time. Captain Maxwell and his crew of seven men were compelled to wheel their boat for two miles before they were able to launch it with the assistance of several fishermen. The oil steamer stood by, and picked up two of the chaser's crew."

Elsewhere it was reported that the USS *Kemah* assisted the tanker in picking up survivors. A sub chaser's usual complement was twenty-seven men.

The two men reported missing were second class machinist's mate Walter Herman Kluth and second class seaman Martin Austin Wilson. Coast Guard boats searched vainly for the missing men. In the Annual Report to the Secretary of the Navy, they were listed as lost: a footnote in the world war then occurring.

The *Thurmond* as the *Colgate Hoyt*, riding high. (Courtesy of the Institute for Great Lakes Research.)

THURMOND

Built: 1890
Previous names: *Colgate Hoyt, Bay City*
Gross tonnage: 1,252
Type of vessel: Whaleback steamer
Builder: American Steel Barge Company, Duluth, Minnesota
Owner: Seaboard Transportation Company, New Jersey
Port of registry: New York, NY
Cause of sinking: Ran aground
Location: 150 feet from the beach at Toms River

Sunk: December 26, 1909
Depth: 8 feet
Dimensions: 276' x 36' x 18'
Power: Coal-fired steam

The *Thurmond* was an unusual and odd-looking vessel, an unorthodox design by any set of standards. Her rounded, cigar-shaped hull made her look more like a submarine than the ore carrier she was. Her low freeboard and circular turrets lent the appearance of a Civil War monitor. Her blunt bow and stern resembled the snout of a wild but friendly boar, and, switching similes, waves washed across her hull and sealed hatches like water off a duck's back. This miscegenation of motifs, this patchwork quilt of architectural components, this radical departure from conventional hull construction, was the pioneering brainchild of Captain Alexander McDougall, a ship builder whose yard spanned the north shore of the St. Louis River where it flowed into Lake Superior and separated Duluth from its twin city, Superior. Between 1888 and 1898, McDougall's company, the American Steel Barge Company, launched forty-three vessels of a similar mold, all successful in their purpose despite initial criticism to the contrary.

The first five hulls were built as barges. McDougall's fertile invention for design was not matched by any imagination for names. These initial vessels were christened simply after their hull numbers. The number given to the first barge was 101, so the vessel was named *Barge 101*. The function of these barges was to transport iron ore from the rich inland Minnesota mines to the smelting plants in Cleveland. In that they succeeded admirably.

McDougall called his unique vessels "whalebacks" or "whaleback barges" after their sleek, black appearance and the way they carved through the water. Contemporary pundits called them "pigboats" because of their snub-nosed ends. The hull was essentially a long tube or cylinder with curvilinear sides and a narrow, flat bottom. The top of the sides tapered inward to form the deck, which was pierced by rounded hatches with tall, external coamings, much like soup cans balanced on top of a loaf of Italian bread. Cargo hatches were fitted with watertight covers.

Instead of bucking the wind and water as conventional vessels did, a whaleback was aero- and hydrodynamic so that air flowed over the upper portion of the hull as if it were a foil, while the underwater portion slid through the waves with the deck awash. Think of a whaleback as a submarine freighter which could not completely submerge.

With a handful of experience behind him, McDougall achieved a higher note of originality in the construction of hull number 106. This whaleback was given a more sophisticated name - *Colgate Hoyt* - and was fitted with two Scotch boilers and a compound steam engine. It was the first of eighteen whaleback steamships that were launched - sideways - over the next eight years.

The turrets provided access to the interior of the hull, much like the trunk in the conning tower of a submarine. Unlike the gun turrets of monitors, a whaleback turret did not rotate. The stationary turret was like a stairwell. The turrets over the machinery spaces doubled as stacks, permitting ventilation and the exhaust of smoke and steam, while serving as foundations for the wheel house, crew's quarters, and superstructure.

The evolution of the whaleback reached its zenith with the launching of hull number 128, the *Christopher Columbus*. This plush model was fitted out as an excursion steamer for the 1892 World's Fair. She sported four decks and seven turrets, each of which contained a grand staircase, allowing passengers to roam freely throughout the ship. On her maiden voyage she carried 7,500 passengers from downtown Chicago to the fair grounds at Jackson Park. The World's Fair ended, but not the career of the *Christopher Columbus*. Over the next forty-four years, she transported more passengers than any other vessel on the Great Lakes, perhaps in the world.

Of all the rancid comments that were made about the whalebacks, the only ones that held any sway were those which dealt with their stability. Because of the rounded hull design, they were known to exhibit excessive roll in more than marginal seas, like a lumbering water-soaked log. They were on their best behavior when they were heavily loaded, in which case the low-slung profile was hidden from the wind. But riding in ballast proved difficult in any kind of a blow, as the high hull was buffeted by gusts which tended to push the bow aside. Aside from their steering problems, whalebacks were staunch and reliable vessels.

More than half the whalebacks constructed eventually saw salt water service. Of these, seventeen were lost in the Atlantic Ocean, two in the Gulf of Mexico, and one in the Pacific. Of the seventeen whalebacks lost in the Atlantic Ocean, five were lost off the coast of New Jersey, three off Long Island, New York, three off Virginia, three off Massachusetts, one off Maine, and two far out to sea. Of the latter two losses, the *Sagamore* was torpedoed by a German U-boat in 1917.

The *Colgate Hoyt*, first of the whaleback steamers, served under half a dozen owners and was known by three names. In 1905, she was renamed *Bay City*. In 1907, when she was purchased by the White Oak Transportation Company and registered in Maine, she officially became a "saltie" (as opposed to a "laker"). In 1909, she was purchased by the Seaboard Transportation Company, of New Jersey, and renamed *Thurmond*. Instead of ore she now transported coal.

On December 24, 1909, the *Thurmond* departed Newport News, Virginia on her way to Providence, Rhode Island. She was heavily laden with coal, as was the barge she was towing, the *John A. Briggs*. Initial foul weather did not portend a storm of the severity which developed. Christmas day found the New Jersey coast in the throes of a winter blizzard, snow lashing the steamer's steel hull practically parallel to the deck. There was nowhere to hide, so the *Thurmond* had little choice but to continue on her way.

Around midnight, the violence of the storm and the crashing seas put too much strain on the tow rope. The rope parted and the barge went adrift to be swallowed up by the snow. Aboard the barge were five freezing men whose lives now hung in the balance. The *Thurmond* turned immediately and went in search of her missing tow. The steamer was taking a terrible beating. As she rolled from the onslaught of a crashing wave, her cargo shifted and her plates sprang. Now with a list, leaking badly, and unmanageable in the heaving sea, she was in trouble. Yet she continued to search in the darkness for the missing barge.

Hours passed. The captain must have gotten disoriented as the night and blinding snow hid both the barge and the proximity to shore. Without warning, the *Thurmond* ran aground on the Toms River bar some two hundred yards from

The *Thurmond* as the *Colgate Hoyt*, deeply laden. (Courtesy of the Institute for Great Lakes Research.)

shore. It was 9 o'clock in the morning on December 26. "There was a strong gale blowing, and the snow and sleet were blinding." Flares fired by the *Thurmond* alerted the men of the Toms River Life Saving Station, three-quarters of a mile away. Henry Ware, keeper of the station, rallied his men to the rescue. He also notified Joel Hulse, keeper of the Island Beach Life Saving Station, and asked him for assistance. A surfman burned a Coston signal to let those on the *Thurmond* know that their plight had been observed. The crews from both stations arrived with the beach apparatus in tow.

The life savers mounted a Lyle gun on the beach opposite the wreck. The first shot was fired accurately across the stranded steamer's deck, but carried away before any of the *Thurmond's* crew members could reach the line. The second shot was as accurate as the first. This time, the men on board managed to grab and hold on to the line. This was just a messenger line. The life savers tied on a heavier line, then signaled for the stricken crew to pull it in. The survivors' fingers were numb from the bitter cold, but at last the job was done. Now their lives were in the frozen hands of the life-saving crews on shore.

The breeches buoy was rigged and hauled out to the ship. Because the *Thurmond* had swung broadside to the beach, the pounding waves caused the ship to roll back and forth. The line from ship to shore alternately sagged and then went taut, one moment dipping the breeches buoy into the surf, the next moment threatening to snap. Both crews as well as onlookers pressed into service took hold of the line. With their combined strength, they ran back and forth as the *Thurmond* rolled on her axis, and managed to keep the line taut while the first man was hauled ashore.

The Life Saving Service report was tauntingly laconic. "At 11:45 a.m. the first man was landed. By 2:35 p.m. the entire crew of 20 had been safely brought ashore. Seaside Park cottagers gave them hot coffee, and they were furnished dry clothing at the station and by the cottagers."

This during a northeast gale and driving snow!

News of the loss of the *Thurmond* was patchy and inaccurate. From Maine to Maryland the storm knocked down communication wires, and heavy snow drifts interrupted train service. Ships at sea struggled to stay alive and reach the relative safety of New York harbor. Schooners tied up at the Battery were dashed against the sea wall by the abnormally rising tide. "Coming on a full moon, the gale rolled a wave along the coast which, in some places, reached a height of more than fourteen feet, and has only been exceeded, according to local records, by that which swept the coast at the time that Minot's Light was destroyed in April, 1851." Basements were flooded, travel was nearly impossible, millions of dollars of damage was done, and several people were killed. Compared to catastrophes of greater, global importance, the stranding of the *Thurmond* was a minor event.

Not until the following day, when the storm subsided, could salvage vessels thrust their bows beyond the protection of New York harbor. By then the *Thurmond* had broken her back on the bar. The weight of the coal in her hold had bent the ship's ends down and had snapped the keel as if it were nothing more

The *Thurmond* aground. (Courtesy of Sharon Reese.)

than a twig. The ship sat in the surf like a giant beached whale. Waves washing over the curved deck smashed against the turrets and superstructure, causing further damage and leakage. The *Thurmond* was given up as a total loss.

Miraculously, the *John A. Briggs* was found anchored off Chadwick, with all five crew men alive and well. They must have had an anxious time until a surf-boat from the Chadwick Life Saving Station brought them ashore.

It was later reported that a "Government derelict destroyer came down the beach and blew up the wreck of the barge which lay between Sea Side Park and Chadwicks, about four miles off shore, with one mast and the stump of another sticking out of the water. The noise of the dynamite explosions were heard plainly at Toms River." The derelict destroyer was the *Seneca*. Her usual duty was destroying and sinking the partially submerged hulls of wooden windjammers which had capsized or wrecked on the high seas, where they posed a hazard to navigation by drifting aimlessly across the shipping lanes.

The *Thurmond's* crew became temporary guests of the Life Saving Service, and were put up at the Toms River station overnight. They left for New York the following day, after communications and transport were re-established. The Seaboard Transportation Company reimbursed the Life Saving Service for the food that the men consumed. The company's president, C.B. Orcutt, sent a letter of acknowledgment to the Service. He wrote:

"We desire to express our appreciation of the good work done by the life-savers at Toms River, N.J., in rescuing the crew of 20 men from our steamer Thurmond, wrecked off Seaside Park on December 26. It was a very bad storm which caused the loss of our vessel, and the life-saving crew certainly did a noble work in rescuing the men on board."

At the time of her loss, the estimated value of the *Thurmond* was $55,000, that of her cargo $6,165. There is no record of attempted salvage, yet the engine is not in evidence. In fact, very little of the wreck has ever been seen.

Joe Paolo remembers that when he dived the *Thurmond* in the mid-1980's, both boilers were exposed and lay in a line at a maximum depth of about 15 feet. Because they were the largest and most distinctive feature on the site, the wreck was called the Boiler Wreck. Each boiler had a relief of about five feet, and at low tide rose to within six feet of the surface. These boilers were originally eleven feet in diameter, so they must have been more than half buried.

Over the years, the wreck has gradually sanded in and gotten closer to the beach. In 1998, one boiler was covered completely, the other was barely exposed, and the maximum depth was only 8 feet. Technically, of course, the *Thurmond* has not moved closer to the beach. Rather, the beach has accumulated sand and grown out toward the wreck. Life-savers noted that the wreck lay stranded some six hundred feet from shore. Paolo recalls having to swim about three hundred feet in the 1980's. Now the distance has shrunk to between one hundred fifty and two hundred feet. Of course, the walk across the beach is longer.

The wreck lies on the back edge of a sand bar. Paolo remembers getting thrown around quite a bit by wave action. He suggests diving when the seas are flat and the tide is slack.

The *Thurmond's* identity has been established by means of strong circumstantial evidence, primarily the wreck's location. No other steamships are known to have been lost in the vicinity.

To find what is left of the wreck, swim straight off the beach and keep the utility pole aligned with the north side of the second house south of E Street.

WESTERN WORLD

Built: 1845
Previous names: None
Gross tonnage: 1,354
Type of vessel: Three-masted, full-rigged ship
Builder: Frederick Fernald and William Pettigrew, Portsmouth, New Hampshire
Owner: Messrs. D. & A. Kingsland & Company, New York
Port of registry: New York, NY
Cause of sinking: Ran aground
Location: 26947.0

Sunk: October 22, 1853
Depth: 35 feet
Dimensions: 183' x 40' x 20'
Power: Sail

43524.0

(Off the boardwalk at Spring Lake)

The Spring Lake Wreck has probably been known to anglers since the beginning of sport fishing and charter boat service. It is likely that the first people to set eyes on her rotting timbers in the twentieth century were skin-divers and spearfishers. The wreck was explored by scuba divers in the 1950's - when scuba was in its infancy and had yet to make the transition in the English language from a capitalized acronym to a lower-case noun and conjugated verb. The remains of this unidentified windjammer generated throbs in the hearts of these early underwater explorers because of the wide assortment of relics that they found buried under the exposed ribs and planks: old English china plates and bowls, brass riding spurs, copper powder flasks, tubes of copper sheet, hinges, drawer handles, files, latches, brass fastening spikes of varying lengths, and at least one silver-plated hand-engraved tray.

In an article published by Bill Scripko and Chuck Tucker in 1962, they reported that after knowledge of the fertile trove of souvenirs was spread in the local community, an average summer week saw as many as forty divers descending upon the wreck in newfangled and largely imported scuba gear. The long hard swim from shore undoubtedly kept away those of weaker constitution.

During this period of intense exploration and salvage, the site was scoured for artifacts by divers who discovered an easier means of access: boats. They also began wearing wetsuits so they could dive in more adverse conditions, when the water was too cold for the naked body to endure for very long.

After doing some research, Scripko and Tucker thought the wreck might be that of either the *Western World* or the *Ayrshire*, both of which were lost in the vicinity. Their efforts to spark archaeological interest came to naught. The wreck's popularity grew among those who were willing to brave the elements, but outside the world of divers the wreck elicited little or negative appeal.

Then came the day of enlightenment. Undiscouraged by the lack of academic curiosity, one group of divers "worked" the wreck consistently. Bearing tools such as crowbars, pinch bars, hammers, and picks, they chipped and chopped their way through thick encrustation and were eventually rewarded with a prize that held a value greater than that of a mere souvenir: the ship's main capstan, on whose brass cover was stamped the name *Western World*. The group who shared this long-sought identification - and who crammed themselves and their gear aboard a twenty-five-foot boat - were Howell Brose, Bill Gage, James Johnson, Gene Kordahl, Mike Krosted, Joe McCloskey, and Ray Wagner.

The *Western World* was a packet ship: a ship whose dates of departure were based upon a strict and published schedule. Previous to the packet ship era, ships delayed departure until their holds were filled with cargo and their cabins allotted. This system of shipboard efficiency made it impossible for merchants to guarantee delivery, and passengers were forced to linger on board for days - even weeks - awaiting passage. By adhering to a timetable, packet companies made transatlantic travel reliable except for the vagaries of the wind. (For more information on packet service, see Manasquan Wreck.)

The *Western World* was built by Fernald & Pettigrew to travel between New York and London. She was rigged with square sails that were hung from perpendicular yards: this because Atlantic winds blew predominantly east and west, and square-riggers traveled fast in a tailwind yet tacked well against a head wind. (By contrast, schooners - whose sails were rigged fore and aft - made poor sailors in such winds. They were designed as coastal transports, and were faster and more maneuverable than square-riggers when the wind came from the beam.) She sported three decks and a man figurehead.

Since the *Western World's* principal occupation was the transportation of people and cargo, she can best be described as a wind-propelled passenger-freighter. In the days before container ships and bulk cargo carriers, the best way to pack cargo was in barrels. Wooden staves were bent and locked together between circular headings or end caps, then braced with outer iron hoops in the same fashion as wagon wheels. Barrels were rolled by manpower along the wharf, up the gangplank, and across the deck, then lowered into the holds by means of tackle and tongs. A skilled stevedore could roll and turn barrels much like today's warehouse worker can twist two compressed gas bottles across a concrete floor. The barrel was the universal shipping container. It held manufactured products, produce, powders, salted meats, even liquids. Delicate items were packed in excelsior (now replaced by bubble wrap and Styrofoam). A person who made barrels was called a cooper.

Many of yesteryear's units of measurement are no longer in use and are not familiar to the modern general populace. The standard barrel was equivalent to 31 1/2 liquid gallons. (This is different from today's barrel used as a measure of petroleum products; a barrel of oil is 42 gallons.) The barrel was also a dry measure of fruits and vegetables, in which case it was equivalent to 105 dry quarts, or 3.9 bushels - unless it was a barrel of cranberries, in which case it was equivalent to 87 quarts or 2.7 bushels. The modern bushel, by the way, is equal to four pecks or thirty-two dry quarts. (A dry quart is slightly larger than a liquid quart. There is no such unit as a dry gallon in the American system of measurement, although there is in the British system.) If this all sounds confusing, pray that someday the entire world goes metric.

The barrel was not only a container but a quantity of measure. Ten barrels of product did not necessarily mean ten individual wooden barrels, any more than ten gallons of gasoline in an automobile's fuel tank means ten individual one-gallon jugs.

It is interesting to note the kinds of trade goods that were imported by England from its one-time colony in the middle of the nineteenth century. According to the British bill of entry, the *Western World* arrived in Liverpool on July 14, 1853 with an assorted cargo consigned to more than a dozen local merchants. This cargo consisted of 637 bales of cotton, 7,636 barrels of flour, 20,900 bushels of wheat, 807 barrels of rosin, 1 tierce of potato meal, 19 briskets of pork, 43 boxes of bacon, 3 casks of sperm oil, and 5 casks listed as "contents unknown." (A tierce is one-third of a pipe or 42 gallons; brisket is the chest of an animal; a cask is a small barrel of indeterminate size intended for liquids, primarily for wine, but which was also used to hold other commodities such as salted meat.)

On what proved to be her final voyage, the *Western World* left Liverpool on September 8, 1853 under the command of Captain John G. Moses, who also owned a large share of the ship. She traveled in company with the slightly smaller *Marmion*, which departed the same day for the same destination: New York. British export records listed only the bonded items, and lumped those items together without distinguishing which vessel was transporting which of those items. There exists no complete manifest of the *Western World's* last cargo.

Aboard the two vessels were the following bonded items: 8 cases of colored paper valued at £200, 1 case of cigars valued at £30, 1 case of otto of roses and 1 case of scammony valued collectively at £150, 1 case of squirrel tails, 100 bags of cubic nitre, and 9 packages of woolen manufactured goods. (Otto of roses is the same as attar of roses, or rose oil; it was distilled from rose petals and, mixed with other ingredients, was used as a fragrance. Scammony is the tropical New World morning glory, or its dried root, or its extracted resin; the resin was used as a cathartic. What merchants would want with a case of squirrel tails is anyone's guess.)

The demise of the *Western World* drew scant publicity. On November 7 the Lloyd's List published this notice: "New York, 25th Oct. The *Western World*, from Liverpool to this port, was stranded on Squam Beach, coast of New Jersey, 22nd Oct., is full of water, and bent up very much amidships; crew and passengers landed - cargo expected to be saved."

On November 28, the Lloyd's List published this additional notice: "New York, 16th Nov. The *Western World*, from Liverpool to this port, which went ashore on Squam Beach 22nd October, broke up during a gale from the Eastward, on the 13th Nov." (What is known today as Manasquan was then called Squam or Squan.)

The lag between the date of each notice and the date within each notice resulted from the time it took for intelligence to reach London from New York by fast steamer. More prompt, if not much more descriptive, was mention of the

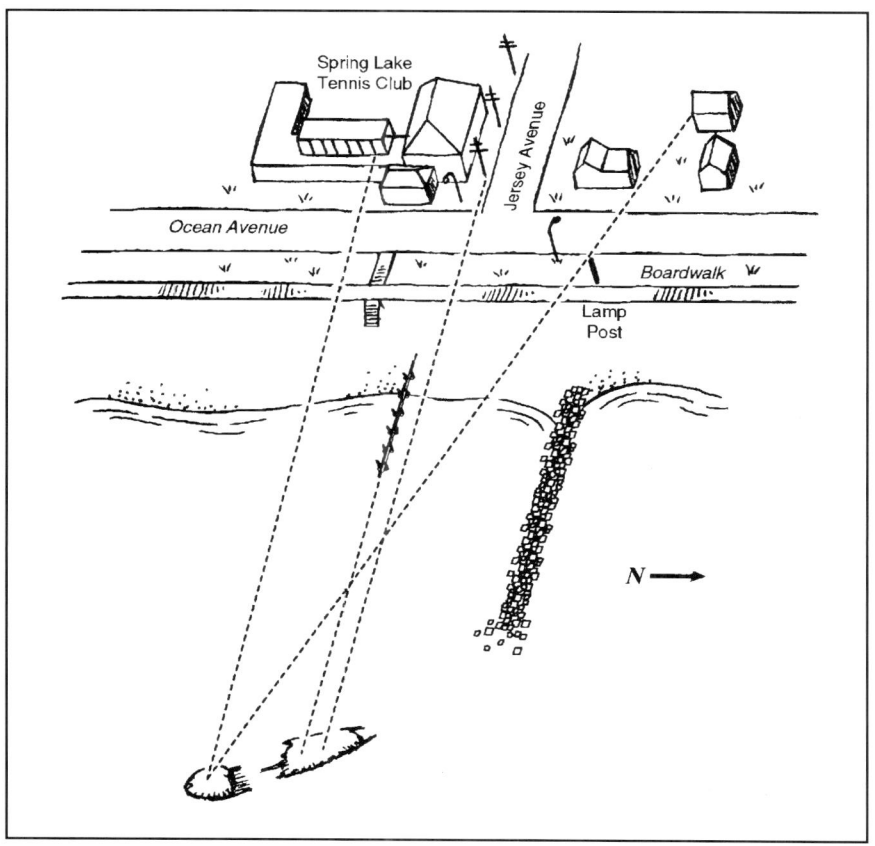

Park on Ocean Avenue as close Jersey Avenue as possible. Suit up by your vehicle, then walk up onto the boardwalk and down the steps to the south and onto the beach. The wreck lies roughly straight out from the pipe in front of the cement structure under the boardwalk. Swim east, keeping the flag pole just to the north of the center of the cement structure, and descend when you see what appears to be the center of the third house north of Jersey Avenue aligned with the light pole cn the street. Note that the third house is actually the second house back from the road, but because of the angle it appears to be the third in the row, only set slightly back. To locate the south piece of wreckage, Howard Rothweiler takes a compass heading due south and counts 55 kicks. If you try this and do not find the south piece, surface and check the ranges, or do a search pattern by working south no more than 5 kicks at a time while traveling east to west at least 20 kicks. Note that the northeast corner of the south piece has a great deal of brass hardware mixed in with the iron or steel ingots. China can be found anywhere on the wreck.

event in New York newspapers on October 23 and 24. "The packet ship *Western World*, from Liverpool to Messrs. Kingsland & Co., went ashore on Friday night, on Squam Beach, about eighteen miles south of the Highlands, and at last accounts was laying broadside to the beach. A steam tug and lighters have been despatched to her assistance. The passengers, six hundred in number, are all safe. They were being landed on the beach as the steamer *United States* passed yesterday afternoon."

Today, the rescue of six hundred passengers would be a major media event, not just a line in the middle of an unremarkable fourth page paragraph.

A postscript noted that "a telegraphic dispatch received last night from the Highlands states that the ship lies with head to the northward, and broadside on. She is reported to have seven feet of water in her hold, and considerably hogged. Part of her keel has come ashore. The steam tug *Achilles*, which went to her assistance this morning, is returning off Long Branch and probably has the greater part of her passengers."

She was last mentioned in New York on October 25: "Ship *Western World*, which we reported yesterday as ashore, has sustained more serious damage than was at first supposed. She went ashore on Friday night near Squan Inlet, about 10 o'clock, and it is said there was a pilot on board at the time. The W.W. was a first class ship of 1,354 tons burden, (three-decker,) built in Portsmouth, N.H., in 1845, owned by Messrs. D. & A. Kingsland & Co., of this city, and valued at about $70,000 or $80,000, the cargo about $100,000. Both vessel and cargo are largely insured in Wall st. We publish the following extract from a letter in relation to her:

"Squan Beach, Oct. 23 - 4 P.M.

"Elwood Walter, Esq., Secretary of the Board of Underwriters 'Although a very high sea, we have succeeded in getting all the passengers from the ship, and from the shore to the *Achilles* - some four or five hundred - and much of their baggage to the *Splendid*. The *Splendid* will leave in the morning with the passengers' baggage. The ship lies broadside to the beach, full of water, so much rounded up amidships, that I have some fear she is badly injured, and that the pumps may not be able to free her of water. The water ebbs and flows freely in her. We are preparing to have the cables in and anchors down in the morning, and the steam pump on board, as a very heavy sea in her present position would most likely make serious work with her. Every package of goods on board are under water, and I have not seen one yet recovered. She has about 400 tons iron, 800 sacks salt, 200 tons dry good, 150 crates &c. The rudder is unshipped and troublesome, and we are striving to get clear of it.' "

Further intelligence was not forthcoming. Perhaps because the *Western World* stranded where she did, Spring Lake later was sometimes referred to as Wreck Pond. That designation has long since been abandoned.

No serious work has been performed on the *Western World* in recent years. The wreck is now covered with sand as a result of the Beach Replenishment Project.

The *Yankee* as the *German*. (Courtesy of the Institute for Great Lakes Research.)

YANKEE

Built: 1890
Previous names: *German*
Gross tonnage: 2,418
Type of vessel: Freighter
Builder: Globe Iron Works Company, Cleveland, Ohio
Owner: United States Shipping Board
Port of registry: New York, NY
Cause of sinking: Collision with SS *Argentina*
Location: 26671.4

Sunk: June 12, 1919
Depth: 110 feet
Dimensions: 296' x 40' x 21'
Power: Coal-fired steam

43574.4

The *Yankee* led a long and productive career as a bulk freighter - a career that spanned nearly three decades. For practically the entire time she was owned by the Pittsburgh Steamship Company. She was launched as the *German* on November 19, 1889 from the Globe Iron Works in Cleveland, Ohio. She was nearly completed during the following winter months, but a slump in the economy forced her lay-up. She did not actually begin service until 1891.

The *German* routinely steamed along the Great Lakes as a reliable work horse until 1917. When the United States entered the Great War, the country had a sudden and desperate need for merchant ships of all types: freighters, tankers, and passenger liners that could be converted to troop ships. The United States Shipping Board was established in order to acquire the necessary tonnage. The Shipping Board purchased many "lakers" - as vessels that plied the Inland Sea were called - and converted them for saltwater service.

"Conversion" in this sense meant merely steaming downbound through the locks into the St. Lawrence Seaway, thence out to sea and south to the eastern seaboard. But many lakers - the *German* included - were too large to fit through the lock in the canal that bypassed Niagara Falls, which presented a barrier between Lakes Erie and Ontario. These ships had to be cut in two. The *German* was bisected at the American Ship Building Company in Buffalo, New York, floated through the canal, towed to Montreal, Quebec, then re-assembled. Once officially a "saltie," the *German* was renamed *Yankee*.

The *Yankee's* ocean career was unfortunately short-lived. The night of June 11-12, 1919 proved to be a bad one for shipping in the New York harbor approaches. "The sea was enveloped in a heavy fog, so dense that it was impossible for the lookouts to see more than 50 feet ahead." Radio waves crackled constantly with calls for help.

First, the steamship *Redondo* rammed the transport *Graf Waldersee* squarely amidship. "The impact was so great that those asleep on both boats were sent flying from their bunks." Four rescue vessels answered the SOS and rushed to the scene of the collision. The *Graf Waldersee* was holed deeply in the engine room. All her passengers and crew were removed without injury, and the transport was taken in tow until she reached shoal water, where she grounded. She was eventually refloated, and lived to cruise the high seas again.

Not so lucky was the *Yankee*. According to one report, the Italian steamship *Argentina* "outward bound for Gibraltar and Trieste collided with the str. *Yankee* off Fire Island Light last night. The *Yankee*, bound from Norfolk for Boston with coal, was reported leaking so badly that she was abandoned by her captain and crew, who were taken aboard the *Argentina*, which proceeded, after transferring

The *Yankee* as the *German*. (Courtesy of the Institute for Great Lakes Research.)

the *Yankee's* crew to the tug *Marshal J. Sanford*, which brought them to port. The *Yankee* sank shortly after being abandoned. The *Argentina* apparently sustained very little, if any, damage."

In another account, the tug's name was given as *Margaret E. Sandford*. "The seamen had been rescued by the *Argentina* and taken to the *Cardinal* Lightship to await a boat from this port [New York]. According to John Gargan, a member of the *Yankee's* crew, there were two distinct crashes. The *Argentina* first struck the *Yankee* diagonally, bow on, and then veered around and struck her again, this time punching a large hole in the port side. He said no warning whistles or signals were given by the *Argentina*, although the *Yankee* had been blowing her fog horn at regular intervals."

Yet another version had both vessels taking evasive action when they became aware of each other's presence. "The engines of the *Yankee* were stopped at once, but as it was seen that a collision was inevitable, the helm of the *Yankee* was brought hard-a-port, and the engines were started ahead for the purpose, if possible, of paralleling the other vessel." The twin screw Italian liner tried to get out of the way by reversing one propeller while going forward with the other.

The two ships glanced off each other's bows, but in passing, the stern of the *Argentina* swung into the hull of the *Yankee*. The *Argentina's* rotating propeller gouged through the freighter's steel hull. The *Yankee* started taking on water at a prodigious rate, quickly outpacing the ability of her pumps to eject it. To no avail, collision mats were thrown over the gaping hole. Captain Dennis Morgan, master, ordered abandon ship. The captain, eight passengers, and twenty-one crew members, got away in the boats none too soon, for the *Yankee* went down within fifteen minutes of the collision. All the people were taken aboard the *Argentina*, then transferred to the tug *Marshal J. Sanford*, which transported them to New York.

It has long been accepted that the remains of the *Yankee* lay at loran coordinates 26609.5 and 43592.0, at a depth of 120 feet. The wreck which lies at that location is that of a very old steamship. Exposed wreckage consists of an engine and boilers surrounded by low-lying debris. The vintage of the wreck can be interpreted from the fact that divers have found deadeyes partially buried in the sand. The presence of deadeyes implies that the ship must have been built in the early days of steam, when reliance upon machinery was not yet taken for granted. Steamships that were built as late as the 1880's were equipped with masts, sails, and rigging. Although the design of the hull may not have been the most efficient for sailing purposes, sails could help stabilize a ship in adverse or contrary winds, add speed to a slow-moving vessel whose engine was insufficient for propelling the hull against strong tidal currents, and provide motive force in the event of fuel depletion or a machinery breakdown.

Brass portholes found on the wreck appear to have been manufactured in the early stages of porthole evolution. A cut glass captain's decanter recovered by the author positively reeked of posh antiquity.

Near the so-called *Yankee* lies a wreck called the "Gloria and Doris." Captain Jay Porter named this wreck after two women who happened to be aboard his charter fishing boat (the *Jess-Lu*) on the day of the wreck's discovery (in the 1960's). "Gloria and Doris" has since been shortened to G & D because it is easier to pronounce. In 1994, John Lachenmeyer recovered from the G & D a dish on whose rim was displayed a shipping line flag. Bill Schell researched the flag and found that it was the logo of the Pittsburgh Steamship Company, the original owner of the *Yankee* when she plied the Great Lakes as the *German*. The discovery that the G & D was the *Yankee* sent a thrill through the wreck-diving community.

Much of the true *Yankee* is exposed. The wreck is circumscribed by a well-defined waist which is covered in only a few spots amidships. A section of the bow is intact with a slight list to port, and can be entered from behind. Abaft this section is a long field of debris with very little relief: generally one or two feet. A spare iron propeller lies flat in the sand. About one hundred feet abaft the bow is a break some ten to fifteen feet wide. Then there is more wreckage leading to two high boilers which lie side by side. Immediately abaft the boilers, the engine rises more than fifteen feet from the bottom. The fantail lies so low that neither the rudder nor the propeller can be seen.

Visibility generally exceeds forty feet. The depth is 110 feet.

The identification of the G & D as the *Yankee* has solved a long-standing mystery, but it has also created a new one: what is the identity of the wreck that was previously thought to be the *Yankee*? Hopefully time and continued exploration will tell.

SUGGESTED READING

Berg, Daniel (1990) *Wreck Valley Vol II*, Aqua Explorers, 980 Church Road, Baldwin, New York 11510.

Berg, Daniel & Denise (1993) *New Jersey Beach Diver*, Aqua Explorers, 980 Church Road, Baldwin, New York 11510.

Berman, Bruce D. (1972) *Encyclopedia of American Shipwrecks*, The Mariners Press, Boston, Massachusetts.

Burton, Hal (1973) *The Morro Castle: Tragedy at Sea*, Viking Press, New York.

Charles, Joan (1997) *Mid Atlantic Shipwreck Accounts to 1899*, privately printed by Joan Charles, 101 Madrid Drive, Hampton, Virginia 23669.

de Camp, Michael A. (1973) *Wreck Diving*, Petersen Publishing Company.

Downey, Leland Woolley (1983) *Broken Spars*, Brick Township Historical Society.

Gallagher, Thomas (1959) *Fire at Sea: the Story of the Morro Castle*, Rinehart & Company, New York.

Gentile, Gary (1995) *The Nautical Cyclopedia*, GGP, P.O. Box 57137, Philadelphia, PA 19111 ($20 postage paid).

Gentile, Gary (1989) *Track of the Gray Wolf*, Avon Books, New York, NY.

Keatts, Henry (1992) *Guide to Shipwreck Diving: New York & New Jersey*, Gulf Publishing Company, Houston, Texas.

Krotee, Walter and Richard (1965) *Shipwrecks off the New Jersey Coast*, privately printed.

Lonsdale, Adrian L. and Kaplan, H.R. (1964) *A Guide to Sunken Ships in American Waters*, Compass Publications.

New Jersey Department of Environmental Protection (1989) *A Guide to Fishing and Diving New Jersey's Artificial Reefs*, Marine Fisheries Administration, CN 400, Trenton, New Jersey.

Price, T.T. (1878) *Historical and Biographical Atlas of the New Jersey Coast*, Woolman & Ross, Philadelphia, Pennsylvania

Raguso, John N. (1992) *Atlantic Wrecks: Book One*, The Fisherman Library, 1620 Beaver Dam Road, Point Pleasant, New Jersey 08742.

Rattray, Jeanette Edwards (1955) *Perils of the Port of New York*, Dodd, Mead & Co.

Sachse, Julius Friedrich (1907) *The Wreck of the Ship New Era*, Pennsylvania German Society, Lancaster, Pennsylvania.

Sheard, Bradley (1991) *Beyond Sportdiving!*, Menasha Ridge Press, P.O. Box 43059, Birmingham, Alabama.

Sheard, Bradley (1998) *Lost Voyages*, Aqua Quest Publications, 486 Bayville Road, Locust Valley, New York 11560.

Thomas, Gordon, and Max Morgan Witts (1972) *Shipwreck: the Strange Fate of the Morro Castle*, Stein and Day, New York.

U.S. Hydrographic Office (1894) *Wrecks and Derelicts in the North Atlantic Ocean*, Government Printing Office.

LORAN NUMBERS - ALPHABETICAL

3 Fairs	26652.1	43605.2	BA Wreck	26874.7	43619.6
3 Sisters	26791.6	43642.1	Bacardi	26308.1	43310.6
6 Minute	26909.1	43149.7	Bad Bottom	26874.0	43180.0
7 Minute	26906.4	43024.7	Bald Eagle	26831.2	43640.3
12 Minute Piece	26844.6	43172.9	Bald Eagle	26061.6	43640.2
17 Fathoms	26889.0	43654.0	Ballast Stones	26813.0	42956.3
54 Fathom Wreck	26205.7	43183.4	Barge	26587.5	43659.8
59 Pounder	26632.4	43601.1	Barge	26883.2	43301.7
120 Lillian	26717.9	43079.4	Barge	26855.1	43134.1
120 Wreck	26873.4	43468.3	Barge #1	26530.0	43865.0
2nd Jump	27949.8	42842.1	Barge #2	26838.1	43538.6
A.C. Wescoat	26915.0	42962.8	Barge #3	26788.5	43716.9
A.H. Dumont	26872.1	43197.6	Barge #4	26870.4	43734.7
A.H. Dumont (pilot house)	26872.0	43197.7	Barge #5	26869.5	43738.5
AC Ridge	26942.0	43920.0	Barge #6	26737.0	43728.5
AC Wreck	26855.5	43113.5	Barge #7	26881.5	43728.5
Acara	26800.5	43750.5	Barnegat Light Reef	26892.3	43280.0
Ace In The Hole	26535.4	42872.7	Barnegat Light Reef	26891.0	43275.0
Across Wreck	26832.8	43550.1	Barnegat Ridge North	26785.0	43240.0
Adelle	26883.4	43478.2	Barnett	26926.8	43771.2
Adonis	26950.2	43598.8	Benson	26859.5	43566.9
Airplane	26855.6	43113.4	Bidevind	26357.6	43280.4
Airplane Engine	26922.6	43768.8	Big Mama	26900.5	42945.7
Akron	26726.7	43076.7	Big Ship	26315.9	43245.9
Akron (tail fin)	26724.9	43076.7	Big Wood	26828.8	43571.3
Alan Martin	26792.0	43482.4	Big Wreck	26742.0	43936.0
Algol	26795.0	43483.5	Billy D	26797.5	43481.7
Almirante	26915.0	43023.8	Blue Box	26814.7	43508.2
Ambrose Light	26910.0	43700.0	Blue Crown	26897.2	42948.1
Ambrose Wreck	26912.5	43703.0	Blue Fish	26812.8	42956.6
American	26896.5	42944.9	Boiler Wreck	26826.1	43089.1
American Oil	26964.3	42952.1	Bomb	26831.2	43620.6
Amity	26945.2	43497.3	Bonanza	26779.4	43363.5
Anastasia	26853.5	43359.0	Bone Ship	26921.5	43287.6
Anchor Chain	26847.7	43320.0	Bone Wreck	26886.7	43289.7
Annex	26891.0	43558.0	Boston	26910.4	42961.8
Antares	26894.0	43274.4	Brant Beach	26931.2	43187.1
Applegate	26877.4	42955.4	Brass Wreck	26917.9	43286.4
Aqua II	26872.5	43195.0	Brick Barge	26875.9	43245.4
Aqua II (barge)	26872.5	43194.7	Bridge Rubble	26906.2	43509.9
Arundo	26796.9	43534.8	Bridge Rubble	26910.6	43506.7
Arundo	26796.3	43534.0	Bridge Rubble	26910.5	43505.1
Arundo (engine)	26791.8	43514.7	Bridge Rubble	26909.5	43505.1
Asfalto	26831.2	43620.8	Bridge Rubble	26910.5	43504.4
Astra	26901.2	43104.5	Bridge Rubble	26911.3	43504.4
Atlantic Beach Reef	26870.6	43735.0	Bridge Rubble	26910.3	43503.7
Atlantic City Tug	26930.5	43061.5	Bridge Rubble	26911.8	43503.6
Atlantic Princess	26508.0	43294.0	Bridge Rubble	26910.4	43495.1
Austin W.	26705.9	43515.9	Broadcast	26752.2	43600.0
Avalon Shoals	27012.0	42848.0	Brunette	26916.4	43476.0
Axel Carlson Reef	26923.0	43470.0	Bumps	26865.5	43561.4
(3 Army Tanks)			Caddo	26890.4	43207.9
Ayuruoca	26842.3	43547.7	Cadet	26916.4	43475.8
B B Wreck	26934.3	43186.8	Caldwell Barge	26900.1	43155.4

Cannon Ball	26883.9	43207.6
Cannonball	26834.0	43207.8
Captain Ed Schmidiger	26918.0	43447.9
Captain Etzel	26907.3	43507.9
Car Float	26953.4	43013.5
Car Float	26992.2	42866.6
Car Float #52	26911.0	43500.7
Carg	26724.5	42963.4
Carlson II	26912.3	43497.6
Carolina	26530.5	42817.0
Cassoon	26895.6	43350.0
Cassoon	26864.1	43343.1
Cedar Creek Wreck	26921.8	43339.2
Chaparra	26847.6	43239.9
Charlemagne Tower, Jr.	26921.8	43339.2
Charles Morse	26507.5	43600.9
China Junk Wreck	27062.9	42866.7
Choapa	26863.4	43590.8
Chuck's New Piece	26909.7	42932.8
Coal Barge	26502.0	42918.0
Coal Barge #1	26932.3	43789.3
Coal Barge #2	26939.7	43793.7
Coal Barge #3	26535.0	42873.4
Coal Schooner	26860.0	43559.6
Coal Wreck	26796.4	43671.7
Coal Wreck (west)	26798.0	43713.2
Coimbra	26204.0	43576.3
Cole	26535.4	42872.7
Coleman Barge	26941.9	43642.4
Colleen	26917.9	43457.5
Collier	26928.2	42991.1
Concrete Rubble	26945.0	43653.0
Concrete Rubble	26945.0	43651.0
Concrete Rubble	26944.2	43650.2
Concrete Rubble	26944.0	43649.0
Concrete Rubble	26945.0	43649.0
Concrete Rubble	26943.0	43649.0
Concrete Rubble	26943.0	43647.0
Coney Island	26792.0	43481.3
Continent	26884.7	43637.4
Cornelius Hargraves	26854.8	43296.8
Corvallis	26538.3	43200.2
Crane	26853.5	43361.0
Crane Barge	26424.3	43516.1
Cranford (ferry)	26906.8	43503.3
Daghestan	26945.2	43497.4
Dan's Wreck	26937.1	42822.3
Darien	26961.5	42987.8
Dead Eye	26917.6	42941.5
Deck Barge	26911.1	43502.7
Deebold's Mountain	26781.3	43034.9
Delaware	26928.4	43467.5
Dodger	26617.9	43673.4
Double East	26894.4	43149.5
Dragger	26806.6	43250.6
Dredge	26957.4	43029.7

Dredge	27040.3	42824.6
Drumelzier	26674.0	43754.0
Dry Dock	26924.4	43126.2
Dry Dock Reef	26908.8	43506.8
Duke	26781.5	43737.0
Durley Chine	26308.1	43310.6
Eagle	26891.0	43531.0
East	26918.6	43150.5
East Ridge	26788.3	43267.3
Edna	26705.8	43516.0
Edna's Bottom	26629.1	43514.2
Edward H. Cole	26535.4	42872.7
Emerald Wreck	26873.5	43394.8
Eugene F. Moran	26936.1	43020.6
Eureka	26772.1	43600.0
Evelyn K	27050.4	42821.2
F.F. Clain	26859.8	43307.0
Fallon	26886.7	43266.5
Farms	26887.0	43595.0
Fatuk	26871.7	43196.1
Fifty-nine Pounder	26632.4	43601.1
Fingers	26661.0	43169.0
First Lady	26897.3	42943.3
Fisherman's Buoy Wreck	26919.9	43677.2
Florence	26680.6	43574.7
Fran S	26874.1	43733.8
Francis Bushey	26896.2	42950.0
Francis Perkins	26915.-	43369.-
Francis S. Bushey	26896.0	42948.7
G.A. Venturo	26908.8	43504.4
Galimore's Cayru	26724.5	42963.0
Galley	26788.0	43484.4
Gas Barge	26912.5	43492.4
George's Snag	26955.1	42834.0
Gloria	26895.9	43078.3
Gloria & Doris	26671.4	43574.4
Glory Wreck	26895.0	43078.0
Golden Eagle	26907.7	43511.2
Gong Grounds	26975.0	43748.0
Good Times	26873.1	43192.5
Goulandris	26853.9	43576.8
Governor Mansion	26926.4	43349.6
Governor Mansion	26918.1	43317.0
Great Egg Bell "GE"	26016.0	42975.0
Great Egg Reef	26956.0	42952.0
Great Egg Reef	26955.0	42949.5
Great Isaac	26840.9	43195.2
Great Lakes #78	26915.6	43683.3
Greek	26863.4	43590.8
Gulftrade (bow)	26887.7	43260.6
Gulftrade (stern)	26821.3	43318.3
Gun Boat	26609.4	43610.2
Gun Boat	26608.9	43609.6
Gunner's Hole	26889.1	42871.5
H C Jump	26895.6	43217.2
H C Lump Bell	26907.3	43222.3

H C Tank	26912.0	43241.7
Halfway	26894.5	43842.8
Hammies Junk Pile	26911.0	43306.1
Hang	26532.0	43568.0
Hang	26558.0	42916.0
Hang	26472.8	42915.0
Hang	26472.5	42914.9
Hang	26536.2	42853.7
Hankins	26884.5	43340.6
Happy Days	26674.9	43602.2
Haskell	26455.0	43163.0
Hebert	26621.3	43313.5
Hole	26872.8	43189.3
Holgate	26899.1	43153.1
Hooper Barge	26770.8	42977.9
Hornet	26934.2	43071.5
Humpty Dumpty	26795.0	43434.0
Hylton Castle	26569.4	43695.1
Iberia	26855.6	43736.0
Ida K	26855.1	43422.5
Immaculata	26801.8	43584.0
Imperial	26873.6	43395.0
Inshore Barge	26846.6	43212.8
Inshore Barge	27051.3	42851.7
Inshore Tug	26846.4	43213.4
Intact Bow	26877.7	43283.5
Ioannis P. Goulandris	26853.9	43576.8
Irene	26871.3	43359.1
Irma C	26661.2	43570.8
Isabel B. Wiley	26558.1	42914.1
Jacob M. Haskell	26455.0	43163.0
Jerry	26870.4	43197.5
Jessie C	26922.6	43101.4
Jewel	26722.9	43183.1
John Dobilas	26873.5	43195.6
Junior	26863.4	43590.8
Junk	27024.0	42894.4
Karen K	26903.0	43727.1
Kathy and Maria	27019.0	42907.1
Kennebec	26895.0	43078.0
Kiley B (trawler)	26908.9	43494.6
King Barge	26910.5	43193.4
Klondike	26914.0	43494.0
Klondike Rocks	26844.8	43473.1
Lana Carol	26859.9	43419.7
Larsen	26813.6	43547.0
Lemuel Burrows	26928.2	42991.1
Leonard Prather	26927.9	42991.0
Libra	27017.1	42907.5
Lightship	26599.0	43644.7
Lightship (WAL 505)	26903.5	43695.9
Lillian	26697.0	43419.4
Linda	26508.7	43601.2
Linda Snow	27019.5	42942.8
Linda Snow	27017.5	42942.3
Little Clam	27050.3	42821.3
Little Egg Bell "LE"	26953.0	43082.0
Little Egg Reef	26920.0	43100.0
Lizzie D.	26829.0	43696.3
Lobster Hole	26900.0	43970.0
Logwood	26856.4	43474.6
Low Barge	27023.3	42870.6
Macedonia	26941.7	43645.3
Magnolia	26853.2	43240.6
Maiden Creek	26198.8	43451.4
Mainship Boat Mold	26912.0	43492.6
Mako Mania	26794.7	43482.4
Manasquan R "2"	26944.5	43493.3
Manasquan Ridge	26891.0	43444.0
Manasquan Wreck	26945.2	43497.3
Margret	26901.1	43756.3
Maurice Tracy	26890.2	43359.0
Maurice Tracy (piece)	26891.4	43361.7
Metal Piece	26847.5	43320.2
Miah Maull Shoals	27238.0	42849.0
Middle	27034.4	42835.6
Mildred	26829.1	43290.0
Miog	26844.0	43546.3
Mohawk (Clyde liner)	26877.8	43440.2
Mohawk (Clyde liner)	26877.8	43439.6
Mohawk (north)	26875.7	43449.5
Mohawk (revenue cutter)	26867.6	43670.7
Mohawk (south)	26881.0	43424.7
Molasses Barge	26874.0	43195.1
Monofilament	26878.5	43602.7
Moran	26936.1	43020.6
Morania Abaco	26896.1	42948.1
Mountain	26781.2	43035.1
Mud	26967.2	42887.5
Mud Digger	26986.7	42986.7
Mud Hole	26755.0	43485.0
North Ridge	26797.3	43286.7
North Ridge	26797.3	43286.3
Northeast Boiler	26793.2	43112.8
Northeast of Tower	26308.7	43210.9
Northeast of Varanger	26721.5	42852.8
Northeast Wreck	26897.1	43287.4
Northwest Barge	26878.9	43925.3
Northwest Barge	26883.2	43301.7
Northwest Barge	26882.8	43301.3
Northwest Barge	26881.9	43293.2
Number 9	26889.8	43275.0
OC Reef (towers)	27015.0	43907.0
Ocean City Reef	27022.0	42900.0
Ocean Wreck Divers I	26895.8	43152.9
Ocean Wreck Divers III	26914.1	43435.1
Ocean Wreck Divers IV	26908.5	43506.7
Offshore Barge	26847.6	43239.9
Offshore Barge	26802.3	43189.2
Offshore Oil	26955.1	42943.6
Offshore Piece #1	26801.4	43190.2
Offshore Piece #2	26802.4	43191.3

Offshore Tug	26831.6	43189.1		Salem	27008.4	42863.3
Oil Wreck	26842.3	43547.7		Sam Berman	26792.8	43482.9
Oklahoma (stern)	26717.9	43079.4		Sambo (tug)	26874.7	43619.6
Oregon	26453.2	43676.9		San Diego	26543.3	43692.9
Park City (tug)	26933.2	43461.2		San Jose	26877.5	42955.4
Patrice McAllister	26930.5	43061.5		San Saba (bow)	26853.8	43239.9
Patris	26930.2	43061.1		San Saba (stern)	26853.2	43240.6
Pauline Marie	26895.4	42944.0		Sandy Hook "R" 2	26959.0	43704.0
Pentland Firth	26921.2	43682.8		Sandy Hook (pilot boat)	26908.3	43700.4
Pentland Firth	26923.0	43682.4		Scallop Barge	26560.0	43860.5
Pentland Firth	26923.3	43682.4		Scallop Ridge	26930.0	43735.0
Pentland Firth	26921.2	43682.0		Schooner	26915.3	43499.7
Persephone	26897.1	43287.0		Schooner (iron wheels)	26672.7	43559.2
Pet Wreck	26944.2	43005.1		Sea Girt Reef	26905.0	43510.0
Phillips Wreck	26915.6	43683.3		Sea Girt Wreck	26860.5	43471.6
Pig Iron	26942.4	43022.8		Sea Hag	26787.2	43286.7
Pilot Boat	26908.3	43700.4		Sea Isle	27042.0	42868.0
Pinnacle	26896.8	43127.4		Second Jump	27949.8	42842.1
Pinta	26880.5	43563.5		Seven Minute	26906.4	43024.7
Pliny	26949.2	43579.8		Seventeen Fathoms	26889.0	43654.0
Post Boat Mold	27016.4	42906.2		Shark River Inlet "S1"	26943.0	43543.0
Post Boat Mold	27023.4	42898.1		Shaw's	26937.8	42831.0
Post Boat Mold	27024.7	42897.0		Shirley Ann	26875.5	43194.1
Punk Grounds	27195.0	42830.0		Shookus	26717.9	43079.4
Queen Mary	26873.3	43193.3		Shrewsbury Rock	26950.0	43635.0
(cabin cruiser)				Six Minute	26909.1	43149.7
R.P. Resor	26638.3	43277.2		Skippy	26609.9	43609.7
Railroad Barge	26910.4	43499.2		Slabs	26895.1	42982.3
RC Mohawk	26867.6	43670.7		Small Metal Wreck	26889.3	42870.9
Red Tank	26927.0	43160.8		Small Tanker	26806.9	43504.3
Reef	26875.0	43195.0		Snag	26853.2	43240.5
Reggie	26594.3	43659.2		Sommerstad	26425.0	43456.1
Relief (lightship)	26903.5	43695.9		South Piece	26894.1	43150.2
Remedios Pascual	26921.5	43287.6		South Ridge Wreck	26779.3	43623.7
Resor	26638.3	43277.2		Southeast of Oil	26806.9	43540.4
Restorer	26906.8	43509.0		Southeast Wreck	26887.8	43260.5
Revenue Cutter	26867.6	43670.7		Southern Lillian	26717.9	43079.4
Reynolds	26989.8	43005.9		Southwest Barge	26853.2	43240.6
Rhino/100 Tires	26897.8	43155.8		Spanish Steamer	26854.3	43285.2
Rhonde Joyce II	26910.9	43494.9		Spanish Wreck	26854.3	43285.2
Ridge Wreck	26934.5	43071.7		Spartan	26910.7	43491.2
Riggy	26906.6	43449.4		St. Rita	26468.0	42912.2
Rio Tercero	26233.9	42963.7		Stacks Reef	26979.5	43965.3
Rio Tercero	26246.9	42963.6		Stainless Steel Drums	26912.1	43497.6
Rockaway Reef	26926.0	43748.0		Starcraft	26898.2	43154.1
Rockland County	26905.3	43508.5		Steamer #1	26424.9	43455.7
Rockland County	26905.5	43508.2		Steamer #2	26530.5	42817.0
Roda	26741.3	43756.7		Steamer #3	26932.4	43707.0
Rosks	26978.8	42880.8		Steamer #135	26724.5	42963.4
Rothenback II	26955.4	42950.0		Steel Wreck	26794.6	43687.3
Rum Runner	26829.0	43696.3		Stolt Dagali	26787.6	43484.4
Rump	26918.9	43435.4		Stone Barge	26782.5	43728.2
Rusland	26950.2	43598.8		Stone Beds	26990.0	42900.0
Sachem	26912.8	43171.0		Stork's Reef	26979.4	42965.5
Sachem Snags	26908.6	43170.2		Sub	26890.5	43208.0
Sailing Ship	26908.0	43243.4		Sub Chaser	26935.0	43649.0

Sumner	26916.8	43271.7	Twin Anchors	26796.4	43533.9
Swanika	26978.9	42968.6	Two Story Wreck	26915.6	43683.3
Swenson Barge I	26911.1	43502.7	U-869	26460.6	43145.2
Swenson Barge II	26911.8	43493.5	U-Who?	26460.3	43144.9
Tanker	26202.8	43576.8	Unidentified	26913.0	43727.1
Tanker (stern)	26803.0	43492.0	Unidentified	26722.5	43622.5
Tar Pit	26894.5	43151.9	Unidentified	26671.1	43557.7
Tarantula	26609.4	43610.2	Unknown	26859.5	43566.4
Tarantula	26608.9	43609.7	Unknown	26883.6	43301.6
Tea Wreck	26800.5	43750.5	Unknown	26492.5	42951.1
Teaser	26913.7	43005.5	USS Turner	26936.4	43725.5
Teaser	27015.3	42884.4	V.L. Keegan	26943.0	43647.1
Ted's Cod Wreck	26793.3	43112.8	VHFC (cutter)	26896.2	43153.7
Teddy Weeks Wreck	26492.5	42951.0	Vicki-Pat	26915.1	42959.7
Texas Tower #4	26313.5	43266.6	Victory	26812.4	43743.5
Texel	26536.4	42854.1	Viking Hull Molds	26900.6	43155.6
Texel	26537.2	42853.6	Viking/50 Tires	26900.6	43153.6
The Fisherman	26905.8	43508.3	Viking/80 Tires	26900.5	43153.4
Thomas Hebert	26621.3	43313.5	Virginia	26425.0	43456.1
Three Fairs	26652.1	43605.2	Vizcaya	26854.3	43285.2
Three Sisters	26791.6	43642.1	Walcott	26518.7	43713.0
Tin Can Grounds	26972.0	43740.0	Wayne	27033.9	42842.2
Tin Wreck	26945.4	43496.8	Weeks 218	26875.7	43196.5
Tire Units (380)	26897.8	43154.9	Wellington	26932.8	43081.1
Tire Units (500)	26898.3	43155.9	West Wreck	26205.2	43183.0
Tires (500)	26894.8	42943.2	Western World	26947.0	43524.0
Tires (100)	26872.3	43197.5	Wiley	26558.1	42914.1
Tires (100)	27024.4	42899.2	William R. Farrell	26912.2	43240.4
Tires (125)	26875.7	43194.1	Winneconne	26492.5	42951.0
Tires (150)	26896.5	43153.3	Wm. R. Farrell	26912.2	43240.7
Tires (250)	26903.3	43153.9	Wm. R. Farrell	26912.2	43240.4
Tires (250)	27021.3	42901.8	Wood Barge	26803.0	43492.0
Tires (26)	26871.6	43199.1	Wood Wreck	26854.0	43486.0
Tires (27)	26896.0	43156.5	Wreck	26456.8	43126.8
Tires (375)	26874.1	43196.4	Wreck	26560.0	42915.0
Tires (375)	27025.0	42896.5	Wreck #1	26349.0	43268.0
Tires (460)	27017.9	42903.9	Wreck #2	26456.7	43234.7
Tires (475)	27025.7	42897.0	Wreck #3	26650.2	43604.4
Tires (50)	26900.6	43155.6	Wreck #5	26279.0	43117.0
Tires (500)	26903.3	43155.8	Wreck #6	26105.0	43492.0
Tires (565)	27023.6	42897.9	Wreck #7	26853.5	43550.9
Tires (570)	27017.0	42905.0	Wreck #8	26851.1	43548.8
Tolten	26815.9	43360.1	Wreck #9	26859.7	43555.3
Tolten Lump	26813.0	43336.0	Wreck #10	26771.2	43557.7
Tower	27016.8	42907.6	Wreck #11	26722.5	43622.5
Tower	27020.8	42900.7	Wreck #12	26913.0	43717.1
Tower & Tower	27020.3	42900.7	Wreck (north)	26797.0	43363.5
Tower/100 Tires	27018.1	42904.9	Wreck (south)	26755.5	43185.0
Tower/150 Tires	27020.3	42902.7	X #1	26848.7	43553.1
Townsend Inlet "4A"	27056.0	42864.0	X #2	26676.7	43580.5
Tug	26846.4	43213.3	X #3	26865.5	43526.4
Tug Boat	26842.1	43539.9	X #4	26855.0	43497.0
Tug Boat	27008.4	42863.3	X #5	26425.0	43456.8
Tug Boat #2	26881.5	43737.3	Yankee (false)	26609.5	43592.0
Turner	26936.4	43725.5	Yankee (true)	26671.4	43574.4
Twelve Minute Piece	26844.6	43172.9	Yellow Flag	26861.5	43230.6

LORAN NUMBERS - DESCENDING 4 LINE

Lobster Hole	26900.0	43970.0	Great Lakes #78	26915.6	43683.3
Stacks Reef	26979.5	43965.3	Phillips Wreck	26915.6	43683.3
Big Wreck	26742.0	43936.0	Two Story Wreck	26915.6	43683.3
Northwest Barge	26878.9	43925.3	Pentland Firth	26921.2	43682.8
AC Ridge	26942.0	43920.0	Pentland Firth	26923.0	43682.4
OC Reef (towers)	27015.0	43907.0	Pentland Firth	26923.3	43682.4
Barge #1	26530.0	43865.0	Pentland Firth	26921.2	43682.0
Scallop Barge	26560.0	43860.5	Fisherman's Buoy Wreck	26919.9	43677.2
Halfway	26894.5	43842.8	Oregon	26453.2	43676.9
Coal Barge #2	26939.7	43793.7	Dodger	26617.9	43673.4
Coal Barge #1	26932.3	43789.3	Coal Wreck	26796.4	43671.7
Barnett	26926.8	43771.2	Mohawk (revenue cutter)	26867.6	43670.7
Airplane Engine	26922.6	43768.8	RC Mohawk	26867.6	43670.7
Roda	26741.3	43756.7	Revenue Cutter	26867.6	43670.7
Margret	26901.1	43756.3	Barge	26587.5	43659.8
Drumelzier	26674.0	43754.0	Reggie	26594.3	43659.2
Acara	26800.5	43750.5	17 Fathoms	26889.0	43654.0
Tea Wreck	26800.5	43750.5	Seventeen Fathoms	26889.0	43654.0
Gong Grounds	26975.0	43748.0	Concrete Rubble	26945.0	43653.0
Rockaway Reef	26926.0	43748.0	Concrete Rubble	26945.0	43651.0
Victory	26812.4	43743.5	Concrete Rubble	26944.2	43650.2
Tin Can Grounds	26972.0	43740.0	Concrete Rubble	26944.0	43649.0
Barge #5	26869.5	43738.5	Concrete Rubble	26945.0	43649.0
Tug Boat #2	26881.5	43737.3	Concrete Rubble	26943.0	43649.0
Duke	26781.5	43737.0	Sub Chaser	26935.0	43649.0
Iberia	26855.6	43736.0	V.L. Keegan	26943.0	43647.1
Atlantic Beach Reef	26870.6	43735.0	Concrete Rubble	26943.0	43647.0
Scallop Ridge	26930.0	43735.0	Macedonia	26941.7	43645.3
Barge #4	26870.4	43734.7	Lightship	26599.0	43644.7
Fran S	26874.1	43733.8	Coleman Barge	26941.9	43642.4
Barge #6	26737.0	43728.5	3 Sisters	26791.6	43642.1
Barge #7	26881.5	43728.5	Three Sisters	26791.6	43642.1
Stone Barge	26782.5	43728.2	Bald Eagle	26831.2	43640.3
Karen K	26903.0	43727.1	Bald Eagle	26061.6	43640.2
Unidentified	26913.0	43727.1	Continent	26884.7	43637.4
Turner	26936.4	43725.5	Shrewsbury Rock	26950.0	43635.0
USS Turner	26936.4	43725.5	South Ridge Wreck	26779.3	43623.7
Wreck #12	26913.0	43717.1	Unidentified	26722.5	43622.5
Barge #3	26788.5	43716.9	Wreck #11	26722.5	43622.5
Coal Wreck (west)	26798.0	43713.2	Asfalto	26831.2	43620.8
Walcott	26518.7	43713.0	Bomb	26831.2	43620.6
Steamer #3	26932.4	43707.0	BA Wreck	26874.7	43619.6
Sandy Hook "R" 2	26959.0	43704.0	Sambo (tug)	26874.7	43619.6
Ambrose Wreck	26912.5	43703.0	Gun Boat	26609.4	43610.2
Pilot Boat	26908.3	43700.4	Tarantula	26609.4	43610.2
Sandy Hook (pilot boat)	26908.3	43700.4	Skippy	26609.9	43609.7
Ambrose Light	26910.0	43700.0	Tarantula	26608.9	43609.7
Lizzie D.	26829.0	43696.3	Gun Boat	26608.9	43609.6
Rum Runner	26829.0	43696.3	3 Fairs	26652.1	43605.2
Lightship (WAL 505)	26903.5	43695.9	Three Fairs	26652.1	43605.2
Relief (lightship)	26903.5	43695.9	Wreck #3	26650.2	43604.4
Hylton Castle	26594.4	43695.1	Monofilament	26878.5	43602.7
San Diego	26543.3	43692.9	Happy Days	26674.9	43602.2
Steel Wreck	26794.6	43687.3	Linda	26508.7	43601.2

59 Pounder	26632.4	43601.1	Arundo (engine)	26791.8	43514.7
Fifty-nine Pounder	26632.4	43601.1	Edna's Bottom	26629.1	43514.2
Charles Morse	26507.5	43600.9	Golden Eagle	26907.7	43511.2
Broadcast	26752.2	43600.0	Sea Girt Reef	26905.0	43510.0
Eureka	26772.1	43600.0	Bridge Rubble	26906.2	43509.9
Adonis	26950.2	43598.8	Restorer	26906.8	43509.0
Rusland	26950.2	43598.8	Rockland County	26905.3	43508.5
Farms	26887.0	43595.0	The Fisherman	26905.8	43508.3
Yankee (false)	26609.5	43592.0	Blue Box	26814.7	43508.2
Choapa	26863.4	43590.8	Rockland County	26905.5	43508.2
Greek	26863.4	43590.8	Captain Etzel	26907.3	43507.9
Junior	26863.4	43590.8	Dry Dock Reef	26908.8	43506.8
Immaculata	26801.8	43584.0	Bridge Rubble	26910.6	43506.7
X #2	26676.7	43580.5	Ocean Wreck Divers IV	26908.5	43506.7
Pliny	26949.2	43579.8	Bridge Rubble	26910.5	43505.1
Goulandris	26853.9	43576.8	Bridge Rubble	26909.5	43505.1
Ioannis P. Goulandris	26853.9	43576.8	Bridge Rubble	26910.5	43504.4
Tanker	26202.8	43576.8	Bridge Rubble	26911.3	43504.4
Coimbra	26204.0	43576.3	G.A. Venturo	26908.8	43504.4
Florence	26680.6	43574.7	Small Tanker	26806.9	43504.3
Yankee (true)	26671.4	43574.4	Bridge Rubble	26910.3	43503.7
Gloria & Doris	26671.4	43574.4	Bridge Rubble	26911.8	43503.6
Big Wood	26828.8	43571.3	Cranford (ferry)	26906.8	43503.3
Irma C	26661.2	43570.8	Deck Barge	26911.1	43502.7
Hang	26532.0	43568.0	Swenson Barge I	26911.1	43502.7
Benson	26859.5	43566.9	Car Float #52	26911.0	43500.7
Unknown	26859.5	43566.4	Schooner	26915.3	43499.7
Pinta	26880.5	43563.5	Railroad Barge	26910.4	43499.2
Bumps	26865.5	43561.4	Carlson II	26912.3	43497.6
Coal Schooner	26860.0	43559.6	Stainless Steel Drums	26912.1	43497.6
Schooner (iron wheels)	26672.7	43559.2	Daghestan	26945.2	43497.4
Annex	26891.0	43558.0	Amity	26945.2	43497.3
Unidentified	26671.1	43557.7	Manasquan Wreck	26945.2	43497.3
Wreck #10	26771.2	43557.7	X #4	26855.0	43497.0
Wreck #9	26859.7	43555.3	Tin Wreck	26945.4	43496.8
X #1	26848.7	43553.1	Bridge Rubble	26910.4	43495.1
Wreck #7	26853.5	43550.9	Rhonde Joyce II	26910.9	43494.9
Across Wreck	26832.8	43550.1	Kiley B (trawler)	26908.9	43494.6
Wreck #8	26851.1	43548.8	Klondike	26914.0	43494.0
Ayuruoca	26842.3	43547.7	Swenson Barge II	26911.8	43493.5
Oil Wreck	26842.3	43547.7	Manasquan R "2"	26944.5	43493.3
Larsen	26813.6	43547.0	Mainship Boat Mold	26912.0	43492.6
Miog	26844.0	43546.3	Gas Barge	26912.5	43492.4
Shark River Inlet "S1"	26943.0	43543.0	Tanker (stern)	26803.0	43492.0
Southeast of Oil	26806.9	43540.4	Wood Barge	26803.0	43492.0
Tug Boat	26842.1	43539.9	Wreck #6	26105.0	43492.0
Barge #2	26838.1	43538.6	Spartan	26910.7	43491.2
Arundo	26796.9	43534.8	Wood Wreck	26854.0	43486.0
Arundo	26796.3	43534.0	Mud Hole	26755.0	43485.0
Twin Anchors	26796.4	43533.9	Galley	26788.0	43484.4
Eagle	26891.0	43531.0	Stolt Dagali	26787.6	43484.4
X #3	26865.5	43526.4	Algol	26795.0	43483.5
Western World	26947.0	43524.0	Sam Berman	26792.8	43482.9
Crane Barge	26424.3	43516.1	Alan Martin	26792.0	43482.4
Edna	26705.8	43516.0	Mako Mania	26794.7	43482.4
Austin W.	26705.9	43515.9	Billy D	26797.5	43481.7

Coney Island	26792.0	43481.3	Durley Chine	26308.1	43310.6
Adelle	26883.4	43478.2	F.F. Clain	26859.8	43307.0
Brunette	26916.4	43476.0	Hammies Junk Pile	26911.0	43306.1
Cadet	26916.4	43475.8	Barge	26883.2	43301.7
Logwood	26856.4	43474.6	Northwest Barge	26883.2	43301.7
Klondike Rocks	26844.8	43473.1	Unknown	26883.6	43301.6
Sea Girt Wreck	26860.5	43471.6	Northwest Barge	26882.8	43301.3
Axel Carlson Reef	26923.0	43470.0	Cornelius Hargraves	26854.8	43296.8
(3 Army Tanks)			Atlantic Princess	26508.0	43294.0
120 Wreck	26873.4	43468.3	Northwest Barge	26881.9	43293.2
Delaware	26928.4	43467.5	Mildred	26829.1	43290.0
Park City (tug)	26933.2	43461.2	Bone Wreck	26886.7	43289.7
Colleen	26917.9	43457.5	Bone Ship	26921.5	43287.6
X #5	26425.0	43456.8	Remedios Pascual	26921.5	43287.6
Sommerstad	26425.0	43456.1	Northeast Wreck	26897.1	43287.4
Virginia	26425.0	43456.1	Persephone	26897.1	43287.0
Steamer #1	26424.9	43455.7	North Ridge	26797.3	43286.7
Maiden Creek	26198.8	43451.4	Sea Hag	26787.2	43286.7
Mohawk (north)	26875.7	43449.5	Brass Wreck	26917.9	43286.4
Riggy	26906.6	43449.4	North Ridge	26797.3	43286.3
Captain Ed Schmiciger	26918.0	43447.9	Spanish Steamer	26854.3	43285.2
Manasquan Ridge	26891.0	43444.0	Spanish Wreck	26854.3	43285.2
Mohawk (Clyde liner)	26877.8	43440.2	Vizcaya	26854.3	43285.2
Mohawk (Clyde liner)	26877.8	43439.6	Intact Bow	26877.7	43283.5
Rump	26918.9	43435.4	Bidevind	26357.6	43280.4
Ocean Wreck Divers III	26914.1	43435.1	Barnegat Light Reef	26892.3	43280.0
Humpty Dumpty	26795.0	43434.0	R.P. Resor	26638.3	43277.2
Mohawk (south)	26881.0	43424.7	Resor	26638.3	43277.2
Ida K	26855.1	43422.5	Barnegat Light Reef	26891.0	43275.0
Lana Carol	26859.9	43419.7	Number 9	26889.8	43275.0
Lillian	26697.0	43419.4	Antares	26894.0	43274.4
Imperial	26873.6	43395.0	Sumner	26916.8	43271.7
Emerald Wreck	26873.5	43394.8	Wreck #1	26349.0	43268.0
Francis Perkins	26915.-	43369.-	East Ridge	26788.3	43267.3
Bonanza	26779.4	43363.5	Texas Tower #4	26313.5	43266.6
Wreck (north)	26797.0	43363.5	Fallon	26886.7	43266.0
Maurice Tracy (piece)	26891.4	43361.7	Gulftrade (bow)	26887.7	43260.6
Crane	26853.5	43361.0	Southeast Wreck	26887.8	43260.5
Tolten	26815.9	43360.1	Dragger	26806.6	43250.6
Irene	26871.3	43359.1	Big Ship	26315.9	43245.9
Maurice Tracy	26890.2	43359.0	Brick Barge	26875.9	43245.4
Anastasia	26853.5	43359.0	Sailing Ship	26908.0	43243.4
Cassoon	26895.6	43350.0	H C Tank	26912.0	43241.7
Governor Mansion	26926.4	43349.6	Wm. R. Farrell	26912.2	43240.7
Cassoon	26864.1	43343.1	Magnolia	26853.2	43240.6
Hankins	26884.5	43340.6	San Saba (stern)	26853.2	43240.6
Cedar Creek Wreck	26921.8	43339.2	Southwest Barge	26853.2	43240.6
Charlemagne Tower, Jr.	26921.8	43339.2	Snag	26853.2	43240.5
Tolten Lump	26813.0	43336.0	William R. Farrell	26912.2	43240.4
Metal Piece	26847.5	43320.2	Wm. R. Farrell	26912.2	43240.4
Anchor Chain	26847.7	43320.0	Barnegat Ridge North	26785.0	43240.0
Gulftrade (stern)	26821.3	43318.3	Chaparra	26847.6	43239.9
Governor Mansion	26918.1	43317.0	Offshore Barge	26847.6	43239.9
Hebert	26621.3	43313.5	San Saba (bow)	26853.8	43239.9
Thomas Hebert	26621.3	43313.5	Wreck #2	26456.7	43234.7
Bacardi	26308.1	43310.6	Yellow Flag	26861.5	43230.6

H C Lump Bell	26907.3	43222.3
H C Jump	26895.6	43217.2
Inshore Tug	26846.4	43213.4
Tug	26846.4	43213.3
Inshore Barge	26846.6	43212.8
Northeast of Tower	26308.7	43210.9
Sub	26890.5	43208.0
Caddo	26890.4	43207.9
Cannonball	26834.0	43207.8
Cannon Ball	26883.9	43207.6
Corvallis	26538.3	43200.2
Tires (26)	26871.6	43199.1
A.H. Dumont (pilot house)	26872.0	43197.7
A.H. Dumont	26872.1	43197.6
Jerry	26870.4	43197.5
Tires (100)	26872.3	43197.5
Weeks 218	26875.7	43196.5
Tires (375)	26874.1	43196.4
Fatuk	26871.7	43196.1
John Dobilas	26873.5	43195.6
Great Isaac	26840.9	43195.2
Molasses Barge	26874.0	43195.1
Aqua II	26872.5	43195.0
Reef	26875.0	43195.0
Aqua II (barge)	26872.5	43194.7
Shirley Ann	26875.5	43194.1
Tires (125)	26875.7	43194.1
King Barge	26910.5	43193.4
Queen Mary	26873.3	43193.3
(cabin cruiser)		
Good Times	26873.1	43192.5
Offshore Piece #2	26802.4	43191.3
Offshore Piece #1	26801.4	43190.2
Hole	26872.8	43189.3
Offshore Barge	26802.3	43189.2
Offshore Tug	26831.6	43189.1
Brant Beach	26931.2	43187.1
B B Wreck	26934.3	43186.8
Wreck (south)	26755.5	43185.0
54 Fathom Wreck	26205.7	43183.4
Jewel	26722.9	43183.1
West Wreck	26205.2	43183.0
Bad Bottom	26874.0	43180.0
12 Minute Piece	26844.6	43172.9
Twelve Minute Piece	26844.6	43172.9
Sachem	26912.8	43171.0
Sachem Snags	26908.6	43170.2
Fingers	26661.0	43169.0
Haskell	26455.0	43163.0
Jacob M. Haskell	26455.0	43163.0
Red Tank	26927.0	43160.8
Tires (27)	26896.0	43156.5
Tire Units (500)	26898.3	43155.9
Rhino/100 Tires	26897.8	43155.8
Tires (500)	26903.3	43155.8
Tires (50)	26900.6	43155.6

Viking Hull Molds	26900.6	43155.6
Caldwell Barge	26900.1	43155.4
Tire Units (380)	26897.8	43154.9
Starcraft	26898.2	43154.1
Tires (250)	26903.3	43153.9
VHFC (cutter)	26896.2	43153.7
Viking/50 Tires	26900.6	43153.6
Viking/80 Tires	26900.5	43153.4
Tires (150)	26896.5	43153.3
Holgate	26899.1	43153.1
Ocean Wreck Divers I	26895.8	43152.9
Tar Pit	26894.5	43151.9
East	26918.6	43150.5
South Piece	26894.1	43150.2
6 Minute	26909.1	43149.7
Six Minute	26909.1	43149.7
Double East	26894.4	43149.5
U-869	26460.6	43145.2
U-Who?	26460.3	43144.9
Barge	26855.1	43134.1
Pinnacle	26896.8	43127.4
Wreck	26456.8	43126.8
Dry Dock	26924.4	43126.2
Wreck #5	26279.0	43117.0
AC Wreck	26855.5	43113.5
Airplane	26855.6	43113.4
Northeast Boiler	26793.2	43112.8
Ted's Cod Wreck	26793.3	43112.8
Astra	26901.2	43104.5
Jessie C	26922.6	43101.4
Little Egg Reef	26920.0	43100.0
Boiler Wreck	26826.1	43089.1
Little Egg Bell "LE"	26953.0	43082.0
Wellington	26932.8	43081.1
120 Lillian	26717.9	43079.4
Oklahoma (stern)	26717.9	43079.4
Shookus	26717.9	43079.4
Southern Lillian	26717.9	43079.4
Gloria	26895.9	43078.3
Glory Wreck	26895.0	43078.0
Kennebec	26895.0	43078.0
Akron	26726.7	43076.7
Akron (tail fin)	26724.9	43076.7
Ridge Wreck	26934.5	43071.7
Hornet	26934.2	43071.5
Atlantic City Tug	26930.5	43061.5
Patrice McAllister	26930.5	43061.5
Patris	26930.2	43061.1
Mountain	26781.2	43035.1
Deebold's Mountain	26781.3	43034.9
Dredge	26957.4	43029.7
7 Minute	26906.4	43024.7
Seven Minute	26906.4	43024.7
Almirante	26915.0	43023.8
Pig Iron	26942.4	43022.8
Eugene F. Moran	26936.1	43020.6

Moran	26936.1	43020.6	Tower	27016.8	42907.6
Car Float	26953.4	43013.5	Libra	27017.1	42907.5
Reynolds	26989.8	43005.9	Kathy and Maria	27019.0	42907.1
Teaser	26913.7	43005.5	Post Boat Mold	27016.4	42906.2
Pet Wreck	26944.2	43005.1	Tires (570)	27017.0	42905.0
Collier	26928.2	42991.1	Tower/100 Tires	27018.1	42904.9
Lemuel Burrows	26928.2	42991.1	Tires (460)	27017.9	42903.9
Leonard Prather	26927.9	42991.0	Tower/150 Tires	27020.3	42902.7
Darien	26961.5	42987.8	Tires (250)	27021.3	42901.8
Mud Digger	26986.7	42986.7	Tower	27020.8	42900.7
Slabs	26895.1	42982.3	Tower & Tower	27020.3	42900.7
Hooper Barge	26770.8	42977.9	Ocean City Reef	27022.0	42900.0
Great Egg Bell "GE"	26016.0	42975.0	Stone Beds	26990.0	42900.0
Swanika	26978.9	42968.6	Tires (100)	27024.4	42899.2
Stork's Reef	26979.4	42965.5	Post Boat Mold	27023.4	42898.1
Rio Tercero	26233.9	42963.7	Tires (565)	27023.6	42897.9
Rio Tercero	26246.9	42963.6	Post Boat Mold	27024.7	42897.0
Carg	26724.5	42963.4	Tires (475)	27025.7	42897.0
Steamer #135	26724.5	42963.4	Tires (375)	27025.0	42896.5
Galimore's Cayru	26724.5	42963.0	Junk	27024.0	42894.4
A.C. Wescoat	26915.0	42962.8	Mud	26967.2	42887.5
Boston	26910.4	42961.8	Teaser	27015.3	42884.4
Vicki-Pat	26915.1	42959.7	Rosks	26978.8	42880.8
Blue Fish	26812.8	42956.6	Coal Barge #3	26535.0	42873.4
Ballast Stones	26813.0	42956.3	Ace In The Hole	26535.4	42872.7
Applegate	26877.4	42955.4	Cole	26535.4	42872.7
San Jose	26877.5	42955.4	Edward H. Cole	26535.4	42872.7
American Oil	26964.3	42952.1	Gunner's Hole	26889.1	42871.5
Great Egg Reef	26956.0	42952.0	Small Metal Wreck	26889.3	42870.9
Unknown	26492.5	42951.1	Low Barge	27023.3	42870.6
Teddy Weeks Wreck	26492.5	42951.0	Sea Isle	27042.0	42868.0
Winneconne	26492.5	42951.0	China Junk Wreck	27062.9	42866.7
Francis Bushey	26896.2	42950.0	Car Float	26992.2	42866.6
Rothenback II	26955.4	42950.0	Townsend Inlet "4A"	27056.0	42864.0
Great Egg Reef	26955.0	42949.5	Salem	27008.4	42863.3
Francis S. Bushey	26896.0	42948.7	Tug Boat	27008.4	42863.3
Blue Crown	26897.2	42948.1	Texel	26536.4	42854.1
Morania Abaco	26896.1	42948.1	Hang	26536.2	42853.7
Big Mama	26900.5	42945.7	Texel	26537.2	42853.6
American	26896.5	42944.9	Northeast of Varanger	26721.5	42852.8
Pauline Marie	26895.4	42944.0	Inshore Barge	27051.3	42851.7
Offshore Oil	26955.1	42943.6	Miah Maull Shoals	27238.0	42849.0
First Lady	26897.3	42943.3	Avalon Shoals	27012.0	42848.0
Tires (500)	26894.8	42943.2	Wayne	27033.9	42842.2
Linda Snow	27019.5	42942.8	2nd Jump	27949.8	42842.1
Linda Snow	27017.5	42942.3	Second Jump	27949.8	42842.1
Dead Eye	26917.6	42941.5	Middle	27034.4	42835.6
Chuck's New Piece	26909.7	42932.8	George's Snag	26955.1	42834.0
Coal Barge	26502.0	42918.0	Shaw's	26937.8	42831.0
Hang	26558.0	42916.0	Punk Grounds	27195.0	42830.0
Hang	26472.8	42915.0	Dredge	27040.3	42824.6
Wreck	26560.0	42915.0	Dan's Wreck	26937.1	42822.3
Hang	26472.5	42914.9	Little Clam	27050.3	42821.3
Isabel B. Wiley	26558.1	42914.1	Evelyn K	27050.4	42821.2
Wiley	26558.1	42914.1	Carolina	26530.5	42817.0
St. Rita	26468.0	42912.2	Steamer #2	26530.5	42817.0

Books by the Author
Fiction

Vietnam
Lonely Conflict

Science Fiction
Entropy
Return to Mars

Action/Adventure
Memory Lane
Mind Set

Silent Autumn
The Time Dragons Trilogy
A Time for Dragons

Supernatural
The Lurking

Dragons Past
No Future for Dragons

Nonfiction

Advanced Wreck Diving Guide
Ultimate Wreck Diving Guide

Track of the Gray Wolf
Shipwrecks of New Jersey

Available (postage paid) from:

GARY GENTILE PRODUCTIONS
P.O. Box 57137
Philadelphia, PA 19111

Nonfiction

$25	*Andrea Doria: Dive to an Era* (hard cover)
$20	*The Nautical Cyclopedia*
$20	*USS San Diego: the Last Armored Cruiser*
$20	*Wreck Diving Adventures*
$20	*Primary Wreck Diving Guide*
$30	*The Technical Diving Handbook*

Civil War ironclad *Monitor*

$25	Book (hard cover) *Ironclad Legacy: Battles of the USS Monitor*r
$25	Videotape (VHS or PAL): *The Battle for the USS Monitor*

The *Lusitania* Controversies (hard covers)

(These two volumes cover the evolution of wreck-diving from 1955 to 1995)

$25	*Book One: Atrocity of War and a Wreck-Diving History*
$25	*Book Two: Dangerous Descents into Shipwrecks and Law*

The Popular Dive Guide Series

$20	*Shipwrecks of New York*
$20	*Shipwrecks of New Jersey: North*
$20	*Shipwrecks of Delaware and Maryland*
$20	*Shipwrecks of Virginia*
$20	*Shipwrecks of North Carolina: from the Diamond Shoals North*
$20	*Shipwrecks of North Carolina: from Hatteras Inlet South*

Wreck Diving Adventure Novel

$20	*The Peking Papers* (hard cover)

Website: http://www.pilot.infi.net/~boring/gentile.html